THE BATTLE OF BHIMA KOREGAON

History of military culture in Maharashtra

Vijay Gaibi More

PEOPLES LITERATURE PUBLICATION
2019

First published in 2019 by
PEOPLES LITERATURE PUBLICATION
http://peoplespublication.com
connect@peoplespublication.com

ISBN 13: 978-81-934856-0-6

Dedicated to

Dr. Babasaheb Ambedkar

Pioneer of Social Justice and Equality in Modern India

Acknowledgements

This book has been prepared under the inspiring supervision of my respected teacher Dr. T. R. Ghoble, Professor and former Head of Department - History, University of Mumbai. He has been my mentor and guide throughout the planning and execution of this research undertaking. The insight he has given into the subject and the Research Methodology has been immensely valuable. His advice, guidance, parental care, and constant encouragement are the sources of inspiration. Words cannot express my debt to him.

Many people have helped in many ways to complete this work. I am thankful to all of them. Yet I must express my deep and heartfelt gratitude to them. I must mention my sincere thanks to Prof. Dr. S. S. Narwade, Dr. Kishor Gaikwad, Dr. Manjari Kamat, Dr. Sushant Pawar, Dr. Anagha Kamble, Prof Anil Bankar and other staff members of the Department of History, University of Mumbai for their good wishes. I must mention Dr. M. D. David for his valuable advice and timely guidance.

I am also benefited by the discussion with Dr. N.G. Bhawre, Late Dr. Gangadhar Pantavane, Professor R. R. Yadav, Dr. S. D. Pawar, Professor and Former Director at Institute of Distance Education, University of Mumbai, I am thankful to Late Professor Arun Kamble, Shrikant Talwatkar, Librarian of Siddharth College of Arts, Science and Commerce Buddha Bhavan, Mumbai. Mr. Sudhakar Khambe, Mr. D. D. Pawar and Subedar Major D.D. Kamble, T. D. Kamble, Captain Pandurang Bansode, Mr. Rajendra Gaikwad - descendent of Veer Govindgopal (Mahar) Ganpat Gaikwad and Rainak Mahar Fort-keeper of Raigad, and also Mr. Pramod Vijaysinh Inamdar descendent of Veer Shidnak of Kalambi. I sincerely record my thanks to them for their advice and best wishes.

I must record my special thanks to Mr. Ramdasji Athawale, Minister of State for Social Justice and Empowerment – Government of India, his constant encouragement is the source of inspiration to complete this work, I am thankful to Mr. Avinash Mahatekar, Minister of State for Social Justice and Special Assistance – Government of Maharashtra, Dayanand Mhaske, Raja Sarvade, Umakant Randhir, Deepak Nikalje, Pappu Kadge, Kantikumar Jain, Gangadhar Ambedkar, Sumantrao Gaikwad, Gautam Sonawane, Balasaheb Garud, Pravin More, Vaibhav Chaya and Sunil Kadam, who also extended their best wishes.

I must mention my friends and well-wishers Savita, Jivan, Santosh, Jaywant, Sunil, Raja Adate, Late Ramesh Dhole, Vijay Sable, Vaibhav Kalkhair, Siddharth Ranpise, Dadasaheb Jadhav, Sada and Suvarna, Vishnu More, Vinayak Mane Jagannath More, Bapu More, Rajaram More, Late Baburao Kharbade, Avinash Kharbade for their moral and material support and encouragement.

I am thankful to Dr. Anuja Palsuledesai, Principle Swami Vivekanand night college of Arts and Commerce – Dombivali, for supporting me in my research and extension work. I am also thankful to my colleagues of the college.

I must mention my special thanks to Mr. N. D. Kamble, Chairman of Parivartan Bank, Mumbai and Mr. Vilas Parab, Maruti Sadaphule for their assistance to complete this research work.

I have received invaluable help from individuals and institutions to whom I wish to acknowledge my sincere thanks. I would like to record my thanks to the staff of the Jawaharlal Nehru Library and Fort Campus Library, University of Mumbai and staff of Siddharth College, Buddha Bhavan Library Mumbai. I also thank to the staff of Maharashtra State Archives and the Asiatic Society, Library, Mumbai, Dr. Babasaheb Ambedkar Marathwada University Library, Aurangabad, Jayakar Library, University of Pune, Maharashtra State Archives, Pune, Bharat Itihas Sanshodhan Mandal Pune, for providing me facilities to refer their material.

I must record my deepest gratitude to my parents Mr. Gaibi M. More and Mrs. Suman G. More and my in-laws Late Prakash Nikalje, Mr. Rajendra Nikalje and other More and Nikalje family members for their encouragement and moral support. An obliged word goes to my late sister Sujata, my younger brother Upali, younger sister Deepa, Chandrakant Kate, my niece Diksha, Pradnya, Sahil and Sharanya for their unstinted support.

And last but not least, special thanks to my wife Priya for her support and encouragement throughout my writing work. I would not have completed this work without her support.

May all those who are mentioned above and rests gain the Merit and Virtues accrued from this work.

Vijay Gaibi More

PREFACE

The History of India is nothing but the socio-economic conflict and struggle between the social groups in the name of caste. Historians, who claimed eminence have not recorded correct history and misled the masses. There are many unknown historical events which need to be re-assessed with new interpretation. The Koregaon battle on 1st January 1818 is one, but one can hardly find any reference of this battle in the History books of India.

The History of Maharashtra has a unique place in Modern India. Geographically the area is located in the western part of India. As Iravati Karve mentions that "Aryans from the Northern India and Dravidians from Southern India joined together in Maharashtra" and it seems that since ages the Brahmin and non-Brahmin conflict is going on in this region.

In the following pages our main concern is to investigate the socio-economic and military culture of Maharashtra. How? Why and who were the Maharashtrian who participated in the battle? The other aspect or the theme is to look into the military culture, in order to understand the spirit or resistance and power to fight against the unjust social order, which fought for equality in society. History of Indian society is nothing but graded discrimination on the socio-economic and political level. Further people were discriminated on the basis of caste, gender, race and color. They kept away from simple human right of equality, knowledge, religion and nationalism. What made them to fight against injustice is the main theme, which the present theme is looking through the Military Culture of Maharashtra.

Similarly, another aspect of caste discrimination forcibly applied, to perpetuate the concept of inequality as a law and keep the oppressed people all time at lowest level is another aspect dealt here with military culture. The local population, their socio-economic life and military culture has been analyzed. Why the Koregaon battle occurred? How Historians viewed this war? And why a section of Maratha society participated in this battle has been discussed in detail.

The Mahars were the original inhabitants of Maharashtra[1]. Etymological version of the word Mahar is derived from Sanskrit words Maha and Ari which means 'terrifying enemy.'[2] As per the records, their ferocious fights

---

[1] Dr.B.RAmbedkar., *The Untouchables,* Amrit Book Co.,NewDelhi,1948, pp.31-55.

wars against aggression labelled them as Maha Ari. The names of the Mahars were suffixed by Nak, which seems to be the corrupt form of the Nag. Mahars were also recorded as Nagas[3].

The Mahars were a central component in Chhatrapati Shivaji's army. He deployed them in his infantry and naval forces, on whose support he established his empire. After Shivaji's death in 1680, his followers did not understand Mahars and left them from military services and considered them untouchable during the Peshwai. This social oppression and exclusion led the Mahars to join the other forces including that of British who made them reliable soldiers against their enemy.

The second part of this book deals directly with the military culture of the people and how they fought actual battle. Thus, the main theme studied by analyzing the Koregaon battle (1st January 1818), in detail.

To established authenticity, direct sources such as interviews are conducted to analyze the result of the battle and the Military Culture of Maharashtra.

The information collected through questionnaire from various cities such as Mumbai, Pune, Satara, Sangli, Kolhapur, Sholapur and other parts of Maharashtra has been useful for my research. The respondent's response has been classified. The book covers the topic of joining military service caste and economic discrimination, non-availability of jobs. This analysis helps in understanding the socio-economic history of Maharashtra.

Many studies have been conducted in order to study the history of Maharashtra but very few are dealing with such a subject. To understand the Koregaon battle the geographical position and historical line re-examined.

The study provides complete texts of British and Indian laws and notifications, documents published by the British and Peshwas in respect of Koregaon battle. The minority community and other select publications have also been placed at the end as an Appendix.

Various speeches and policy decisions passed and signed are also consulted. The study also makes use of relevant books, articles, newspapers, and government documents.

---

[2] R.E. Enthoven, *The Tribes and Castes of Bombay,* Inter Documentation Co., Switzerland, 1922 , pp.401, 418. Phule, Jyotiba, Gulamgiri, Mahatma Phule Samagra Sahitya Ani Vangmaya , Maharashtra Rajya, p.83

[3] Kosare, H. L., *Prachin Bharatatil Nag*, Shodhgranth, Dnyanpradeep Prakashan, Nagpur, 1989, p.vi.

For completing this book various libraries have been consulted and the subject has been discussed with learned academicians, experts and the people whose services were related to the military have been conducted. Information and sources have been collected from the University of Mumbai, Fort and Vidyanagari Campus Libraries, Maharashtra State Government Archives, (Elphinstone College, Mumbai), Government of Maharashtra Mantralaya Library, Asiatic Society, Mumbai, British Council Library, and Siddhartha College of Arts, Science and Commerce Library at Fort, Mumbai.

In this collection of the source material, Pune is an important place where most of the sources like, Peshwe Daftar, Shahu Daftar, Tarabaikalin Kagadpatre (Marathi) are available and have been extensively consulted. Source material related to Koregaon battle has also been consulted at the Pune University Library. Recently a Subhedar Dharmaji Khambe National Museum of Mahar Regiment has been founded in Pune at Dr. B. R. Ambedkar Sanskritik Bhavan which is very useful.

In a cross-reference questionnaires have been prepared and collected by way of oral source from people with direct knowledge and whose ancestor's services related with the battle of Koregaon, in and around Pune and Koregaon area. This material supports as a primary source and the final conclusion has been drawn.

Also, material published in local languages and in the Western Press has been consulted. This material and my personal visit to various places like the Triumph Monument at Koregaon built by the British in memory of the soldiers who died on the spot has helped in clarifying various issues involved in the subject.

The second chapter deals with the nature of village society and military culture. How it originated from village community to the State level. The chapter further gives an account of the village life, their administration and socio-economic disparities. The entire historical development and important events that took place in the area have been discussed. The main theme of the discussion in this chapter has been constructed on the fighting spirit of the men_against nature and manmade concept of caste and society.

Third chapter deals with historical aspects of the Mahar and their traditions and contribution in military services. It also discusses their service to village society. This chapter traces the military services that the Mahars performed during the reign of various rulers

Forth chapter deals with the Koregaon Battle and its aftermath. The Maratha Empire led by Peshwa Baji Rao II was gradually diminishing due to internal dissents and setbacks in the previous Anglo – Maratha wars. Maharashtrian society under the Peshwa had followed the worst kind of social discrimination wherein the lower strata of society such as untouchables were confined to stringent Brahmanical laws and subsequently, their mobility and development were impaired.

With the help of social and political background this chapter directly deals with the Koregaon Battle (1st January 1818) and has emerged as the main theme in which the main focus is emphasized on the Koregaon battle.

The British erected a victory pillar monument in 1821 as a tribute to the valour and loyalty of the Mahars after the Battle of Koregaon. This cenotaph had the names of 23 Mahar soldiers who fell in action. In fact, in the Battle of Koregaon, the British force of 774 men, of which at least 500 were Mahars, fought non- stop without food and water to defeat the Peshwa army consisting more than 30,000 Army men of all the Prominent Maratha Sardars of Maharashtra. This victory pillar at Koregaon village serves as a focal point in the legend of Mahars Military culture and this monument serving as an inspiration for a modern struggle for self-respect and achieving human rights under the leadership of Bharatratna, Dr. Babasaheb Ambedkar who is the Chief Architect of Modern India and its Constitution.

In the final analysis of this chapter various reactions through the questionnaire have been analyzed to arrive at the right conclusion. After nearly two hundred years how the Koregaon battle has been viewed by the people. The issues emerging out of this chapter and its impact on the present generation has been analyzed in short.

Finally, it concludes issues and clarified in more detail as a part of the conclusion. Understanding the growth of military culture among the different communities of Maharashtra, whose participation in military culture has been brought out successfully.

CONTENTS

INTRODUCTION

This book deals with the Battle of Bhima Koregaon and also the history of Military Culture in Maharashtra. Maharashtra has been a unique place in the Asian Sub-continent and has played a vital role in the making of Modern India. It is located in the western part of India, and Marathi speaking people reside in this state. The state has been surrounded by four states and occupies a center stage in India.

According to census report the setting for the Mahar in Maharashtra (as formed in 1960), which today has a population of over fifty million. Out of this figure, Buddhists (almost exclusively Mahars) and Scheduled Castes account for roughly 6.3 million, this is 12.5% of the total population. Of the 3 million Scheduled Castes in Maharashtra, Mahars represent some 35% of the population, or roughly 1 million. Hence, Mahars are the most populous Scheduled Caste in Maharashtra, followed by the Mangs and the Charmakars. Counting the Buddhists, Mahars number roughly 4.3 million or 8% of the total population. The overwhelming majority of the Scheduled Castes are rural dwellers (84.36% rural, 15.64% urban for the Mahars; 81.81% rural, 18.19% urban for the Mangs; and 68.84% rural, 31.96% urban for the Chambhars). Moreover, of the total Scheduled Caste workers, roughly 67% are represented in agriculture, with agricultural labourers accounting for over 54% and cultivators 13%.

The population of the areas comprising Maharashtra at the height of the Maratha Empire in 1750, may be estimated to have been 2 million. By 1832, the population of Maharashtra was estimated to be 3.2 million, and by 1872 it had become 5.2 million. If we assume that the proportion of Mahars has remained approximately the same relative to the total population of Maharashtra, then in 1750 Mahars must have numbered around 160,000; in 1832, 260,000; and in 1872, 410,000.

As per the 2001 census the Buddhist (Mahar) population has grown upto 56,40,785 i.e. (6.39%). Buddhist (Mahar) derived their livelihood from their traditional occupations such as tanning of hides. They performed agricultural labour for their living and earnings. This community is living along with the other communities in this area. And also how they entered in government as well as private sector higher positions.

Geographically, the land consists of 1/10 part of India, and 1/11 of its population. Fertile soil and abundant agricultural resources have made Maharashtra a rich region. The land has been geographically divided into four parts into (a) Konkan (b) North Central Maharashtra (c) Central Maharashtra and (d) Vidarbha.

a) Konkan: Thana, Ratnagiri and Colaba, Mumbai.

b) North Central Maharashtra: Pune, Kolhapur, Solapur, Satara, Sangli, Ahmednagar, Nasik, Dhule and Jalgaon.

c) Central Maharashtra: Regions consisting of Marathwada, Aurangabad, Beed, Parabhani, Nanded, Osmanabad and Latur.

d) Vidarbha: Nagpur, Akola, Amarawati, Yavatmal, Vardha, Chandrapur, Buldhana, and Bhandara.

Since the Ashokan period this region became famous for trade activities. Though village Panchayat rule was established, local Government became popular and rulers began to give land as Watan to tillers. The Satvahanas established contact with Maharashtra and Northern India. Later on Chalukyas and Rashtrakutas established their power, and from here onwards Brahminism increased.

In the 13th century Muslim rulers turned towards Maharashtra. During 15th and 17th century most of the powerful Deshmukhs and Jamindars belonging to the Maratha group were appointed as Sardars in the court of Muslim rulers. Similarly, at the same point, Kulkarni Brahmins were appointed as accounts officers and administrators. By this time, caste system and economic system evolved, on the basis of caste and religion almost all the powers were held by the Brahmins and the ownership of land by the landlord. In between landless labour class, and bonded labour class system developed and increased. Brahmin and non-Brahmin differences continued to increase as seen in the 17th century A. D. The saint movement tried to reunite the caste differences but could not achieve the desirable success.

In the year 1647, Chatrapati Shivaji rose to power, he established his own kingdom around, Pune, Nasik, Satara and Kolhapur and western part of Karnataka, but officially during his time caste differences never surfaced. Chhatrapati Shivaji opposed traditional Watan System. After his death (in 1680) Maharashtra was ruled by Peshwas from 18th Century.

Peshwas promoted caste-based system in Maharashtra. By identifying Mughals as enemy, Peshwa brought Saranjamshahi and established their own political system. In the early years Chhatrapati's heir apparent, Chatrapati Shahu became the Chief and Peshwa became the Prime Minister. They legitimized their power from administration and some of them reached the status of Army Generals.

This change brought new equation in the political and social system of the Marathas which created a new outlook towards economic and military system. Services were taken from the local population in Maharashtra.

Our main concern is to look into the military culture of Maharashtra. How the Maharashtrian people specially Mahars participated in it. The military culture, here, has been mentioned in order to understand the resistance power against the unjust war fought by the people of Maharashtra for justice and against inequality in society. The Varna System and caste has not been taken here as the main cause of discrimination but also the socio-economic and political condition of the people, on which they were discriminated along with caste, gender, race and colour. They kept away from eqauality, knowledge, and religion and nationalism concept. What made them fight against this inequality has been the main theme of this book, which we are looking through the Military Culture.

Similarly, the dominant high caste whose power and knowledge was forcibly applied, to perpetuate the concept of inequality and keep the oppressed people at the lowest level is one aspect of military culture.

The second aspect of the military culture has been dealt herein as it happened in the war on various actual battle grounds. In this book most of the famous battles have been taken into account in order to show the culture of the people on the basis of the geographical background. The social and cultural tradition for fighting just and unjust wars, in Maharashtra have also been touched upon. This book studies the fighting cause of the people and its justification on the basis of primary and secondary sources.

Finally, the main theme has been supported by studying the Koregaon battle (1st January 1818), in detail with geographical and historical background. The special features of this chapter is that, the oral knowledge of the battle has been analysed by collecting information through questionnaire and interviews to arrive at the result of the battle and the Military Culture.

On the basis of their response an analysis is put forth. The main theme of the research work is specially their joining military service and the discrimination on the basis of caste, non-availability of jobs and economically poor background has been discussed. It has been observed that nowhere else has this unemployed low caste group been accommodated in the economic system of Maharashtra. This phenomenon continued through the Peshwa period to the Koregaon war. The oral sources also show that many of the low caste youngsters were ready to die by joining military services. This analysis helps us to rebuild the history to understand the social and economic situation in Maharashtra. This community study is an example to study the other economically weaker communities (including Brahmins) in Maharashtra. I am confident that this analysis will help to increase the knowledge of history.

The local population, their socio-economic condition and military culture has been analyzed in this book with all available primary sources. Why the Koregaon battle occurred? How Peshwas viewed this war? How the British judged it? And why a section of Maratha society participated in this battle has been discussed in detail.

While concluding it can be stated that there are different methodologies to narrate and analyze history. The Maratha History has been studied by very few historians most of them are interested in warfare and political history of the Marathas, some of them even identified this area as regional history. My aim is different than the traditional historians. I have tried in this research to give judgement to the area which was neglected.

Similarly, many people have studied the military history in the world but very few people have analysed the regional culture which in the final stage promote the military culture as per our hypothesis. We feel that we are successful in proving our hypothesis correct. The Military Culture in Maharashtra developed in particular situation when there was social political suppression of the people. The Military Culture of Maharashtra developed clearly due to this factor.

First two chapters we have devoted to the development of Military Culture taking Geography and history in mind. The village community also has been discussed in order to understand the local security aspect which ultimately helped in building up the strong base and a fighting ability and military culture. The final two chapters third and fourth we have discussed about various theoretical self-level and development of military technique in short actual warfare technique, taking into account to understand the military culture. This chapter also helps to reorganize the book. The fourth chapter is very important. It is considered the main backbone of the entire book. This chapter has been built upon the direct discussion and the oral interviews of various people staying in the vicinity of Koregaon battlefield. In fact, I am thankful to those who responded to my call and specially helped in answering my questionnaire. Through the questionnaire, people from Bombay, Pune, Sangli, Solapur and those who had the slightest information about Koregaon Battle came forward and added new and authentic information to this research on which I am able to build this book with full confidence.

The Importance

Many studies have been conducted in order to study the history of Maharashtra but very few are really dealing with such a subject.

After Grant Duff hardly anyone has gone through the social, military and cultural study in Maharashtra.

Geographically, Pune and Koregaon are agriculturally rich areas. This richness of the area has been highlighted as one of the causes of the resistance, in the making of a strong Maharashtra. With this goal in mind, this study has brought out the real conclusion. The growth of military culture and understanding among the different communities of Maharashtra whose participation in the military culture to re-constitute people's history has been brought out successfully.

Hypothesis

In this study, the tentative hypothesis put forth was, why the events of Koregaon battle occurred, what was the military culture, how this culture is seen time and again in this part of the land and how socio-economic situations contributed to this event.

While dealing with this as a hypothesis, why events occurred on this area, the geographical position and historical line has been re-examined from ancient times to date in order to understand the Koregaon battle. Satisfactorily, this has been answered in the book. The hypothesis has helped us to rebuild tentatively a new history, i.e. the military culture and the war efforts that occurred during that period.

Theoretical framework

Today, past history is studied with an analytical and narrative approach. The behavioural theory states that people, who were staying together in the area, were automatically developing enmity on caste, class, religion and social differences which, ultimately turned into conflicts. The present book has been developed on this line to pinpoint the cause and to apply a remedy. Therefore, in this research to formulate the theoretical frame work of history; traditional caste, ideology, economic dependence, has been analyzed relating to military culture and the Koregaon battle. The subject has not been identified to reconstruct the history.

Research design and methodology:

The research methodology is adopted on historical lines chronological and analytical approach. The issue has been described on the basis of primary and factual source of information. The approach towards the study has been purely analytical and diagnostic and objectivity in research has been maintained. Various hypothesis and premises have been put forth to testify the primary source material. The entire study has been organized on a scientific method of research.

Chapter Scheme

Chapter 1 – Historical and Geographical Background of Maharashtra:

This chapter deals with the History and Geography of the area from ancient to the end of the Maratha power. The entire historical development and important events that took place in the area has been discussed. The main theme of the discussion in this chapter has been constructed on the fighting spirit of the men_against nature and manmade concept of caste and society. An economic force, political settlements, resistance of people, and religious position has been taken into consideration.

Military culture has been identified and discussed in depth up to the end of Peshwai, which formed in itself as the main theme in the rest of the chapters.

Chapter 2 – Maharashtra Society and Military Culture.

This chapter deals with the Military Culture. How it originated from village community to the State level. The chapter further gives an account of the village life, their administration and socio-economic disparities. By relating this, we are able to discuss defence activities through which military culture has been identified. This chapter also deals with issues, such as, low castes men who participated in the war and militant activities against suppression in Maharashtrian society.

While discussing the above issues, the history of military organizations and its development has been kept in mind throughout the book. The Military, Infantry and Cavalry; its working and their services have been discussed as part of the military culture in detail. The rewards and grants which gave them support to fight for the state and nation has been discussed.

On the basis of this theoretical framework the rest of the other chapters have been co-related and rebuilt to bring out the truth in the book in the final analysis.

Chapter 3 – Mahar Military Culture.

This chapter deals with the Mahar's origin, growth and tradition. It also discusses their service to village society. This chapter traces the Military services that the Mahars performed during the reign of various rulers. What battles they fought and the cause behind the fighting capabilities has been touched upon. The social suppression under the Peshwai has been discussed in detail in order to understand the resistance power of the community.

This chapter deals with the Mahar's military services in British Army, and how the British employed and used them. Their removal from military service and how they fought for re-enlistment in the army is discussed. Their movement for re-recruitment in army and finally the establishment of Mahar Regiment has been touched upon.

Chapter 4 – Koregaon Battle and its Aftermath.

This chapter directly deals with the Koregaon Battle (1st January 1818) and has emerged as the main theme of this book in which the main focus is emphasized on the Koregaon battle. This chapter is divided into the following parts.

The background, the cause of conflict behind the Peshwa and British. Specific emphasis lay upon the internal social situation under the Peshwas. Chapter further deals with direct analysis of war, taking into account the geographical location of the battle and the events leading to the war. Further why the Peshwas were defeated and why the British built the Koregaon monument is discussed in the final analysis of this chapter.

After two hundred years how the Koregaon battle has been viewed by the people. In the final analysis of this chapter various reactions through the questionnaire have been analyzed to arrive at the right conclusion. The issues emerging out of this chapter and its impact on the present generation has been analysed in short.

Chapter V – Conclusion

This chapter concludes the entire arguments. Some issues like Maharashtra's Mahars have been clarified in more detail as a part of the conclusion in this research work.

To support the sources and argument, standard bibliography also has been at the end of the book.

HISTORICAL & GEOGRAPHICAL BACKGROUND OF MAHARASHTRA.

The present chapter is to investigate the military culture and society in Maharashtra. To find out the history, geography and environmental conditions of the region, it should be clear to set-forth a logical link between military culture and society in the region.

Geography of Maharashtra

Maharashtra lies in the central and western part of India. Maharashtra is inhabited by Marathi language speaking people.[1] They possess a distinct historical and socio-cultural tradition, which sets them apart from the rest of the subcontinent of India.[2] Maharashtra covers an area which is bound by the Arabian Sea on the west.[3] The unique qualities of Maharashtra as stated by Sir Richard Temple, the Governor of Bombay in 1870. Speaking of the extent to which the high culture of Hinduism had influenced the religious traditions of the region, Sir Richard Temple observed:

> "*But despite (the values which they share with the rest of India) the Marathas have always formed a separate people or nation, and still regard themselves as such.*"[4]

After 1960, politically Maharashtra is divided into four regions: Konkan, Deccan, Marathwada and Vidarbha. Konkan lies on the western seacoast. An area comprising of the districts of Thana, Ratnagiri, Raigarh, Sindudurg, Colaba and the City of Mumbai. The Deccan on the Island plateau including Pune, Kolhapur, Satara, Sangli, Solapur, Ahmednagar, Nasik, Dhule, Nandurbar and Jalgaon and Marathwada including Aurangabad, Jalna, Latur, Hingoli, Beed, Osmanabad Parbhani and Nanded; In other side Vidarbha comprising Akola, Amaraoti, Yeotmal,

---

[1] Iravati Karve, *Maharashtra Land and its People,* Directorate of Government Printing Central Press, Mumbai, 1968, p.1.

[2] Ravindra Kumar, *Western India in the 18th Century, A Study in the Social History of Maharashtra,* Routlege & Kegan Paul, London, 1968, p. l.

[3] Map of Maharashtra.

[4] R. Temple, *The Maratha Nationality, in Shivaji and the Rise of Marathas,* K.P. Bagachi & Co., Calcutta, 1953, p. l.

Buldhana, Nagpur, Wardha, Chandrapur Bhandara Washim, Gadchiroli, and Gondhiya.[5]

Maharashtra, the homeland of the *Mahars* is the Central and Western portion of Peninsular India. The Vindhya and Satpura mountains and the Narmada river separate the huge wedge-shaped mass of land from Northern India. The Krishna divides the mass of land from Northern India into two unequal halves, the Deccan or the Dakhan of Muslim times and South India, the home of the Dravidians. Tapti river runs through the north-western edge of the Satpuras, commences the main Sahyadri range stretching in a southerly direction, parallel to the Western sea coast, nearly eleven hundred miles. The Sahyadri separates the long but narrow coastal strip from the Central Deccan plateau. Maharashtra divided into three distinct regions.[6]

1. The Konkan – subdivided into North and South Konkan.
2. The Ghatmatha and the Mavals.
3. The Desh including Khandesh and Berar.

Politically Maharashtra was seldom coextensive with the Marathi speaking belt. Maharashtri Prakrit supplied a bond of union as it was the language spoken in Vidarbha, Ashmaka (from Khandesh to the Godawari), Mulaka (South of the Godawari) and Kuntala (Kolhapur and Southern Maratha States). Few great monarchs ruling in the Central Deccan succeeded in uniting these regions under a single administration. The mountain and river system of the land determined the provincial boundaries and fostered love of regional independence.

---

[5] Iravati Karve, n. l. pp. 5-6.

[6] M.B. Deopujare, *Shivaji and the maratha art of war*, Vidharbha Sanshodhan Mandal Nagpur, 1973, p.5. The fifth Rock Edict of Ashoka Maurya mentions the Rastikas, the Petenikas and the Aparantas. The Ceylonese Chronicle Mahavamsha of 5th century A.D. records that Mahadhamma Rakshit was sent as a Buddhist missionary to Maharatta. In the Aihole inscription of Satyashraya Pulakeshin II of the year 634 A.D. there is a reference to three Maharashtrakas. This expression has been taken to refer to Vidarbha, Ashmaka and Kuntala. Some scholars hold that Kuntala was a Kannnada speaking region. It was generally not included in Maharashtra. Although Maharashtra was not a compact unit, its different regions shared a common culture. As has been shown by recent excavations at Paoni in Bhandara district, such cultural and religious contacts were close and continuous.

Konkan

The Konkan is bounded on the north by the Damanganga beyond which lies the Gujarati coast. At the southern end lies Karwar. The total length of the strip is four hundred miles and its breadth vary from twenty-five to thirty miles. It enjoys a copious rainfall. The western spurs of the Sahyadri reaching up to the sea provided bases to build sea-forts upon.[7] The coast possessing as it does many a safe anchorage for sailing ships attracted traders from abroad from early times. The various passes of the Sahyadri connected to the seaports with the hinterland. The Naneghat via Junnar, the Kasur via Igatpuri, the Borghat between Kalyan and Poona, the Kumbharli between Chiplun and Karhad were even then the most frequented routes.[8] Sopara, Thana, Kalyan, Chaul, Dabhol, Rajapur and Ratnagiri were the chief emporium of trade. Long before the advent of the Portuguese, the Kolis, the Bhandaris, the Abyssinians and the Arabs had settled down in the Konkan.[9] When Allauddin Khilji defeated Ramchandra Yadav, he sent his son Bhimdev to Konkan. In 1347 Naiku Malik of Gujarat invaded North Konkan which ultimately passed into the hands of Bahamani kings. The Local rulers like the Raja of Rairi and the chiefs of Khelna and Sangamehswar maintained their independence till they were subdued between the years 1436-1469 A.D.[10]

At the opening of the seventeenth century, North Konkan (Thana and Kolaba districts) and the Abyssinian principality of Janjira formed part of the Nizamshahi Kingdom (1490-1636). South Konkan was under the Adil

---

[7] James G. Duff, *History of the Mahrattas*, Reprint, Karan Publication, Delhi, 2000, p. 4.

8 S.N.Joshi: *Aitihasika Sankirna Sahitya*, Vol. IX, Anath Vidyarthi Griha Prakashan, Pune, 1953, pp. 11-13. A list of ghats – 125 of the Sahyadri, 10 of the Satpuras and 10 of the Vindhyas – is given there.

9 P.B. Joshi: *History of Ancient Konkan*, pp. 47-49. S.M. Edwardes The Rise of Bombay, a retrospect, Times of India Press, 1902, pp. 13, 14, 15. The seven islands of Bombay were called Heptanesia by Ptolemy in 150 A.D. Marco Polo records that the Lad Brahmins settled in the Konkan engaged in trade and were men of adventurous spirit.

10 J. Scott, *Ferishta's History of the Deccan*, Shrewsbury, London, 1784, pp. 122, 123, 155, 156, 346. Raja ShankarRay of Khelna and the Shirke chief annihilated a large Muslim force sent against them under malik-ul-Tujjar in 1347.

V.K. Rajwade: *Mahikavatichi Bakhar,* II nd ed. Varada Books, Pune, 1991, pp.69, 102. Nagardev was the ruler at the time of Naiku Mallik's invasion of the Konkan.

Shahi Sultans. The Portuguese held Goa, Salsette (Sashti), Bassein (Vasai), Chaul, Bombay, Daman and Dieu. The Portuguese were dominant of the coast which was obnoxious to the Muslim rulers as it was to the Hindus. Indeed, Akbar's Deccan policy comprehended annihilation of the Portuguese power. In 1582 the Mughals made an unsuccessful attempt to capture Bassein and Daman.[11] The Dutch and the British appeared, before long to challenge the ascendancy of these so-called 'Lords of Indian Navigation'. The emergence of Chhatrapati Shivaji introduced by the new factor in the political situation. The exposed condition of his kingdom in the Desh made the possession of Konkan of vital importance for him as a place of refuge. The Konkan could provide the food-grains, salt and its ports giving access to outside places.

Ghatmatha

The Ghatmatha is the plain land on the main Sahyadri range extending from Harishchandragad in the north to Phondaghat in the South for a distance of two hundred miles. Its average height from the sea level is two or three thousand feet. A few of its peaks reach up to five thousand feet. The Ghatmatha provided natural sites for building strong forts like Raigad and Sinhagad. The region was in ancient times a centre of varied religious activity. Numerous Buddhist, Jain and Brahmanical monasteries were situated near the highways connecting the hinterland with the seaports. Rainfall in the region being heavy, the forests were then occupied by the haunts of wild animals, the wolf, the leopard the tiger and other dangerous creatures.

Mavals

The valleys of Sahyadri to the east of group round Junnar and Poona are known as Mavals or the 'Sunset Land'. The area was colonized in the fourteenth century. Each valley was named after the river flowing through it. Thus Gunjan Maval was the valley watered by the Gunjan which rises at the near of Raigad region. 'Khyore' and 'Ner' were other names for such fertile valleys.[12]

The settlers in the valley formed an active, industrious and hardy community of farmers. They were inured to fatigue and had to be

---

11 V. Smith: *Akbar the Great Mogul*, Clarendon Press, 1919, pp.264-265. The author dilates on the tortuous policy of Akbar towards the Portuguese.

12 V.K. Rajwade: *Marathyanchya Itihasachi Sadhane*, Vol.VIII, Granthamala, Kolhapur, 1903, p.78. See also, Vol. XII, Bharat Itihas Samshodhan Mandal, Pune, 1912, p.5.

watchful of the wild animals and highwaymen. The Mavals were under the administration of Maratha Deshmukh rulers who acted as royal revenue collectors and the guardians of people. However, they did not form a united group. The more powerful among them wielded considerable influence at the Muslim courts. They helped preserve the martial tradition of the Country. The Muslim rulers exercised control over the Ghatmatha and the Sahyadri passes through them.[13]

Desh

The Desh is considered as a proper Maharashtra region, it comprised Nasik, Ahmednagar, Pune, Satara, Sholapur and Kolhapur districts. The Sahyadri slopes from the west to the East and from the South to the North. The tableland became habitable centuries ago as the lava overspreading the Deccan which gradually cooled down. The fraction of heat, air and water shaped the irregular configuration of the Deccan terrain. The Satmala, Ajanta, Chandor, Balaghat and the Mahadev offshoots of the Sahyadri divided the tableland into relatively separate units. The river system of the Deccan accentuated local differences. The Narmada and the Tapi flow East-West to the Gujarat coast, whereas the Godawari . and the Krishna with their tributaries flow West-East across the entire breadth of the tableland. The Harishchandragarh hills forms the watershed between the Godawari and the Bhima river. The Wardha and the Wainganga rising in the Satpuras flow North-South and join the Godawari. The Painganga river rises in the Ajanta range near at the Babhulnaghat and after flowing North-South turns East to meet the Godawari. The Balaghat range forms the eastern border of Maharashtra. The sloping country to the East of it was known as the Payanghat which was a part of Telangana.[14]

The Central portion of the tableland was in historical times the meeting place of Marathi, Telugu and Kannada cultures. The Satvahanas had their capital at Paithan near Aurangabad.[15] Their connection with Andhra Pradesh was close.

---

13 V.K.Rajwade, *Marathyanchya Itihasachi Sadhane*, Vol.XV, Atmaram Chhapkhana, Dhule, 1912, p.87. The Jedhe and the Khopde Deshmukhs had a long feud. Khopde turned hostile to Shivaji and went over o the Mughals because he did not get a share in the Vatan village of Nazare. The history of Jagdale family of Masur whose Vatan was taken by Shahji Bhonsala.

14 James Grant Duff, Ibid., n.7, pp.6,7.

15 C.A.Kincaid, Parasnin, *Comprehensive History of the Maratha Empire*, Anmol Publication, Delhi, 1986, p.11.

Khandesh Berar and Vidarbha

Khandesh lying in the alley of the Tapti formed a buffer state between Gujarat, Malwa and Vidarbha, Vidarbha was a separate political and cultural unit from very old times.[16] As early as the 6th Century A.D. Vidarbha poets were known for all over India for their literary excellence. The two main routes of invasion from the North through Malwa and Nimad converged on Ellichpur (now called Achalpur) the capital of the Kingdom of the Imadshah. The first led from Mandleshwar, Burhanpur and across the Tapti to Ellichpur; the second from Handiya, Harda, Betul to Ellichpur. Rohankhed s near Buldhana district, just below the Balaghat range occupied the same position in the Deccan as Panipat did in Northern India.[17] The Tapti, the Purna, the Penganga and the Wardha marked the territorial limits of Berar. The Chalukyas of Badami, the Rashtrakut. of Malkhed and the Yadavas of Devgiri wielded sovereign power in Vidarbha in succession before the advent of the Muslims.

The whole of Maharashtra came under a single administration by the Yadavas rulers of Devgiri (1187-1294 A.D.).[18] The Yadava was ruling over Maharashtra for longtime. The well to do dynasty was uprooted by the Khalji invaders, who inflicted untold misery on the Hindu Kings of the Deccan and South India. The failure of Harpala Deva's bold attempts to expel the Turks from his country led to the annexation of the kingdom. Muhammad Tughlaq organized Deogiri rulers into a centre of Muslim power. He helped thousands of Muslim families in Northern India and foreign countries to settle down in the Deccan.[19] The Sultan put down with a heavy hand rebellion of local chiefs like that of Naga Nayaka, the Koli chief of Kondana. But centrifugal forces proved too strong even for the Tughlaq. The Muslim nobles dissatisfied with the Sultan's Policies broke out in rebellion and the Deccan region fell apart.[20]

---

16 R.G. Bhandarkar, *Early History of the Deccan*, Asian Educational Services, New Dlehi, 1985, p.3, 14.

17 Ibid., p.10, S.N. Hodivala: *Studies in Indo-Muslim History*, Vol.1, S.N. Hodiwala, Bombay, 1939, p.621.

18 Ibid., n.7, p.37.

19 Ibid., n. 7, pp. 33, 34.

20 Ibid., p.34. The Maratha country was divided among four officers who found it difficult to control the Yuzbashis, remnants of the New Mussalmans and Afghan adventurers. Muhammad Tughlaq called Devgiri 'Qubbat-at-Islam' meaning the 'Cupola of Islam.'

The Bahamani kingdom of Gulbarga was founded by Allauddin Hasan Bahaman in 1347 A.D. during the lifetime of Muhammad Tughlaq.

The Bahamani Sultans found it politic to assign mountainous tracts to loyal Maratha chiefs ready to submit to the new masters. The employment for foremost communities like the Marathas, Brahmins, Kshatriyas and Prabhus in the civil and military departments was continued on an extended scale by the Sultans of the succession states of the Bahmani Kingdom.[21]

Climate

The atmosphere of Maharashtra comes under the monsoon type of climate. There are four clear cut seasons, summer, rainy, autumn and winter season. The maximum and minimum temperature during winter range between 10 and 30 degrees Celsius. Rarely in some places light frost may be observed for a day or two. The summer temperatures reach 40 degrees or even more in Vidarbha, but in the coastal regions, the temperature does not exceed above 20 to 25 degrees, although the humidity is very high prior to the beginning of the monsoons. When the monsoons are over the temperature rises during the month of October.[22]

Rainfall

Maharashtra gets heavy rainfall from the South-East monsoons during the period June to October. The Western Konkan coastal strip gets rain as much as 250 to 350 centimetres. As the moisture laden winds cross the Sahyadri ranges, the rainfall becomes less, and the area falls in the rain shadow area. Some parts of eastern Maharashtra gets rain from the North-West monsoon during winter. Amboli gets 720 cm. of rainfall.[23]

Soil

Different kinds of soil are found in various parts of Maharashtra, depending upon the rainfall and natural vegetation. Black cotton soil or regular soil is found in areas where the rainfall is less than 100

---

21 J.D.B. Gribble: *A History of the Deccan, Vol.I*, Luzac and Co., London,1896, pp.44, 52, 141, 183. Selections from Peshwa Daftar, Vol. 31, No. I, Apte D.V.: History of the Ghorpades of Mudhol, p.31. The career of Sajjansingh is an interesting case.

22 Santosh Dastane, Santosh, *Glimpses of Maharashtra*, Dastane Ramchandra & Co., Pune, 1993, pp.14-15.

23 *Maharashtra 1969,* Directorate of Publicity, Government of Maharashtra, Sachivalaya, Bombay, 1969, pp. 4-5.

centimeters. The Deccan Plateau is formed by oil from lava. It is rich soil; it is helpful for cotton cultivation. It is mainly found in the plains and on the banks of the river.

Red soil is found where the rainfall is heavy. The red colour is developed due to the presence of Iron oxides and Aluminum. As the soil is acidic, it is not suitable for agriculture, it is found in Western Maharashtra. Brown sandy soil is found in Chandrapur area – Saline soil is found at the mouths of the rivers in the Konkan area.[24]

Mountains

The most dominating feature of Maharashtra is the Sahyadri range on the Western Ghats, running north-south close to the Western Coast. The great divides of Maharashtra, the rock of Sahyadri claimed to be older than the snowcapped Himalayas, and as influential on the lands of the Marathas as is the Nagadhiraj.[25] The rivers and the forests all depend upon the presence of the Sahyadri. The Western Ghats have provided many hills and forts which played an important role in the history of Maharashtra. The holy places on the banks of streams and rivers, temples and sacred places on the top of adjoining hills are the gifts of the Western Ghats to the people of Maharashtra. The caves, temples, Chaityas and Viharas are owe their existence to the trap rock of the Sahyadri.[26] The Thal and Bhor Pass provide routes from Nasik and Pune respectively to Bombay. While Kumbharli, Amba and Ponda are gaps further south, providing access across the steep hills to the coastal towns.[27] One striking feature of the Sahyadri is the large plateaus on hilltops at many points. In olden times, these became the famous hill forts while today they are famous as hill-stations. Mahabaleshwar is a significant example of such a plateau at top of the Western Ghats.[28]

In the physical features of Maharashtra like the Western Ghats are seen shooting eastwards in between the river valleys between the Krishna and

---

24 Dastane, n.22, p.15.

25 S.R. Tikekar, S.R., Maharashtra. *The Land, its people and their culture*, Maharashtra information center, New Delhi, 1966, p. 6.

26 B.G. Gokhale*, Buddhism in Maharashtra*, Popular Prakashan, Bombay, 1976, p.3.

27 James Grant Duff, n.7, p.5.

28 Deshpande, C.D., *Western India, A Regional Geography*, Student's own Book Depot, Dharwar, 1948, p.128.

Bhima intervene the Mahadeo ranges, as between the Bhima and the Godavari, are the Balaghat ranges. The Satmala and the Ajanta ranges separate from the Tapi and Purna valleys from the Godavari basin.[29]

Danda Karanya

Maharashtra region was also known as Dandakaranya – The Dandaka forest with a lot of aboriginal people living in it. It seems that they were a long-headed, medium statured people with noses ranging from extremely broad to medium broad. The region extends southwards beyond the Krishna and northward forest till Central India.[30]

Rivers of Maharashtra

The major rivers[31] of Maharashtra have the Tapi, Godavari, Krishna and the Bhima with their numerous tributaries.

The rivers in Maharashtra fall in two distinct categories. Rivers that originate in the Sahyadri ranges and flow westwards and meet the Arabian Sea and others that flow eastwards and meet the Bay of Bengal.[32]

Rivers flowing in the Deccan plateau may be divided into the two categories of Rivers such as Narmada and the Tapi, flows westwards travelling through Madhya Pradesh and Gujarat state. The Narmada flows through Dhule district for about 54 km., while the Tapi flows among of Maharashtra and Gujarat. Similarity out of these two regions as well. The main tributaries of the Tapi are Purna, Girna, Bori, Anar. River Tapi and her tributaries have enriched the soil of Khandesh. The Narmada and Tapi in the North, and the Malaprabha in the South, while its eastern boundary limits the Andhra Pradesh. Apart from the narrow coastal strip which lies between the Arabian sea and the Ghat difficult passage through hill, Maharashtra comprises a plateau which slopes gradually to the east but descends precipitously to the east towards the coastal plain and the Arabian sea. From, which stretch roughly north to south, long tongues of higher ground run east and divide the plateau into

---

29 Karve, n.1, p.8.

30 Maharashtra State Gazetteers, History, Part I, Ancient Period, The Director, Government Printing Stationery and Publication, Maharashtra State, Bombay 1967, p. 5.

31 See rivers in map of Maharashtra.

32 Imperial Gazetteers of India, Provincial Series, Bombay Presidency, Vol. V, Superintendent, Government Printing, Calcutta, 1909, p. 178.

compartments like the plains of Berar and Nagpur region, the basin of the under the Godavari and of the Bima between Poona and Sholapur.

The location of Maharashtra has conferred certain advantages upon there people, which reflects in their history, politics and cultural traditions. The Narmada and Tapi, which define the northern boundary of Maharashtra, act as formidable barriers in the path of any invader who proceeds towards the Deccan[33] from the North. Besides, such obstacles, the terrain of Maharashtra offers ideal conditions for sustained resistance against an alien authority. Both the Ghats, which run parallel to the coast, and the tongues of higher ground, which branch off eastwards from the Ghats, are flanked by rich valleys and plains in which are located many towns and villages. The uplands of Maharashtra, therefore, constitute an ideal base for armed resistance against the invader, since they possess abundant sources of supply and numerous sites for military strongholds, where power can be organized both for aggression and for defence. The region is considered to be one of the most inaccessible parts of India by military strategists.[34]

Because of the location of Maharashtra and the identity of the people, the region possesses a political and a historical convention which distinguishes it from other parts of the subcontinent of India. In referring to these unique qualities of Maharashtra State, for instance, has summed up the land and the people with remarkable acumen and perception. 'The entire region', he points out, bears the imprint of the Marathas: a tough, hardworking, and cheerful peasantry, ably served by an adroit Brahmin elite which maintained close touch with the people.[35]

The Godavari, Krishna and the Bhima are the main rivers of Maharashtra. The Godavari which is the longest takes its origin at Trimbakeshwar in Nashik district.[36] Nashik, Kopargaon, Paithan, Gangakhed and Nanded are important towns situated along the bank of the River Godavari. Her tributaries are Darana, Pravara, Sindfana,

---

33 Deccan: The word Deccan expresses the country watered by the upper Godavari and that lying between that river and Krishna. Deccan – The word "Dakkhan" represents the vernacular pronunciation of the Sanskrit work Dakshina meaning " Southern" used to designate the portion of the Indian Peninsula. Ibid, n.15, p.3.

34 Ravindra Kumar, n.2, p.2.

35 O.H.K.Spate, *India and Pakistan*, Methuen & Co.Ltd., London, 1954, p. 644.

36 B.G.Gokhale, *Buddhism in Maharashtra*, Popular Prakashan, Bombay, 1976, p.4.

Dakshinpurna, Pranhita, Dudhana and Indrayani, Sangamner and Newase are situated on the banks of the Pravara. A dam has been constructed on this river at Bhandardara. The Purna, Wardha and Vainganga are important rivers in Maharashtra. River Bhima takes her origin at Bhimashankar. Some of her tributaries are Kukadi, Pawana, Indrayani, Mula-Mutlang, Neera, Karha, etc. Dehu, and Alandi are situated on the Indrayani and Pandharpur is within a crescent shape of the Bhima, which is why the river is known as Chandrabhaga in that area. The Bhima finally joins river Krishna at Raichur in Karnataka confluence between the two major rivers. River Krishna takes her origin at Mahabaleshwar. Her main tributaries are Venna, Koyana and Panchaganga, wai, Sanghi Miraj and Narsobawadi are important places on this river.

These peculiar geographical features have produced a race of sturdy people who have to labour hard for a meagre subsistence.[37]

Society of Maharashtra in 18th century

Two distinguishing features marked the organization of the 18th century society and gave it security and stability – religion of the mass of the population of Maharashtra and the caste system and the village. Hinduism advanced in the south with the march of Indo-Aryan Civilization, but the movement was slow and many of its concepts though accepted superficially, did not obtain the same hold in this region. The Hindu theory of mankind is divided into four varnas or group of races like, Brahmin(worshiper), Kshatriya(warrior), Vaishya(traders) and Shudra (the lower caste). The only distinction in society was between Brahmins, the general mass of people known as Marathas and the untouchable Mahars.[38]

The forest dwelling tribes like Bhills, Ramoshis, Kolis, Varlis and Katkaris were outside the pole of civilized society. They were literally hewers of wood and were not disturbed so long as they confined themselves to the jungle and remained quiescent. Whenever for some reason or other the forest dwellers raided villages on the border, punitive expeditions were sent against them and they were hunted like wild beasts.[39]

---

37 A.R. Kulkarni, *Maharashtra in the age of Shivaji*, 3rd Revised edition, Prabha Prakashan, Pune, 2002, p.3.

38 Maharashtra State Gazetteer, History III, *Maratha History*, Government Central Press, Bombay, 1967, p.210.

39 Ibid., p. 210.

Brahmins

The Brahmins were a priestly class and enjoyed social privileges. They engaged in religious duties. They studied the shastras, acted as temple worshippers and preached the traditional religion to the masses by reading Puranas and by holding religious concourses.[40] The class which strictly followed the tenets of the faith and devoted their lives to the study of divine ordinance was held in esteem, but otherwise there was no special veneration for the Brahmin character. Many of them had taken to mundane activities and were working as merchants, bankers and soldiers. But the profession in which they excelled their services were the clerical one. The Brahmin who acted as an accountant in village and district they were keeping records. They had a also charge of land measurement and assessment, as well as they acted as Divans to Jagirdars. The Brahmin clerks and accountants nearest to the king became ministers of the realm.[41]

In those times there were several sects of Brahmins in Maharashtra, the more important were the Desastha Brahmin from Central Maharashtra and Kokanastha or Chitpavan from Konkan. In the early days of the Maratha state, Desastha Brahmins were in greater prominence in administration, but with the rise of Balaji Vishwanath Peshwa they lost their pre-eminent position to the Chitpavans.[42]

Thus the Brahmin was an important factor in the population though the percentage of Brahmins to the general population was barely five the small minority wielded much greater political power than could be warranted by its strength. The Peshwa's court in Poona in its later days came to be known as "Brahmans Daulat", Brahmins dominated the state and roused feelings of jealousy among the masses owing to the favoured position of the Brahmin Class.[43]

---

40 Ibid., p.211.

41 Ibid., Shivaji's peshwa or chief minister Moropant Pingle, was a Brahmin. His Finance Minister Annaji Datto was a Brahmin Ramchandra Amatya and Naro Sankar sachiv and Balaji Vishwanath who founded the family of the Peshwa which later usurped royal authority was a Brahmin.

42 Ibid. n.38, p.211.

43 Ibid. p.211.

The Marathas

The villagers residing at the mountain areas joined as army man for Chhatrapati Shivaji. The Peshwa and other princes of the Maratha confederacy.[44]This class was important to the Marathas. The term had a much wider connotation that at present included not only the peasantry but the shepherds and cowherds. With the exception of a few prominent families they were looked on as shudras, the fourth class in society.

The Maratha is eminently qualified for a military life.[45] His caste by which he belongs to the labouring population of the country endures him to fatigue and the vicissitudes of weather. The Marathas are the most numerous races of the Hindu people, which circumstances promises hope of success in every military undertaking.

The simplicity of manners of the Marathas, their democratic feeling of equality surprised strangers, who had seen servility of conduct of Muslim courts. The ruler was from a Maratha family. The big confederates like Shinde, Bhosle, Gaikwad and Pawar. were all Marathas. The Maratha peasantry was the dominant element in the army. Marathas in every village of Maharashtra were Patil of village and Deshmukh were chief land holders in district. Their total strength was about one third in the entire population, and besides the Brahmins, they were a powerful element in the population.[46]

The Mahars

The Mahars are one of the most populist caste in Maharashtra, almost there is no village in the region where Mahar is not there. Their mother tongue is Marathi and they are hereditary village servants.[47] Mahar had no

---

44 Hiralal and Russel, *The Tribes and Caste of the Central Provinces of India*, Remint Cosmo Publication, Delhi, 1971.

The Marathas are divided into 96 exogamous clans, p.20l.

45 Ibid, n. 38, p.198.

46 Ibid. p.212.

47 Iravati Karve, Maharashtra State Gazetteers, *Maharashtra Land and its people*, The Director, Government Printing and Publications, Maharashtra State, Government Central Press, Bombay, 1968, p.32.

specified work of his own. He was really a worker for the whole village where the work involved no contact with the house or people.[48]

The hereditary work of the Mahars is to remove the dead cattle[49] from the village, to sweep the streets, to run errands for the village officers and to keep watch on the village property. The Mahar is generally the principal witness in disputes about boundaries of fields etc. It is said that the Mahar walks more than all the villagers put together.[50] As village watchman, it was his duty either to find out the thief and identify the real identity of fellow villagers that the thief did not belong to the village and was an outsider, in which case his suspicions were communicated to the headman of the next village, and the Mahar of that village had to prove either that the villager was innocent or to produce the offenders.[51]

The Inter-village contact of Mahars in pursuit of their duties and the participation of Mahars in Tamasha and Jalsa (while travelling the full of entertainment from singing groups) may have created the channels of communication of new ideas, but the ideas and the impulse for organization came from non-village factors.[52]

While the new economic opportunities presented to the Mahars undoubtedly encouraged a movement up from their inferior position, another factor that contributed both to their economic and social progress and to their caste spirit was the Mahar clan (Military service). Even before the arrival of the British, the Mahar had an outlet from traditional work in the time of Shivaji as guards in the hill forts and soldiers in the artillery.[53] It is fairly clear that they had their own units in the later armies of the Peshwas. But it is from the records of their service

---

48 Maharashtra State Gazetteers, *History, III, Maratha period.*, Government Central Press, Bombay, 1968, p. 213.

49 T.N. Atre, *Gao-Gada* (in Marathi), published by H.V. Mote, Bombay, 1959, p.98.

50 Karve, n.1, p.32.

51 Karve and Damle, *Group relations in village Community*, Deccan College, Monograph series, No.24, Poona, 1963, p.26.

52 Eleanor Zelliot, *Caste in Indian Politics*, (ed.)Rajani Kothari, Orient Longman Ltd., New Delhi, 1970, pp.31-32.

53 S.N.Sen, *Military System of Marathas*, Bagachi & Co., Calcutta, 1928, p. and also see, Thorat, S.P.P., Regimental History of the Mahar Machine,Sun Regiment, Army Press, Dehra Dun, 1958, p.3.

in the armies of the British that the Mahars draw the contention that they are a martial race.

A military monument at Koregaon a small village near Pune serves as a focal point in the legend of Mahar, heroism, and a number of Mahar gatherings have been held at the pillar of victory. The Koregaon pillar commemorates the soldiers of the British Army who fell during a battle on 1st January 1818 with Peshwa forces,[54] of the forty-nine names of the 2nd/1st regiment recorded there, twenty-two are Mahar,[55] or Parwari, as Mahars were known then.[56]

From the record of military services dates back to the pre-British period and may lend some plausibility to their claim to the status of a martial group.

Thus, the society in Maharashtra was divided into three main castes, and all the social functions had been divided between these three castes. Caste within itself was a bond of union but considering the society as a whole it was a force of disuniting as it split the society into hereditary groups making marriage,[57] dining,[58] and drinking possible only within the caste group. Any social contact with the member outside the caste was prohibited.

Maharashtra was the last country occupied by the Aryans from the northern countries. Here as there, they drove some of the aborigines to the fastness of mountains and jungles and incorporated the rest into their own society.[59]

At the time of the Aryan invasion, the condition of the country must have been similar to that of Ramayana as a forest infested by Rakshas or wild

---

54 Identifiable by the Nak ending of the names a designation used for Mahars into the early years of this century.

55 Sir Patric Cadell, *History of the Bombay Army*, Longman's Green and Co., London, 1938, pp.154-55.

56 Eleanor Zelliot, n.52, p.33.

57 S.N. Sen, (Ed), *Foreign Biographies of Shivaji*, K.P. Bagachi & Co., Calcutta, 1931, Vol.II, p.61.

58 N.C. Kelkar, & D.V. Apte, (ed), *Shivaji Nibandhavali*, Part II, Shivcharitra Karyalaya, Pune, 1929, P.11.

59 R.G.Bhandarkar, *Early History of the Dekkan*, Asian Educational Services, New Delhi, 1985, p.4.

tribes who disturbed the religious rites of the Brahmin sages. Sanskrit literature was referred the Aryas were gradually progressing from Punjab. The wild tribes, they met with are spoken of under the name of Dasyus, Rakshas and others.[60]

Early History of Maharashtra

Maharashtra has a long cultural and historical tradition. The history of this region goes back to the third century B.C. The first known rulers of Maharashtra were the Satvahanas (1st century B.C. to 250 A.D.) who were succeeded by Abhiras (3rd century A.D.), Vakatakas (25 A.D. to 510 A.D.) Kalachuris (5th to 6th century A.D.), Western Chalukyas (560-750 A.D.), Rashtrakutas (750-950 A.D.) and Silaharas (10th to 12th century A.D.).

The Marathas came into limelight during the Yadava period, i.e. from the 12th century onwards.[61]

Satvahanas

The foundation of the Satvahana Empire in 220 B.C. is an important milestone in the History of the Maharashtra which begins with the foundation of the Satvahana Empire.

Before the foundation of the Satvahana Empire, Maharashtra was ruled with a large number of petty kingdoms, who often fought war with one another. The Satvahanas for the first-time wielded Maharashtra into a powerful and gave a cohesion and integrity to the region. The Satvahanas for the first time wielded the Deccan into a powerful state.[62] Trade and industry prospered in the Deccan under the Satvahanas, Economic life was given cohesion by the guild organization which had permeated almost every profession.[63]

The Satvahanas were orthodox Brahmans,[64] they established Deccan as a connecting link in terms of politics and the emerging Brahmanic cultural system. Their kings had uprooted the Shakas and destroyed the pride of

---

60 Ibid., p.5.

61 A.R. Kulkarni, *The Marathas*, Books and Books Publishers, New Delhi, 1996, p.4.

62 Maharashtra State Gazetteer, I, n.30, p.57.

63 Ibid.

64 Ibid.

Kshatriyas.[65] As part of this process, the Satvahanas patronized Sanskrit and despised their native Dravidian language as a "global language".[66]

The Satvahana dynasty consisted of 25-30 kings. The names of the Satvahana kings who ruled over the Deccan or Maharashtra[67]

Abhiras

After the breakup of the Satvahana Empire about the middle of the 3rd century A.D. several small kingdoms came up in different parts of Maharashtra. Abhiras rose to power in northern Maharashtra is shown by the inscription of the Abhira Rajan Isvarsena in a cave at Nasik.[68]

The Abhiras were an ancient race whose original habitant lay in the north-western parts of India. They are classed with the people of the southern countries like Maharashtra, Vidarbha, Asmaka and Kurtala. Gradually Khandesh became their stronghold. Even now the Abhiras or Ahiras predominate in that part of Maharashtra.

The Abhiras generally followed the profession of cowherds. They were consequently associated with the Sudras. Patanjali discusses in his Mahabhasya whether Abhira was a sub-caste of the sudras and concludes that it is a different caste. In the Kasika, a commentary on Panini's Astadhyayi, the Abhiras are called Maha- sudras or superior-sudras. A Mahasudra was one of the functionaries at the coronation ceremony of kings. Commentators explain the term Mahasudra as "a commander of the Sudra Army."[69] Some Abhiras are known to have occupied high

---

65 Bombay State Gazetteers Poona District, Government Central Press, Bombay, 1954, pp.101-2.

66 Ibid., p. 122.

67 Ibid, n.28, p.74.(1) Satvahana (2) Simuka (3) Krsina c.199.189 B.C. (4) Satkarni I c.189-179 B.C. (5) Purnotsanga c.179-161, B.C. (6) Skandastambhi 161-143 B.C. (7) Satkarni II 143-86 B.C. (8) Skandavati, (9) Mrgendra (10) Svatikarna, (11) Puloma I (21 B.C. – 22 A.D.) (12) Arishtakarna, (13) Hala (14) Montalaka (15) Purindrasena (16) Sundara (17) Satkarni (18) Cakora (19) Svatikarna and Sivasti (47-86 A.D.) (20) Gautamiputra Satkarni (86-110 A.D.) (21) Vasishthiputra Pulumavi (110.138 A.D.) (22) Sivasri Satkarni c.138-145 A.D.) (23) Sivaskanda Satkarni 145-175 A.D. (24) Gautamiputra Yajna-Sri, Satkarni (174-203 A.D.) (25) Vijaya Satkarni (26) Candra Sri Satkarni (27) Pulumai III.

68 Maharashtra State Gazetteer, n.30 p.102.

69 Ibid.

political position under the Western Chalukyas. Isvarsena founder of the Abhira dynasty which continued in use for nearly a thousand years.

Traikutakas

They derived their name and ran Triakuta, the three-peaked mountain or the district in which it was situated. The Traikutakas have been found only in South Gujarat, North Konkan and Maharashtra. The province of Aparanta (north Konkan) was included in the kingdom of the Traikutakas.[70] From the inscriptions and coins we gather the following genealogy of the Traikutas kings. Inamdatta - (son) -Maharaja Dahrasena (k 207 A.D. 456-57) -(son) MaharajaVyaghrasena (K241 A.D. 290-91) Traikutakas kingdom was invaded by the mighty Vakataka king, Itarisena.[71]

Rashtrakutas

The Rashtrakutas were powerful in Kuntala[72] or Southern Maratha Country. The history of the Early Rashtrakutas has been unfolded during the last few years.[73] Early Rashtrakutas ruled over Kolhapur, Satara and Solapur district. Their capital Manapara, which was plainly founded by Manaka and named after himself is probably identical with the town Man the headquarters of the Man Taluka of the Satara District.[74]

Vakataka

The Vakatakas were equal to the Guptas in the North India. Their empire extended from Malva in the north to the Tungabhadra in the South and from the Arabian sea in the west to the Bay of Bengal in the east. They were great patrons of art and literature. The liberal patronage which they extended to Sanskrit and Prakrit poets made the Vaidarbhi and Vachchomi ritis famous throughout the country.

Viharas and Chaityas at Ajintha were excavated and decorated by Vakutakas ministers and feudatories. Their profound influence on the

---

70 Ibid., n.30,p.108.

71 Ibid., P.107

72 Kuntala was the name of the Upper Krishna Valley.

73 Ibid., n.30, p.132.

74 Ibid., p.134.

culture and civilization of the Deccan or Maharashtra.[75] Vakataka dynasty ruled over the Deccan from 25 A.D. to 510 A.D.[76]

Kalachuris

Kalachuris connected with Mangalisa of the early Chalukya dynasty.[77] Aparanta[78] was included in the dominion of the Kalachuris.

The Kaluchuris ruled from Mahismati. The city is usually identified with Omkar Mandhata which from very early times has been famous as a holy place. The early Kalcuris rose into prominence of the downfall of the Traikutaka. The only powerful dynasty to which he may have owed allegiance was that of Kalcuris. The Kalhcuri king ruling at the time must have been the father of Krsnaraja. Krsnaraja father, using Mahismati as his base, seems to have extended his power in the east, west and south. The time of krsnaraja was used by several later dynasties. His territory was included in Gujarat, Konkan and Maharashtra including Vidarbha were comprised in it.[79]

Krsnaraja's son and successor of Sankargana is known from several records.[80] Sankargana was succeeded by his son Boddharaja. After his accession, Boddharaja had to face an invasion of his territory by his southern neighbour Mangalesa of the Early Chalukya dynasty of Badnauj. In this struggle, Bodhiraja completely routed and led away leaving his whole treasure behind him, which was captured by Mangalesa. Mangalesa became supreme in the South.[81]

Mauryas

Western India was placed under the prince governor of Ujjain. Missions spread Buddhism among the traders of the coastal towns and the western

---

75 Maharashtra State Gazetteer, n.30, p.107.

76 A.R. Kulkarni, n. 61, p.4.

77 Ibid., n.30 , p.107.

78 Ibid., p.140, Aparanta name of ancient North Konkan.

79 Ibid., p.137.

80 Ibid., p.138, Abhona place issued from his camp at Ujjaini and record the donation of some land in a village in the Marathwada region of Maharashtra, p.138.

81 Ibid, p.140.

Deccan, which by that time was more or less completely Aryanized, and Jainism also seems to have first reached the south at this period.[82]

The first notice of the Maurya family ruling in North Konkan occurs in the description of the conquest of the early Chalukya King Kirtivarma I (A.D. 566-598).[83]

The Mauryas were ruling over North-Konkan for about seventy-five years.[84]

The magnificent cave temple of Siva at Elephanta was probably carved out of solid rock during the reign of the Maurya kings.

Chalukyas

The Chalukyas who are famous in history for evolving a distinctive style of temple architecture, now known as Chalukyan architecture. Chalukyas ruled over Maharashtra for a period of well over two hundred years.[85]

Kirtivarman was the first king of this dynasty to have established his sway over parts of present Maharashtra.

In this dynasty, Mangalga was a great warrior and described in the Ailhole inscription as having led successful campaigns to the limits of the eastern and western seas.

The famous Chinese Pilgrim Hi-uen-Tsang travelled in India between 629-645 A.D. he visited parts of Chalukyan king Pulkesin's kingdom apparently Maharashtra, which he called Mo-ho-la-cha.[86]

In this dynasty the last king was Kirtivarman II, he ascended to power in 744-45 A.D. It was in Kirtivarman's reign that the Chalukyan sovereignty was overthrown by the Rashtrakuta prince. Dantidurga sometime before A.D. 754 and the Rastrakutas gained possession of the Chalukya dominions. The decline of the Chalukya power was evidently due to their

---

82 Imperial Gazetteers of India, *Provincial Series, Bombay Presidency, Vol. V,* Superintendent of Government Printing, Calcutta, 1909, reprint, Usha Publication, New Delhi, 1985, p.15.

83 Maharashtra State Gazetteers, n.30, p.140.

84 Ibid., p.142.

85 Maharashtra State Gazetteers, n.30, p.201.

86 Ibid., p.216.

constant conflicts with the Pallavas and other southern rulers which had considerably weakened the Chalukyas.[87]

Rashtrakutas (750-950 A.D.)

Rashtrakuta was the name of an office and not of an individual. Rastra was the name of a territorial unit, corresponding roughly to the modern district and its administrative officer was called Rastrauta, a Rashtrapati, or Rastrika or Rathika or Rathi in different periods and provinces.[88]

The Rashtrakuta family was in all likelyhood the main branch of the race of Kshatriyas named Rattas who gave their name to the country of Maharashtra and were found in it even in times of Ashoka the Maurya. The Rashtrakuta were the real native rulers of the country and were sometimes eclipsed by enterprising princes of foreign origin, such as the Satvahanas and the Chalukyas who established themselves in the Deccan and exercised supreme sovereignty but were never extirpated.[89]

Dantidurga the founder of the Imperial Rashtrakuta family.[90] Dantidurga defeated the army of Chalukyas with a handful of soldiers,[91] which hitherto had achieved very great glory by vanquishing the forces of the kings of Kanchi, the Keralas, Cholas and Pandyas, Sriharsena. The Lord paramount of northern India.

Rashtrakuta dynasty had fourteen kings from Dantidurga to Karka,[92]among them 9 kings were powerful and warriors, two had no powers and they ruled for short periods.

Rashtrakuta dynasty ruled for 200 to 250 years. Rashtrakuta kings fought battles with infantry only and they did not have a navy.[93]

---

87 Ibid., p.229.

88, Maharashtra State Gazetteers, Ibid no.30 p.233.

89 R.G. Bhandarkar, n.58, p.62

90 Maharashtra State Gazetteers, n.30, p.237.

91 R.G. Bhandarkar, n.58, p.62.

92 V.K.Bhave, *Musalnampurva* Maharashtra, (Marathi), Modern Printing Press, Pune, 1946, p.76.

93 Ibid., p.77.

Silharas

The Silharas were one of the most royal feudatories of the Rashtrakutas. There were three families of the Silharas, one ruled over the north Konkan comprising of the modern Kolaba and Thana District. The second family of the Silharas ruled over Kolhapur and Satara district. Its capital was situated at Valivada at Kolhapur with the strong fort of Pannhala in its vicinity.[94] The third family governed south Konkan. It was also known as sapta Konkan and comprised of the modern territory of Goa and the former Savantvadi state and the Ratnagiri district. Its capital was Balli Pattana.[95]

Silharas of North Konkan ruled from 825-1265 A.D. there were nineteen kings who ruled north Konkan. They ruled for three hundred and fifty years.[96]

Silharas of Kolhapur ruled from 1109-1218 A.D. there were twelve kings who ruled over Kolhapur for a period of hundred years.[97] According to V.K.Bhave, the capital of the Silharas of North Konkan was Rajpuri.[98]

Yadavas of Deogiri

The early Yadavas were feudatories of the Rashtrakutas, who were the rulers of Deccan. Seunacandra was regarded as the real founder of the dynasty.[99]

Yadava dynasty ruled the area belonged to them from 860 A.D. to 1315 A.D. Yadava history becomes obscured during the 50 years from 1125 to 1175 A.D. The feudatory Yadavas of Deogiri had been steadily enlarging their boundaries and strengthening their armies for the final struggle. The Yadavas under Singhama remained masters of the Deccan (1212). The

---

94 Maharashtra State Gazetteers, n.30 p.259.

95 V.K.Bhave, n.92, p.157.

96 Ibid., p.158.

97 Ibid., p.159.

98 Ibid., p.166.

99 According to Dr. Bhandarkar, Dridhaprahana the founder of the family, please see Bhandarkar R.G., n.58, p.99.

Konkan chiefs, however, maintained their independence for some time longer.[100]

Kingdoms of the Deccan

The Kingdom of Khandesh (1370-1599 A.D.) founded by Malik Raja Faruqi, an officer of Muhammad Tughlaq lay in the valley of the Tapti enclosed between the Vindhya, the Satpura and the Sahyadri ranges. The chief fort Asirgad dominated the route from the North across the Satpuras. Burhanpur was the Capital of the Kingdom. The Western portion of Khandesh called the Dangs or Baglan was ruled by a Rathod Rajput family. At present Kolvan included in the Nasik District, is the southern region of the Dangs (the word Dang literally means a hilly ascent) and Bhilwada forms its northern portion. It had close political connection with Gujarat.

The Kingdom of Berar (1484-1572) founded by Fathullah Imad Shah, a Hindu Convert, extended from the border of Khandesh eastwards to the Warda river. The Ajanta range has two branches one going up to Bhandara and the other upto Parbhani. It commanded the route into the Deccan.

The Ahmadnagar Kingdom (1489-1633) comprised Nasik, Poona, Ahmadnagar, Thana, Kolaba districts and Janjira. Murtaza Nizam Shah conquered Berar in 1572 A.D. The southern boundary of the kingdom extended up to the Nira. From that river to the Krishna and the Tungabhadra lay the kingdom of Bijapur separated from the Kutbshahi Kingdom by the Manjra. Satara, Solapur, Kolhapur and Talkonkan were included in the Adil Shahi kingdom. In 1592 Bidar ceased to be a separate State having been conquered by Ibrahim Adil Shah II. There was unceasing struggle among the five Sultans to achieve a paramount position. It was no easy task to hold together the various regions under one administration. Religious considerations did not weigh with the Sultans, who made war upon one another. The Marathas, scattered as they were in several warring States, ceased to think and act as one people. Maharashtra was only a geographical expression.[101] The economic condition of the people under Muhammadan rule deserves a passing notice. At the opening of the seventeenth century, the population of India consisted of a small but wealthy and extravagant upper class, a small

---

100 Imperial Gazetteers of India, n. 32, p.21.

101 G.S. Ghurye, *Caste and Class in India*, Popular Prakashan, Bombay, 1957, p.106, remarks "The saints of Maharashtra produced a revolution without the uproar of a rebellion…"

and frugal middle class and a very numerous lower class. [102] Foreign trade was controlled by the Europeans and their Indian monopolists like Virji Vora, then thought to be the richest merchant in the world. The Sultans depended upon foreigners for regular import of horses for their cavalry and for sword blades. The coast was infested by pirates who preyed upon commerce and the precarious hold of the Muslim rulers on the ghats of the Sahyadri encouraged hill tribes to commit robberies. The Maratha peasant earned his bread by the sweat of his brow. Land was the main source of wealth. The Desh region was deficient in economic resources; famines were not infrequent.[103] In the sum, several regions of western Maharashtra were economically not less than politically depressed under alien rule. History would take a turn if some new force got in.

Sultanate period

The Pune, Nasik and Satara districts and particularly the tract around the Nira, Bhima and Krishna rivers formed the cradle land of Maratha independence. The situation of the Maval land away from the centres of Muslim government allowed the political movement to take root and grow strong as the conquerors lost their original vigour. During the period of Turko-Afghan dominance of the Deccan, the Vijayanagar Kingdom (1336-1565) played the historic role of acting as a bulwark of Hinduism.[104] In 1565 it suffered a catastrophe at Talikot from which it did not recover. But the Sultanates also were left exhausted. On the eve of the first Mughal invasion, the Muslim States were plagued with party strife. At Ahmadnagar a fatal succession dispute following the death of Burhan Nizam Shah in 1594 divided the leading nobles into hostile camps. The Muslim invasion coincided in time with the thought ferment in Maharashtra and created favourable conditions for giving a shape and content to the vague stirrings of Swarajya. As Mughal imperialism triumphed over the Deccan States and posed a threat to Hinduism, the Marathas rose in its defence even as their forbears, the Satavahanas and their neighbours the Andhras, had done. The geography of western Maharashtra lent a helping hand in carrying the political revolution to success. A nucleus of Maratha power was built up in the tracts which, as

---

102 Moreland: *From Akbar to Aurangzeb A study in Indian Economic History*, Macmillan & Co., London, 1923,pp.153, 197.

103 Purandare: *Shiv Charitra Sahitya*, Vol.I, For details of a great famine lasting for 12 years.Bharat Itihas Samshodhan Mandal, Pune, 1926, p.2.

104 Dr. B.A. Saletore, Dr. S. Krishnaswami Aiyangar, *Social and Political Life in the Vijayanagar Empire, Vol. I,* B.G. Paul & Co., Publishers, Madras, 1934, p.1.

has been remarked before, were administered through the agency of Maratha chiefs.

The Swarajya Self-government, from its very inception, had to organize itself for war. Ruin of the Yadav Kingdom before the Turkish onslaught had given the Marathas a foretaste of the terrible efficiency of the Turkish methods. The bold offensive strategy of Allauddin and his lieutenants, their discipline, the rapid manoeuvres of horse archers and the religious zeal of the warriors of Islam had proved irresistible. It was realized that the ascendancy of the Turks could not be challenged successfully unless the art of war was reorientated and dynamic social forces asserted themselves.[105] The Vijayanagar Bahamani warfare in which the Maratha chiefs fought under the Muslim region and the wars of the five sultanates intersperse made the Marathas thoroughly familiar with the Muhammedan art of war. The military profession attracted young men of good families in search of the means to improve their material prospects. They distinguished themselves as Shiledars and the commoners enlisted as Bargirs. The Maratha was more powerful Jagirdars maintained their own stables.

The Muhammendans had introduced several improvements in fort architecture. The use of lime and mortar as the binding medium construction of gates fitted with iron pikes, sidewalls with embrasures for the use of musketeers, provision of earthen glacis, cannon platforms and towers at strategic points were built. Among others, innovations calculated to render siege warfare a specialized art. The employment of Portuguese and Turkish gunners for casting cannon pieces had become common.[106] The siege weapons of the day made the task of reducing strong forts difficult. The Sultans built or the forts and relaced also on the

---

105 M.B. Deopujari, *Shivaji and the Maratha Art of War*, Vidarbha Samshodhan Mandal, Nagpur, 1973, p.13, Ramchandra Yadav has been wrongly called an unmilitary king. He, his son Shankar and his son-in-law Harpal Dev fought to the bitter end.

106 'Elliot and Dowson: *Akbar Nama of Abul Fazal*, pp.146-147. F.M.. Elliot, j. Dowson, History of India , as told by its own Historian, Akbarnama of Abul Fazal, Trubner & Co., London, 1867, pp. 146-147. Abul Fazal was amazed to behold Asir. He writes, "Old soldiers and men who had seen the fortress of Iran and Turan, of Rum, Europe of the whole habitable world, had never beheld the equal of this." The fort of Golkonda for its arrangement of acoustics, Ahmadnagar for the earthen glacis and Asirgad for its military works are examples of fort architecture in the Deccan.

Ibid.

flat-topped hills of the Sahyadri. The Marathas being at home in the hills, their services in reducing such forts by stratagems were valued. The Sultans, like the Hindu kings, employed war elephants in sieges as in field warfare.[107]

Changes in the Military Sphere

The Maratha fighting class imbibed the new discipline of arms and fighting technique. The Muslim expansion into the Deccan gave them an opportunity to play a decisive role in politics and warfare, first as auxiliaries and later, as fighters for their own freedom. The spirit of regional independence expressed itself in a general anti-mughal line up. The participants unconsciously paved the way for the creation of an independent State of the Marathas.

Mughal

Allauddin Khilji was the first Muslim who established his power in the Deccan in 1296, and occupied the area of the Godavari, Krishna, Kaveri and Pravara.[108] Later on, Qutab-ub-din Mubarak Shah,[109] marched on Devgiri in 1318, and crushed the rebellion.[110] The Deccan passed completely under Muslim rule.

Later on Malik Yaklakhi became the Governor of Deccan.[111] The south was unsettled and was in an unhappy condition ultimately resulted in the

---

[107] Ishwari Prasad, *Qurannah Turks*, Ibid, pp.291, 292, The Tughlaq Sultans had 3000 caparisoned elephants with howdas (towers) each carrying from six to ten fighters. The elephants were placed in front of the centre and foot soldiers with swords marched in front of them clearing theway for the elephants. The Deccan Sultans used elephants to stiffen the ranks, convey heavy guns and to break open fort-gates. The commander rode a tall beast to keep an eye on the entire battlefield.

108 S.G. Malshe, (ed), *Marathi vangmayacha Itihas (Marathi) Part II, Vol.I*, Maharashtra Sahitya Parishad, Pune, 1st edition 1982, p.18.

109 V.V. Mirashi, *Satavahana and Prachin Kshatrapa Yanchya Itihas Ani Kcriv*, lekh (Marathi & English) Maharashtra Rajya Sahitya Mandal, Bombay, 1979, pp.129-131.

110 B.G. Kunte, Maharashtra State Gazetteer, *Maharashtra Language and People*, Government Printing Press, Bombay, 1971, p.9.

111 Devgiri was the capital of Yadavas. Maharashtra State Gazetteer, History, Part I, Ancient Period, Directorate Government Printing, Stationery and Publication, 1967, p.374.

rise of an independent Hindu Dynasty at Warangal. An effort was made to establish a separate Hindu Kingdom at Vijayanagar. This Kingdom of Bahamani dynasty continued till 1538.[112] When the provincial governors declared their independence. Bahamani kingdom disintegrated into the five sultanates such as Nizamshahi, Ahmadnagari, Adilshahi of Bijapur, Imadshahi of Berar, Gutabshahi of Golconda and Baridshahi of Bider. Sultan of Bahamani became a puppet in the hands of Quasim Barid, who became an independent ruler of Khandesh and dynasty was called Faruqshahi. After that Berar and Bidar Sultanates annexed Ahmed and Bijapur Sultanates in 1574 and 1619.[113]

Rise of the Marathas

By the beginning of 17th century Maratha feudal knights working under Adilshahi of Bijapur, were getting Watan, Inam, or Jagirs,[114] from Adilshah. The Maratha sardars spread into different parts of Maharashtra. Jadhavas of Sindkhed (Berars), the Nimbalkars of Phaltan (Satara), the Desai's of Savantwadi, the More's of Javali, the Ghorpade's of Mudhul (Karnataka), the Surves of Shrinngpur, Bhosle of Nagpur and others like Gaikwad, Shirke, Nai, Angre.[115] All these Marathas served at Adilshahi court, and their main purpose was to get hold of watan. Ghadges, Ghorpades, Jadhavas, Nimbalkar, Mores, Shindes, Dafles, names were enjoying property of Jahagiri (small region) and Inam (reward) and the Mores, the Shirkes, the Mahadik ruled over Konkan and Ghatmala and the Gujars and Mohites in lower Mavals. The Bhosle, ancestors of Shahaji were the chief supporters of the Bijapur rulers. Shahaji was also given

---

112 The sultan selected as Governor of Devgiri, Malik Yaklkhi, an old servant of Alluddin.

113 Ibid, Part II, Bombay, 1972, p. IX, Ibid. pp.7, 10-11; Ibid., pp.265-66.

114 Watan: Country, Native country, place of residence, hence amongst the Marathas it has come to import any hereditary estate, office, privilege, property or means of subsistence, a patrimony. Please see, H.H.Wilson, Glossary of Judicial and Revenue Terms, East India Company, London, 1855, p.556, S.G. Malshe, Marathi Vangmayacha Itihas, Maharashtra Sahitya Parishad Pune, 1982, p.26.

115 Setu M, Pagadi, *Shivaji and Swarajya*, Indian Institute of Public Administration, Maharashtra, Orient Longman, Bombay, 1975, pp.7-8. M.G. Ranade, The Rise of Maratha power and other Essays, Publication of Bombay University, 1961, pp.30-32.

Jahagiri (by the Adilshahi Court. Parts of Poona, Chakan, Indapur and frontier parts of Wai and supa.[116]

Chhatrapati Shivaji

The rise of the Maratha power under the leadership of Shivaji (1646) coincides with the rising of the first bodies of sepoy troops by the East India Company for the defence of their factories, whilst the Maratha power embraced all castes and creeds in their army. Chatrapati Shivaji employed Mahars to watch jungles at foot of the hill forts, act as scouts to keep the forts supplied with wood and fodder.[117]

Shivaji organized the Maharashtrians and established a strong force by taking help from officers like Babaji Avaji Chitnis, Ramji Nilkanth who were given watan and also faithful persons, like Bakaji Farjad.[118] Watan was given a special task or work done by the people. When watandars were not loyal to Shivaji their watans were also annexed. During the famine people sold their watan,[119] when watandars had no descendant, then their watan was annexed by the Government.[120] When there were hereditary person watan was regularized. In this regard, Shivaji had given information. "Do not disturb the village people or farmers. You give security to them, try for agriculture developing."[121] After the death of Shivaji, watan system was changed, people became covetous about the watan. Sambhaji did not give Jahagiri. Jadhav and Nimbalkar left him and joined Nizam. Hence for the sake of securing watan the Marathas joined the Mughals. During the period of Rajaram only four forts had remained with the Maratha Power.

---

116 Yadunath Sarkar, *Shivaji and Shivkal,* Njarat Governors, Granthmala, Bombay, 1930, pp.10-14. Maharashtra State Gazetteers, Maratha Period, Part III, Government of Bombay, Bombay, 1967, p.5.

117 S.P.P. Thorat, *Regimental History of The Mahar Machine gun Regiment,* Army Press, Dehra Dun, 1958, p.3.

118 S.N. Joshi, *Shivkalin Patra-Sar-Sangraha*, Vol. III, BISM, Poona, 1932, p.2706. Joshi S.N., Shivcharitra Sahityakhanda, Vol.III, Lekh, 417, Chitrashala Press Pune, 1930, pp.22-30.

119 S.N. Joshi, *Shivkalin Patra-Sar-Sangraha*, Vol.I, Raighad Smarak and B.I.S.M., Poona, 1930, Letter No.95, p.83, and letter No.292-293, p.77.

120 Datta Vaman Potdar, *Shivcharitra Sahitya,* Chitrashala Press, Pune, Vol.II, 1930, p.239.

121 S.N. Joshi, n.119, p.246.

In 1700 Tarabai (Rajaram's wife) captured power and established her rule in Kolhapur for seven years. After Aurangzeb's death (1707) the Mughal power became weak. In the Maratha kingdom too Shahu and Tarabai fought for the throne. Shahu started distributing watan to the Mughals and Maratha sardars.[122]

Rise of Peshwa

After the death of Aurangzeb in 1707, Nizam-ul-Mulk became the governor of Bijapur and Bahadur Shah was the leader of the Mughals. All the Deccan Governors were appointed by Mughal court of Delhi. The famous Sayyed brothers Farrukhsiyar dominated the power at Delhi. Nizam-ul-Mulk, was offered vice-royalty of the Deccan of February 1713. In the same year (17th November 1713). Shahu gave viceroy authority to Balaji Vishvanath. This gift was rendered to Balaji Vishwanath because of his help to Sayyids brothers for getting Delhi throne and Sanad (Right of dominion state) was brought from Sayyid brothers.[123] This Sanad was given to Balaji by nominal king Rafi-ud-darjat.[124] Day after day the power of Chhatrapati reduced to the nominal Prime Minister, Peshwa became powerful.

After Balaji, his son Bajirao I (1720-40) occupied the Maratha Power. Geographically, Maharashtra was extended in his, Bajirao I period.

From 1740 to 1761 Balaji, Bajrao alias Nanashahib and from 1761 to 1771, later Madhavrao ruled. He extended the boundaries of Maharashtra to the Northern India. Madhavrao Peshwa personally solved the social and economic problems of the people specially the conflict between farmers about land and their watan, revenue, tax, army, religion, etc.[125]

After the Battle of Kharda, Nana Fadnis gave the authority of Maratha State to Peshwa Bajirao II. The internal upheaval was not liked by the

---

122 N.G. Pawar, *Letters of Tarabai, Vol. I,* Shri Siddheshwar Printing Press, Kolhapur, 1st ed. 1969. Letter No.188, p.260.

123 Irvin William, *Letters of Mughal, Vol. II,* M.C., Sarkar and Sons, Calcutta, 1922, p.100.

124 Shejwalkar, S.S., *Nizam-Peshwa Relations*, Poona University Press, Pune, 1959, pp.22-24.

125 R.V.Oturkar, *Peshwekalin Samajik Va Arthik Patra-Vyavahar*, B.I.S.M. , Poona, 1950, Letter No. 31, 47, 110-112, 114, 119, 123.

Maratha Sardar, Tukaji Holkar, Nagpur Bhosle, Tipu Sultan and Bombay British.[126]

Bajirao II, assumed power and began to extort money from the people by imposing a special new tax 'Santosh Patti'[127] on people for which discontent increased among the people.

Conflict Between Peshwa and British

Along with the Marathas, East India Company, also began their rule under Lord Wellesly, on 17th May 1798. Pamar was a British resident. Wellesly tried to establish relations with Peshwa with the help of Parmar.[128] The British had also been helping Bajirao with money. Bajirao developed a soft corner for the British. At this point, all the Maratha Sardars were politically divided, from the regime of Balaji Vishwanath. Shinde, Jadhav, Nimbalkar joined the Mughals. During Balaji Bajirao (I) Chimnaji (Appa) Damodar, Senapati Dabhade, an Army officer, and Chhatrapati Sambhaji (son of Tarabai) these Marathas helped Nizam during Nanasahebs regime. Tarabai, wife of Rajaram, Dabhade, Gaikwad, Pawar, Raghuji Bhosle, Bapuji Naik did not join Nizam.[129] During Madhavrao (1761-71) representatives such as Bhosale, Gaikwad and Peshwa as (servants) Shinde, Holkar and Patwardhan were included in Nizam and British. Already this conflict was created between Marathas, Raghoba Raghunath Rao and Madhavrao, Nizam's, British and Marathas. Govindrao Sayajirao Gaikwad, Manoji-Mahadji Shinde, Tukoji-Ahillyabai Holkar. Janaji-Mudhoji, Bhosle, Aba Nana Purandare was developed.[130] The conflicts were complicated day by day among the Sardarsx up to 1801. To overcome the internal problems Bajirao signed Vasai Treaty

---

126 V.V. Khare, *Aitihasic lekh Sangraha* B.I.S.M. Poona, 1941, Letter No.3856, p.5021.

127 Santosh Patti, A cess levied upon the cultivators by the King or zamindars on an occasion of rejoicing as the birth of a son.

Please see, H.H. William, *Glossary of Judicial and Land Revenue Terms*, East India Co., London, 1855, Vol. II, p.464.

128 Colonel G.B. Malleson, *Administration of British India under Lord Wellesly*, Daya Publishing House, Delhi, (Reprint) 1989, pp.13-28, 42.

129 A.R. Kulkarni, N.61, pp.166-172.

V.G. Dighe, *The Maratha Supremacy, Vol. VIII, The History and Culture of Indian People,* Bharitya Vidya Bhavan, Bombay, 1977, pp.502-507.

130 V.K. Purandare, *Purandare Daftar*, Vol.I, B.I.S.M., Pune, 1929, Letter No.287.

(See Appendix No. VI.), with British on 31st December 1802.[131] Pendharis people from the area challenged against the Vasai Treaty. In this revolt Mahar, Mang, Ramoshi, Balutedars were also joined. For the safety from Pendharis (plunder tribes) Bajirao took the help of British. Gaikwad, Holkar and Shinde also took help from British against Pendharis and the Treaty was signed with British for safety. And thus the British came to Maharashtra on 16th May 1817, Deccan British resident, Elphinstone, gave an order to Bajirao, "you accept the new treaty otherwise be ready for war." Helpless Bajirao signed the treaty on 13 June, 1817.

Elphinstone shows the carving eagerness about the treaty. Bajirao ceased the war against British. Then British marched on Poona, Bapu Gokhale fought against the British, and at once Bajirao ran away in the evening from the Battlefield. Bajirao came under the control of British. In this way, Maratha power was abolished[132] after the Battle of Koregaon on 1st January 1818.

Geography of Pune

Pune lies between 17^0 51^0 and 19^0 24^0 north latitude and 73^0 19^0 and 75^0 10^0 east longitude, has an area of about 6,027.5 sq. miles. (See Appendix No. VII).

The district has the shape of a triangle with its base in the Sahyadri mountains on the west, and its apex in the extreme south-east corner near the point of confluence of the Bhima and Nira rivers.

In the west along the Sahyadris, Pune has a breadth of nearly eight miles. From this, it stretches about 130 miles. Southeast sloping gradually from about 2000 to 1000 feet above the sea and narrowing in on irregular

---

131 G.S.Sardesai, *Selection from Peshwa Daftar, Vol.38, Letter No.152.* G.S. Sardesai, The Main Currents of Maratha History, Phoenix Publications, Bombay, 1949, pp.137-156. See Appendix No. VI.

132 G.S. Sardesai, *Poona Residency Correspondence*, Vol. X, P.37, Vol.XIII, Part II (1816-1818), Letter Nos. 133, No.47, ed. By Government Central Press, Bombay, 1958.

P.C.Gupta, *Bajirao II and the East India Company*, Oxford University Press, London, 1939, p.203.

Secret Political Diary, Maharashtra State Archives, File No.148, pp.6078-79.

132 Gazetteers of India, District Series, XX, Poona District, Bombay Presidency, Government Central Press, Bombay, 1954, p. 1.

wedge-shape to about 20 miles in the east. It is bounded on north by talukas of Akola, Sangamner and Parner in Ahmednagar district, on the east by Parner, Shrigonda and Karjat also in Ahmednagar district and Karmala in Sholapur district, on the South by Malshiras in Sholapur district and Phalton and Wai in North-Satara district, and on the west Roha, Pen and Karjat in Kolaba district and Murbad in Thana district.[133]

Climate

The height of the Pune plateau (1,800 feet) its freedom from alluvial deposits and the prevalence of westerly breeze, makes it dry. The air is lighter and the heat less oppressive and the cold more bracing than in almost any other district of the presidency (state). Pune has cold season from November to February, March to June hot season and June to October rainy season.

During the cold season the cool land winds prevail, with sea-breeze mostly after sun-down. The hot winds, the chief characteristic of the hot season are over by the middle of May. During the hot season the air is occasionally cooled by severe thunderstorms, bringing heavy rain and occasionally hail.[134]

Rivers

Pune is crossed by many rivers and streams which take their rise in and near the Sahyadris and bound by the east-stretching spurs flow east and south across the district. The chief river is the Bhima which crosses part of the district and far more than a hundred miles from its eastern boundary. The main tributaries of the Bhima are the Vel and the Ghod on the left, and the Bhima, the Indrayani, the Mula or Mula-Mutha and the Niva on the right. During the rainy season all the rivers flow with a magnificent volume of water and during the hot season shrink to a narrow thread in broad stretches of gravel. At intervals barnes of rock cross the beds damming the stream into long pools.[135]

---

[133] Gazetteers of India, *District Series, XX, Poona District,* Bombay Presidency, Government Central Press, Bombay, 1954, p. 1.

[134] Imperial Gazetteer of India, *Provincial Series, Bombay Presidency,* Vol. I, Government Printing Press, Calcutta, 1909, p.487.

135 Gazetteer of India, n. 133, p.6.

Agricultural

Agriculture is the predominant occupation of the area.[136] In Poona all arable land comes under one or other of three great heads 'dry-crop', water crops and rice land. The Kharif or early crops are brought to maturity by the rains of the south-west monsoon. The rabbi or spring crops depend on dew, on irrigation and on the small cold-seasonal showers which occasionally fall between November and March. The principal Kharif crops are spiked millet (Bajra), mixed with the hardy tur, and Jowar. [137]

The agricultural operations vary according to the crops, the rainfall and the soil of the tract. These operations consist of the opening of the land by digging or ploughing, further pulverising the soil, cleaning the fields spreading the manure and mixing it with the soil, sowing the seed or planting the sets or seedlings, inter culturing, weeding, earthing up, irrigating, applying quick-acting manures as top dressings. Spraying or dusting of insecticides watching to protect the crops from birds, stray cattle and wild animals, harvesting, threshing and preparing the crops for the market, and storing. In addition to this, occasional operations for permanent improvement of the soil, such as bunding, levelling trenching, draining the excess water from the soil and reclaiming lands for cultivation are also undertaken by the farmers.[138]

History

The earliest reliable reference to the Pune region is to be found in the copper plate inscriptions of the Rashtrakuta kings. A reliable account of the Pune region before the Rashtrakutas is not available.[139] In the village of Kazad in Indapur Taluka in Pune District, some coins of the Traikutaka King Dahragana (A.D. 465) were discovered.[140] The silver coins discovered at Junnar show that the region was also under the Andhra Kings.[141] A gap of many centuries between the kings and the

---

136 Gazetteer of Bombay State, District Series, Poona District, Government Central Press, Bombay, 1954, p.167.

137 Imperial Gazetteers of India, Ibid., n.134, p.492.

138 Ibid., n.136, p.217.

139 D.R.Gadgil, *Poona A Socio Economic Survey Part I, Economic*, Gokhale Institute of Politics & Economics, Poona, 1945, p.2.

140 *Progress Report of the Archaeological Survey of India*, Western Circle, 31st March, 1907,-8, p.24.

Rashtrakutas. The Rashtrakutas seems to have conquered this region from the Chalukyas in the year A.D. 754.[142]

The Rashtrakutas were overthrown in 973 and Pune passed under the Yadav kings of Daulatabad. That the Pune District was held by the Yadavas, after the Rashtrakutas, is indicated by several monuments of that period still to be seen in the district.[143]

In 1294, Raja Ramdeo, the last Yadava king was attacked by Ala-ud-Din-Khilji. The Yadava king had to submit and to accept the suzerainty of the Delhi sultans. In subsequent expeditions, Sultan Ala-ud-din conquered the whole of the Deccan, Pune and its surrounding parts thus came to be governed by the Mohammedan rulers of Delhi.[144]

Meanwhile, in 1320, the Khalaji sultans at Delhi had been displaced by the Tughlaqs. In the reign of Muhammad Tughlaq,[145] one Hasan Kango Bahamani, a Sardar of Muhammad Tughlaq, raised the standard of rebellion and founded the Bahamani Empire in 1347 and the whole of Deccan came under the rule of the Bahamani kings.[146]

From 148l the Bahamani kingdom began to decline in a few years time it broke up into five different kingdoms. Of these ones was the Nizamshahi of Ahmednagar founded by Malik Ahmad in 1490. Another was the Adilshahi at Bijapur also founded in 1490. Poona and the surrounding territory came under the Nizamshahi kingdom of Ahmednagar.[147]

During the latter part of the sixteenth century, the Bhosles rose to power and eminence under the Nizamshahi kings, Maloji Bhonsle the grandfather of Shivaji and his brother Vithoji, rose from mansabdar to

---

141 Paranis, *Poona in Bygone Days*, The Times of India Press,1921, p.8.

142 A.S.Altekar *Rashtrakutas and their times*, 1934, p.39.

Please see, Rehm C&A, "*How old is Poona?*" *The New Review*, Calcutta, July, 1940, pp.34-41.

143 DR. H.D.Sankaliya, "*Monuments of the Yadava Period in Poona District*", Bulletin of the Deccan College Research Institute, June 1941.

144 D.R. Gadgil, Ibid., n.139, p.4.

145 Prof. Chaghtai, *"Poona in the Muslim Period"*, Bulletin of the Deccan College Research Institute, June 1941, Also recorded by Ferishta.

146 Ibid., n.136, p.219.

147 Ibid., n.141, p.4.

great positions by sheer dint of valour and ability. In 1595, generously Nizam Shah conferred on Maloji and Vithoji the Jagir of Poona and Supa.

Shahaji Bhosle the son of Maloji, who had come to man's estate in the meanwhile had become a prominent Sardar of the Nizam Shahi and had been then serving under Malik Amber. In 1621, Malik Amber ordered him to conquer Poona. In 1620 Poona was governed by one Rayrao on behalf of Bijapur. It was governed from the fort of Bhuleshwar on Daulatmangal. At the news of the termination of the friendly relations between Adilshahi and Nizamshahi Rayrao began to collect money by oppressing the subjects. Shahaji was dispatched against him by Malik Amber to turn him out of the district. On the performance of this service, Shahaji obtained the Mokasa or the Superintending powers of the Parganas of Pune and Shirwal from Nizam Shah.[148]

Shahaji fell out of favour with Malik Amber. Then he began to act as an independent chief in his Jagirs of Pune, Shirwal and Karyat Patas. Initially he suffered and defeated at the hands of Sabaji Anant, the Commander of the Nizam Shahi forces, but soon retrieved this defeat by successfully resisting the forces of Malik Amber which had been sent to out him from his Jagir, Shahaji, then became a Sardar under the Adilshahi kings of Bijapur.[149]

After the death of Ibrahim Adilshah in 1627, the political conditions at Bijapur altered unfavourably for Shahaji. Nizam Shah sent out an invitation to Shahaji requesting him to join him. Shahaji accepted this offer and in 1628 went over to Nizamshah.[150]

Shahaji fought against the Mughals bravely. In 1630, however, Nizam Shah traitorously murdered Lakhoji Jadhav, Shahaji's father-in-law. Shahaji then broke of his connection with the Nizamshah and retired to the districts of Pune and Chakan. He raised the flag of revolt against Adilshahi and Nizamshahi dominions. From several grants it appears that Pune was in his possession up to 1630.[151] Then Murar Jagdeo Pandit, a Sardar of the Adilshahi attacked Pune in 1631 and captured it. He

---

148 K.V. Purandare, *Shiv-Charitra Sahitya, Vol.I*, Bharat Itihas Samshodhan Mandal, Pune, 1926, p.9.

149 PatraSar Sangraha, *Letter No.226, 227*, Bharat Itihas Samshodan Mandal, Pune, 1930.

150 D.R. Gadgil, n.139, p.6.

151 Patrasar Sangraha, *Letter No. 274, 269, 282, 285,* Bharat Itihas Samshodan Mandal, Pune, 1930.

plundered the city and literally raised it to the ground. An Ass driven plough was driven over the whole place.[152]

In December 1636, Adilshah confirmed the Shahaji's Jagir of Chambhargunda, Supa, and Pune, Shahaji served in southern Karnatak under Adilshahi. Shahaji was thus prevented from staying in Pune and managing his own Jagir. In 1637, he appointed Dadoji Konddeo, one of his trustworthy assistants as his representative in Pune. He was in-charge of the management of the Jagir and was assisted by one thousand horsemen under the commander of the Abyssinian Shiddi Halal. It appears that Shahaji's son, Shivaji and Jijabai, Shivaji's mother were sent to Pune three or four years later.[153]

The territories around the city were dilapidated and had gone barren, Dadoji Konddeo, with consummate skill, restored law and order in the land. The fields that had remained fallow for years were again brought under cultivation. The city of Pune again became a habitable place and Dadoji Konddeo constructed a palace in the city, known as Lal Mahal, for his young master, Shivaji. Pune became the central place of the Jagir and began to acquire importance.

Shivaji embarked his activities with the aim of establishing the Maratha Empire only and succeeded in founding a small independent kingdom within a few years. Pune was too open for attack and was bare of any natural defences. Shivaji moved his capital to Raigad.

In 1665 a treaty was signed between Shivaji and the Mughal emperor and Shivaji surrendered a large part of his territories.[154] In 1666, Shivaji had to go Delhi at the imperial behest. Aurangzeb conferred on him his old Jagir of Pune and supa excepting the forts of Kondhana and Chackan.[155] After the death of Shivaji in 1680, Aurangzeb revived his plans of conquering and subjugating the whole of the Deccan. In 1685, Pune was stormed and conquered by Khan Zahan and this time it remained under the Mughals for a long period.[156]

---

152 Selection from the Peshwa Daftar, Vol.31, pp.5032-33.

153 Jadaunath Sarkar, *Shivaji and his times,* Orient longman ltd. Bombay 1973 p .25

154 A.R. Kulkarni, n.61,p.29.

155 S.N. Joshi, *Sabhasad Bakhar,* Chitrashala Press, Pune, 1960, p.43-51.

156 Grant Duff, *History of the Mahrattas, Vol. I*, Reprint, Karan Publication, Delhi, 2000, p.241.

Balaji Vishwanath, who later became the Peshwa, was the subedar of Pune Prant or district in 1699.[157] He was evidently administering the district on behalf of Queen Tarabai. Pune during this period was under a double government. Both the Marathas and the Mughals claimed sovereignty over it. In 1707, Rambhaji Nimbalkar, a subordinate of Nizam-ul-Mulk, captured Pune.[158] For eight years the city was under Rambhaji Nimbalkar. In 1713, the Mughals conferred on him the Jagir of Pune district.

In November 1714, Balaji Vishwanath was made the Peshwa or the Prime Minister.[159] Peshwa became the undisputed master of Pune. According to the grant made by the Mughal Emperor in 1720, Pune became one of Shahu's eight swaraj districts.

In 1720, Balaji Vishwanath died and his son Bajirao I became the Peshwa.[160] He felt a pressing need for a central place or capital from which he could conduct his far-flung affairs. Bajirao I fixed on Pune and Shahu approved the choice. In 1725 Shahu conferred on Bajirao- I the Jagir of Pune.[161] Pune as the capital of the Marathas now began to expand and grow. In 1730 Bajirao built for himself the Shaniwarwada (Palace) in Pune.[162] In the reign of Balaji Bajirao, son of Bajirao- I, with the growing prosperity of the Maratha realm the city expanded still more.

In 1761 however, the Marathas sustained a mortal defeat at Panipat.[163] The Peshwa died of this severe shock in the same year. He was succeeded by his young son Madhavrao. Taking advantage of the disorganization after the death of the Peshwa, the Nizam attacked the Marathas. The chaos and the disorganization of the Maratha forces helped the Nizam

---

According to Jedhe Shakavali, Poona was captured in 1683.

157 Bharat Itihas Samshodhan Mandal, Third Conference, Pune, 1838, p.150.

Selection from Peshwa Daftar, Vol.7, p.793.

158 Grant Duff, n.156, p.316.

159 Ibid., pp.314, 316.

160 A.R. Kulkarni, n.61, p.89.

161 G.C. Vad, D.B. Parasnis, (ed*), Selection from the Satara Rajas and Peshwa Diaries*, Vol.I, p.47.

162 Grant Duff Grant, n. 156, p.506-530.

163 Jadunath Sarkar, *Fall of the Mughal Empire*, Vol. II, K.P. Bagachi & Co., Calcutta, p.360.

directly attack and overwhelmed Pune in 1763.[164] Madhavrao however, was a man of ability and soon turned the tables by inflicting a crushing defeat on the Nizam at Rakshas Bhavan in1765. The last two decades of the eighteenth century witnessed the rise of Nana Phadnavis who ably governed the realm for the young Peshwa, Sawai Madhavrao.[165]

In 1795, Sawai Madhavrao committed suicide and was succeeded by Bajirao- II. After him, the Peshwas were incapable of controlling and organizing the various Maratha Sardars. Sardar Yeshwantrao bore down on Pune and captured it in 1802. He plundered and looted Pune. The Peshwa fled away to Bassein and signed a treaty with the English. This treaty was practically the end of the independent Maratha Empire.

According to this treaty, the English were to restore the Peshwa to the throne. So the English forces under General Wellesley invested and captured Pune on 20 April 1803, and the Peshwa was reinstalled. The Peshwa began to feel the growing burden of the English yoke. His attempts at throwing it away were unsuccessful and in November 1817, the English forces occupied Pune and deprived the Peshwa of whatever power he had.[166]

British came to Maharashtra on 16th May 1817, the Deccan British resident, Elphinstone gave an order to Bajirao, "you accept the new treaty otherwise be ready or war." Helpless Bajirao signed the treaty on 13 June 1817. Bajirao came under the control of British. In this way, the Maratha power was abolished in Pune after the Battle of Koregaon on 1st January 1818 in Pune District.[167]

Koregaon Village

Sirur Taluka of Pune District, Maharashtra, lying between 18^0 29' and 19^0 2' N and 74^0 35'E, with an area of 601 sq. miles. It contains one town,

---

164 Selection from the Peshwa Daftar, Vol. 38, Letter Nos. 87, 94,95.

165 Ibid., n.141 p.10.

166 Grant Duff, n. 156, p.306.

167 G.S. Sardesai, *Poona Residency Correspondence, Vol.X, p.37, Vol.XIII, Part II, (1816-1818). Letter Nos, 133, 47,* ed. By Government Central Press, Bombay, 1958.

P.C. Gupta, *Bajirao II and the East India Co.*, Oxford University Press, London, 1939, p.203.

Secret Political Diary, Maharashtra state Archives, File No.148, pp.6078-79.

Sirur the headquarters and 78 villages including Talegaon-Dhamdhere. Sirur consists of stony uplands seamed towards the centre by rugged valleys but towards its river boundaries sloping into more open plains. The chief features are low hills and uplands the low hills are occasionally rugged and step; the uplands, in some parts are poor and stony while in other parts have rich tracts of good soil. In the south-east corner of the country opens out with gentle undulations into a fairly plains. It is throughout sparsely wooded. The prevailing soil is a light friable grey, freely mixed with gravel. The best upland soils are very productive, even with a comparatively scanty rainfall which averages only 22 inches annually.[168]

Koregaon village situated in the Sirur Taluka of Pune district, Maharashtra, situated in 18^{0} 39" N, and 74^{0} 4'E, on the right bank of the Bhima river 16 miles Northeast of Pune city.

This area has witnessed the last three battles in the neighbourhood, which led to the collapse of the Peshwa power, fought on January 1, 1818.[169] Captain Stauton on his march to strengthen Colonel Burr arrived at Koregaon on the morning after a fatiguing night march with a detachment of 500 Bombay native infantry, 300 irregular horse and 2 six-pouders manned by 24 Madras artillerymen. He found the whole army of the Peshwa,[170] some 20,000 strong, encamped on the opposite bank of the Bhima river. The Maratha troops, mostly Arabs, were immediately sent across against the exhausted handful of soldiers, destitute of both provisions and water. The engagement was kept up throughout the day and resulted in discomfiture and retreat of the Marathas. The remarkable feature of this engagement was that the British troops were all natives,[171] without any European support, excepting the 24 artillerymen, of whom 20 were killed and wounded, of 7 officers engaged, 4 were killed and

---

168 Imperial gazetteers of India, Provincial series. Bombay Presidency, Vol.I, Government Printing Calcutta, 1909, Reprint Usha Publications, New Delhi, 1985, p.503.

169 Secret Political Diary, *Maharashtra State Archives, file No.148*, pp.6078-79.

170 G.S. Sardesai, Ibid., 167, p. 37.

171 Source material on Dr. Babasaheb Ambedkar and the Movement of Untouchables Vol. I, Dr. Babasaheb Ambedkar source material publication committee, the Education Department, Government of Maharashtra, Bombay, 1982, p.227.

wounded, total casualties 276 killed, wounded and missing. The gallant fight is now commemorated by a stone obelisk.[172]

This chapter helps in understanding the remote culture and military background of the Maharashtrian society. In the final stage of my book in-depth discussion about geography and society of Pune district has been discussed while dealing with the Koregaon battle. This discussion justifies understand the culture, the working conditions and socio-political history to establish the line between military and culture of the region. This chapter helps to understand the Military Culture in Maharashtra.

172 See Obelisk at Koregaon, Pune, Maharashtra, India.

MAHARASHTRA AND IT'S MILITARY CULTURE.

The present chapter deals with the village communities in Maharashtra, their relationship with the defence activities related to the state administration. By analyzing the activities of the Military Culture in Maharashtra.

To understand under the investigation of the Military Culture, it is necessary to know the various background like races, their nature and duties in order to know and understand military services in Maharashtra and military culture of Maharashtra.

Military organizations and services in village society

Economically a village was a self-sufficient unit. Military culture began from the village being the main centre of the socio-economic activities.[1] Village land was divided into many units such as Gram, Dehe, Mauja, Pargrana called Budruk or Brahak and Khurda or Lagghu.[2] There were village officers looking after the village administration.

Hawaldar, Majumdar, Komavisdar, Karkoon (clerk) Deshmukh or Desai, Deshpande, or Desh-Kulkarni, Patil, Kulkarni, Chaugula, Shete-Mahajan, Mirasdar (a holder of hereditary property), Upari (stranger, outsider) called Darshak were also village officers.[3] As per the religious guideline the Maharashtrian society developed and reorganized into Grams, watans, and castes. The division of the society was made on the basis of caste and were settled in a particular area in villages. The low caste communities such as Mahars, Mangs and Chambhars lived outside the village. They were considered as untouchables.[4] The upper caste lived in the centre of

---

1 Goodine, *A Report on the Deccan Village Communities*, Bombay, 1852, p.4.

2 T.N.Atre, *Gao-Gado* , Published by H.V. Mote, Bombay, 1959, p.1.

3 Jadunath Sarkar, *Shivaji and his Times*, Orient Longman, Bombay, Reprint, 1992, pp.21, 27-66.

J.G. Duff *The History of Maharattas*, Vol.I Karan Publication, New Delhi, 2000, p.22.

4 Sudha V. Desai, *Social Life in Maharashtra under the Peshwa*, Popular Prakashan, Bombay, 1980, p.37, also see, V.K.Rajwade, Marathyanchya Itihasachi Sadhane, Vol.XX, Bharat Itihas Samshodhan Mandal, Pune, 1915, p.54.

the village. They were the Brahmins, Patils, Kulkarnis, Deshmukhs and Deshpandes, Chaugulas and other Vatandars.[5] Thus further division was created. Alutedars and Balutedars Carpenter, Blacksmith, Shoemaker, Milkman, Koli, Leatherworkers and their sub-castes were Mochi, Chambhar, Dhor, Barber, Tailor, Oilmen, Weavers, Mali, Washermen, Goldsmith. There were also nomadic tribes wandering like Garudi (Juggler), Kolhati (entertainment class), Bhilla, Pardhi (Hunter) tribes. Mahar and Mang were also there. Merchant class people lived by the side of the road.[6] Society was built upon the occupation and occupation was divided into castes. Each caste produced their own saint.[7]

Watan was given directly from the king,[8] against the services rendered by the individuals. The Brahmans were given watan for their religious services, but they were not allowed for agriculture. They had to give their land to tillers for cultivation, out of which Khoti system emerged. Khots were called Mirasdars in Deccan.

Under the hereditary system of work the low caste people suffered. After Brahmins the Marathas were placed in the second position, they considered themselves as Kshatriya and were also divided into different Maratha family and most of them were holding a watan.[9] Watan was considered as original identity. They were divided into different sub-castes known as 96 clan classes.[10] Though they had the right to use the Vedas, all the religious ceremonies were performed under the guidance of

---

5 Duff, Grant, Ibid., n.3 P.23.

6 S.G., Tulpule, *Lila-Charitra, Ed., Part 2*, Suvichar Publication Mandal Pune, 1966, p.7, 53, 76, 83, 84.

7 M.G. Ranade *The Rise of the Maratha Power and other Essays*, Bombay University Press, 1961, p.10.

8 K.M. Shrimali., *Agrarian Structure in Central India and the Northern Deccan, A.D., 300-500, A Study of Vataka Inscriptions*, Munshiram Manohar Publication, New Delhi, 1987, p.6.

9 Nirmal Kumar, Phadkule, *Lokhitwadi- Karya ani Kartutva* (Marathi), Continental Publication, 1973, p.125.

10 C.G. Vad, *Peshwa Diaries,* Vol.III, Under the order of the Deccan Vernacular trans Society, Poona, by D.B.Parasnis, published by the Society under the permission of the Government of Bombay, 1970, letter No.11139, p.103; letter No.137, p.101.

Brahmins.[11] Marathas believed in superstitions and placed themselves superior to the lower castes.

In the Indian social system, the Vaishya comes under third category they belong to trading community they were known as Wani. The fourth class was (Shudra, Chaturvarna,). Thus, the society was divided on caste with watertight compartments in the villages of Maharashtra, twelve Alutedars and twelve Balutedars mostly belonging to Shudra caste. Thus, Brahmin and non-Brahmin communities are co-existed in Maharashtra. Caste system was observed strictly in the social life. Defaulters were punished by throwing them out of the caste. The position of the Shudras was pitiable.

Out of Shudra caste untouchable class was created. They were treated worse than animals.[12] They were legally prevented from education and were not allowed to perform any religious practices by the Brahmins[13]. Society was forced to lead and believing the importance of God, Manu and Vedas, people became ignorant, illiterate and became totally dependent on Brahmins.[14]

Unequal development in villages

The village communities were developed on the basis of caste system accordingly economy was distributed and closely related to caste. Share of Baluta (Baluta is the system of yearly payment in form of grain in response to the duties taken from the low caste people) was distributed on the basis of caste which was unchangeable. It was the duty to do traditional work of the ancestors and not take up any other professions.[15]

Untouchables: This caste has existed at the lowest of the low and most illiterate and neglected group. They are identified as Ramoshis, Mahars, Mangs and Dhors. They were also called Atishudras or Antyajas and were the most despised caste, not permitted even to live within the outskirts of

---

11 Bal Krishna, *Shivaji, the Great, Vol. II, Part I, Shivaji's Coronation*, Arya Book Depot, Kolhapur, 1939, p.5.

12 Ibid., n.11, letter No.155, p.111.

13 Mukund G. Marajkar, *Manusmriti*, Chirashala Press, Pune, (Shake 1849), 1927, p.14.

14 G.S. Ghurye, *Caste, Class and Occupation*, Popular Prakashan, Pune, 1932, p.110.

15 Sudha Kaldate, , *Bharatiya Samaj Rachna, (Marathi)*, Bharat Prakashan, Aurangabad, (lst ed.), 1976, p.160.

the village, they had to take their residence outside the village wall. It has been recorded that Mahars were not allowed to enter within the gates of Poona between 3 p.m. and 9 a.m. their long shadows of caste in the street should defile the persons of the high caste. They were even required to carry an earthen pot tied around their neck into which they had to spit, for their sputum was defiling and a thorny branch in their hand, with which they had to sweep off their defiling footprints.[16]

Caste was also related to the occupation. According to Nesfield:[17] "Occupation as the exclusive basis of caste distinctions, while others thought hereditary occupation to be, if not an exclusive basis of caste, an important contributing factor to the emergence of the caste system. Be that as it may, one cannot deny the close association between caste and occupation".

Over the period of time caste-based occupation was considered traditional and rightful occupation and abandoning one right for another perhaps for being more lucrative, was not considered due to caste right. Furthermore, no caste would allow its members to follow any calling which was degrading or impure.[18] Besides such moral restraints and social check of one caste followed strictly as Dr. Ghurye seem to rightly observe:

> "*Restrictions put by other castes which did not allow members other than those of their own to follow their calling also acted as a restraint on the choice of one's occupation*".[19]

---

16 Ibid., p.11.

M.P., Mangudkar, *Maharashtratil Samaj Prabodhan Ani Chhatrapati Shahu Maharajanche Karya,* Pune University, Pune, 1975, pp.118-119.

For details please see, Ambedkar B.R., Annihilation of castes, Thakkar & Co., Bombay, 1944.

Who were the Shudras and how they became the fourth varna, Thakkar & Co., Bombay, 1946, p.xi-xxii.

17 G. S. Ghurye *Caste class and occupation* Popular Prakashan, Pune 1932. P. 14.

18 J.H. Hutton, *Caste in India: Its nature, function and origin*, Oxford University Press, London, 1946, p.15.

19 G.S. Ghurye, *Caste, Class and Occupation,* Popular Prakashan, Pune, 1932, p.15.

The twelve Balutedars and eighteen Alutedars (artisans) were regarded as servants of the village communities and their dues to serve communities and in return, they were paid in grain and land in lieu of their duties.

This system helped to carry out the traditions which formed internal rules strictly. Those who refused to obey this order were punished heavily. This system was controlled and followed by every member of society.[20]

Economically, the village community in Maharashtra was self-sufficient. There were two principal tenures by which the village land was held. The Mirasi or Thalavahika (landholders) and Upari people came from other villages and called themselves outsiders.

The villages were divided and identified on the strength of population as Deha, Manja and Kasba. Kashba was a bigger village with a marketplace. Generally, there were two natural divisions in a village, the one known as Pandhar or Pandhari, the residential site, and the other known as Kali, which covered the agricultural land and pastures. The Peth is known as the big market town, had two seperate divisions called Munjeri and Mohatarfa, the latter representing the urban parts. This division was not only physical but also functional, the representatives of the cultivating classes, whereas the Mohatarfa or the market area was under the headship of Shethe and Mahajan who also representatives of the trading community.[21]

The village land was divided into fields, Gayran(The wasteland), and useful for agriculture. Every village had wasteland which was used by all as common grazing ground for the cattle by the villagers. The small villages were known as Majre, Pada, or Wadi. The entire set-up of village organization was mainly based on land. A village was essentially a community of farmers, with the addition of a few traders and artisans required to satisfy their daily needs and a small administrative staff. Thus, there were mainly three types of people (a) The Cultivators, (b) Artisans, (c) Village officials.[22] Moreover, the status and position of members of

---

20 V.S., Shinde, *Dharma, Jivan, Jatvadnyan (Marathi)* Maharashtra government Social, Cultural Department, Bombay, 1979, p.228.

21 Iravati Karve, *Pune Nagar Samshodhan, Vol.XXIV, Issue I*, Bharat Itihas Samshodhan Mandal, Pune, Published Quarterly, Vol.XXIV, issue I, p.116-117.

22 Sudha V. Desai, *Social Life under the Peshwa*, Popular Prakashan, Bombay, 1980, p.3.

the village community depended on the nature of their relationship to the land which was represented in the case of the cultivating classes.[23]

The property was acquired by hereditary is right and by sale. The landholder mirasdar could not sell land and dispose of his land while he continued to pay the land tax. If disposed, he had a right to reclaim the estates, even after a gap of a long period.[24] Uparis acquired the land on a temporary and lease basis. An Upari was only a tenant and not an owner of the land he cultivated.

In those time village had fixed boundaries and were carefully marked. The pattern of the organization of village communities and the function of its officers remained unchanged during the Yadavas, Chalukyas, (the Hindu dynasties which ruled over the Deccan before the advent of the Muslims) and continued the same during the Maratha period. The nature of the duties of the village the officers like the headman, clerk and watchman remained unchanged. In the Maratha, period justice was dispensed through a Panchayat held in a village at the common place – Chowdi.[25] The decision of the Panchayat was binding, and all villagers were held responsible to follow the decision for good or bad.

Officials of the village communities

The Village community was administered by their own officers under the paternal and tax supervision of a set of government officers. The work of these officers again was supervised by the officers of Huzur Daftar[26] supposed to be under the direct control of the Peshwa through his Karbhari. This system (daftar or secretarial) was therefore considered as base of the village communities. Under this system, the village communities worked in a chain of hereditary and non-hereditary government officials.[27]

---

23 Iravati Karve and Y.B. Damle, Y.B., *Group Relations in the Village Community*, Deccan College, Pune, 1963, pp.25-28.

24 M. Elphinston, *Territory Conquered from the Peshwa*, Reprint Oriental Publishers, Delhi, 1973, p.18.

25 Chowdi, A public meeting place for village center. Moreland, W.H., Agrarian system of Moslam India a historical essay, Central Depot, Allahabad, 1929, pp.11-19.

26 Ibid n.4 p.41,

27 S.N. Sen, *Administrative system of the Marathas,* K.P. Bagachi and Co., Calcutta, Second reprint in 2002, p.128.

Patil

Patil was the chief of the village. He was also called as Headman, the Chief Revenue Officer, the Chief Police Magistrate, and also use to perform the job of Chief Judicial Officer. He acted as an intermediary between the villagers and the government of Peshwas and served as a link between the village and the suzerain state. In the village, he had the advantage of acting as the exponent of the Peshwa's authority. The other officers like Kamavisdar or the Mamlatdar were below his power thus he appeared as the authorized representative of his village.

As a judicial officer, it was the duty of the Patil to induce the parties in a suit to come to an amicable settlement and if an amicable settlement or arbitration suite failed, he referred the case to the Panchayat.[28]

As a police officer, he inquired into cases of theft and robbery with the help of his assistant the village watchman.

Thus Patil was, however, not an elected official, nor could he be appointed by the government, it has been continuing job since as professional occupation of caste. The office which could be sold and purchased, and sometimes under pressure for money, unable to retain, yet reluctant to part with all the rights and perquisites of his office. The Patil disposed of some of them by selling and retained others.

The Patil under the Marathas was responsible for the discovery and restoration of all stolen properties within his jurisdiction, failing which he had to make adequate compensation for the loss. He could, however, escape by tracing the thief to the next village when responsibilities were transferred to the headman and inhabitants of that village.

Kulkarni

The position of Kulkarni was next to the Patil. Kulkarni invariably belongs to a Brahman caste was working as a clerk under the guidance of Patil. He was also known as a village record keeper. He shared with the Patil the risk of imprisonment and oppression at the hands of the enemy and unprincipled government officials.[29]

Maharashtra State Gazetteers, *History of Maratha Period*, Part III, Directorate of Government Printing Stationery and Publication, Bombay, 1968, p.215,

28 Bharat Itihas Samshodhan Mandal, Tritiya Sammelan Vrita, Pune, 1927, p.521.

29 A.R. Kulkarni, *Medieval Maharashtra*, Books & Books, New Delhi, 1996, p.170.

Chaugula

In the hierarchical position, Chaugula stands in the third position below Kulkarni. Chaugula assisted Patil in his duties and also had to take care of the Kulkarni's records.[30]

Mahar

Mahar, low caste village official was an important person in the village. He always helped Patil in revenue collection, summoning up the villagers to the office of the Patil or chawdi. He was also called a yeskar (watchman).[31]

Potdar Sonar

The fifth rank of village officer was the Potdar, known as a sonar or goldsmith by caste. His duty was to test the genuineness of the coins, and gold or rather to see whether the coins really had the prescribed weight and proportion of metal. The Potdar services were more necessary to the Central Government than to the villagers.[32]

Militant Races

Military is required to serve the military. It is related to the self-defense and state defence. We have discussed them. The Following communities in Maharashtra served for Military services.

Brahmins

Brahmins basically perform the priestly duties under Hindu religion. In Maharashtra, Brahmins are divided in Charak Brahmins and Konkan Brahmins.

Charak Brahmins: They belong to the Krishna Yajurveda and found in Nagpur region only. They are landholders, professionals like Doctors and Teachers.

---

30 Grant Duff, *History of the Mahrattas, Vol.I*, Karan Publication, New Delhi, 2000, p.23 also see, Ibid, n.4, p.44, also see V.K.Rajwade, Marathyanchye Itihasachi Sadhane, Vol.XV, Atmaram Chhapkhama, Dhule, 1912, p.241.

31 Grant Duff, *History of the Mahrattas*, Vol.I, Karan Publication, New Delhi, 2000, please see, footnote p.23.

32 S.N.Sen, *Administrative system of the Marathas*, K.P. Bagachi & Co., reprint, Calcutta, 2002, p.139.

Konkan Brahmins: The Sarasvat, the Karhada, and the Citpavan were all originally dwellers of the West Coast. The Saraswats are found from Malvan to South Kanara. The Karhada is a comparatively small number of sub-caste of Brahmins. Their home is the region between Malvan and Sangameshwar near the West Coast.[33]

The Citpavans: The Citpavans have their home in the region from Malvan to Bombay. They migrated to Deccan plains during the period of Shivaji and Peshwas and are now found in almost all the upland districts of the Maratha country. Their number decreased during the Nizam's Dominions and eastern central provinces.[34]

The Deshasta Brahmins[35] are divided into two great endogamous groups (a) The Rigvedi Desastha, and (b) the Sukla Yajurvedi Brahmins. The appellation Desasthan means that they belong to Desa i.e. the upland plateau of the Maharashtra and not to the Konkan. The Rigvedi Brahmans seem to be the older in the population of the Maratha country. They are found all over in Maratha country from the river Tapi to Krsna along with the Western bills and inside country into the Nizam's dominion and Bearers.

Prabhu

The full name of the caste is Candraseniya Kayastha Prabhu (CKP) this is to distinguish it from the Pathare Prabhu.[36]

The Kayasthas are found all over northern India and are most influential caste. They played a prominent role in the field of education, law, medicine and writing. Being professional writers, they were always engaged in the court services of the Hindu kings of India and later on at the court of the Islamic rulers.[37]

---

33 *Maharashtra State Gazetteers, History III Maratha Period* , Government of Maharashtra, Bombay, 1967, p.210.

Arthur, Crawford, *Our Troubles in Poona and the Deccan*, Archibald Constable & Co., Westminister, 1897, p.115.

34 Ibid., p.125.

35 Ibid., p.115.

36 Prabhus worked in Military service of Marathas and as well as in the British army. They filled most of the Military post in the British period.

37 Ibid., n.34, p.137.

The Kayasthas during the Maratha fought against Aurangzeb and distinguished their loyalty and staunch support to the ruler such as Shivaji, Sambhaji and Rajaram became great warriors during the period.

Prabhus

The Prabhus are known for their excellent secretaries and accountants' services, and they were also soldiers in the Maratha Army. Baji Prabhu Deshpande and Balaji Avji were the distinguished members of this caste. Baji was soon won over by Shivaji and was appointed commander of his personal retinue. In 1660 he immortalized his name in the battle of Ghodkhind.[38]

They are mostly concentrated in the region north of Bombay and are found in great numbers in the cities of Bombay and Poona. Some families are found in the villages near the Western Ghats where they hold Inam lands. Thus, a Brahmin took to the profession of arms in Maharashtra.

Marathas

The Marathas are the most important caste. They are numerous and widely spread in Maharashtra. Castewise they differ, not only in appearance and language but even physics observance. They all acknowledge each other as caste fellows and this unity and sympathy must have contributed greatly to their success as a united force in building the nation.

Generally, Maratha served themselves in the military as well as in civil service of Government were called Kshatriyas. They wear a sacred thread and perform Hindu rituals.[39]

The overwhelming majority of officers and soldiers hailed from Kulin Marathas. The Shilharas, Chalukyas, Mauryas, Kadambas, Parmars and Yadavas were of the families and well known in India. They had in their veins, the blood of the Kshatriya race. Hereditarily were determined to make efforts and struggle hard in life to rise.

In Marathas, the martial spirit is seen all through history. They disinclined to take up the service in the British Army. Their young men eagerly

---

38 *Sulabha Vishwa Kosha, Part IV*, , p.16, Madya Yugin Charitra Kosha, p.547, Prabhu Ratna Mala, p.56.

M.B. Deopujare, *Shivaji and the Maratha Art of War*, Vidarbha Sanshodhan Mandal, Nagpur, 1973, p. 262.

39 Herbert Risley, Herbert, *The People of India*, 2nd ed. Oriental Books, Delhi, 1969, p.87

sought and readily obtained employment in the forces maintained by the principal Maratha States.[40]

Rajput

The Rajputs of Deccan are few in number and are mostly descendants from soldiers who accompanied with Muhammadan conquerors.

The general name for them is Dekhani Pardesis. They are serving mostly as peons and sepoys and few of them are some of them, cultivators. They are very good policemen, uniting the smartness and dash of the Rajput with the shrewdness and hardihood of the Marathas.[41]

Dhangars and Hetkari

The Dhangars of Maharashtra have maintained their separate identity and also do not mix well with other castes. They maintain distance with other castes and neither eat nor intermarry with other caste.

The Dhangar community produced great soldiers. The famous Malharrao Holkar was a Dhangar by caste. Herdsmen by profession, these people had a thorough knowledge of the provinces. The jungle tracts were familiar to them. Their wandering habit and knowledge of the fauna and fauna of the country had the effect of making them good hunters and marksmen. Endurance was their outstanding quality.

The Hetkaris made good musketeers. They fought obstinately under Baji during the siege of Purandar.

There are several divisions of Dhangar's or shepherds. Dhangars are chiefly inhabited in Talukas of Indapur, Bhimthadi, Purandhar lying between the Bhima and Nira Rivers. They gave up pastoral life became cultivators, and performed their services to Patils and became soldiers at need. The royal family of Indore belongs to this race and derives the name of Holkar.[42]

Mahar

The Mahar are most important martial race in Maharashtra. The term Maharashtra means "country of the Mahars".[43]

---

40 Crawford Arthur, *Our Troubles in Poona and the Deccan*, West Minister, Archibald Constable and Co., London, 1897, p.144.

41 *Journal of Indian Antiquity*, Vol. II Swati Publication, Reprint, Delhi, 1985, p.54.

42 Crawford Arthur, Ibid., n.40, p.203.

Mahar's played an important role in Medieval and Maratha History of Maharashtra. In due course of time, Mahars were pushed into untouchable class and did the lowest work in the society. They actively participated in military services during the reign of Malik Amber, Shivaji, Peshwa and British.[44]

Mahars duty was to guard the village boundaries. He participated in maintaining the public peace, order and health, as watchman.[45] He performed the role of the scavenger or messenger, he guided travellers and did road repair work and guided public treasure and correspondence.[46]

Matanga

Mang is also an untouchable caste[47] scattered all over the region and they are numerous in numbers. They live in a quarter called Mangvada separate from the Mahars and all others. They are ranked lower than the Mahars, rivalry exists between them.[48]

The Mang's are hard-working community, having no permanent source of livelihood. They fear as sorcerers. They make and sell ropes from sisal.[49] They also play music and singing song; they weave bamboo baskets and perform the duties of scavengers and hangmen. They eat flesh of dead cattle and hogs and are held as unclean by all.

---

43 N.D. Kamble, *Deprived Castes and their struggle for equality*, Ashish Publishing House, Delhi, 1983, p.l.

44 C.B. Khairmode, *Ashprushyancha lashkari Peshwa.* Maharashtra Rajya Sahitya Ani Sanskriti Mandal, Mumbai, 1992, p.l.

45 Molesworth, *Marathi English Dictionary*, Preface, Shubhada Saraswat 3rd ed. Pune, 1975, p.23.

46 Khairmode, Ibid., n.45, p.1.

V.K.Rajwade, *Marathyancha Itihasachi Sadhane*, Vol.XV, Chirashala Press, Pune, 1921, p.272.

47 R.V. Russell and Hiralal, *The Tribes and castes in Central Provinces of India,* Vol.IV reprint Cosmo Publication, Delhi, 1975, pp.184-85.

48 Ibid.

49 Maharashtra State Gazetteers, *Part III, Maratha Period*, Directorate of Govt. Central Press, Bombay, 1968, p.215.

Mangs were also recruited in the army by Chattarapati Shivaji and later on in the Peshwe and British army.[50]

Charmakar

Charmakar is an important community in Maharashtra,[51] those we find rare reference of their services to the military establishment. Their main job was to provide durable shoes to the soldiers to walk into the jungles. This community basically was economically self-sufficient by their own profession. Hence their attraction towards military was not found in the earlier literature, but in the period of Chhatrapati Shivaji they fought in battles with enemy one important fort found name Chambhargad in Mahad near Raigad.

However, at the end of the 17th and 18th century, we do find their references with British Military services.[52]

Agris

The Agris are mostly found in Konkan, they appear to be on terms of equality with the Marathas of the Dekhan.[53] Agris are also known as Agale or Kharpatil. They are mostly found in Thana, Kolaba and Janjira. They have no exogamous subdivision's abele families who have the same surname and who observe common mourning.[54]

Agari's claim to be Kshatriya, but their small size and dark colour, their habit of drinking liquor and their belief in un-Brahman gods are marked enough to make them rank as a local or early tribe.

Bhandaris

The Bhandaris were organized under their chiefs called Bhongle. They were enlisted by the English to form the bodyguard of the Governor. The Bhandaris were good seamen. Maya Nayak Bhandari was one of Shivaji's

---

50 C.B.Khairmode, Ibid. n.44, p.1.

51 Russell and Hiralal, Ibid., n.47, Vol. II, pp.407-408.

52 Khairmode C.B., Ibid., n.44, p.1

53 Indian Antiquity, Vol.II, Swati Publication, reprint, Delhi, 1985, p.54.

54 Iravati Karve, *Group relation in Village Community*, Deccan College, Pune, 1963, p.19.

chief naval officers, who took part in the war with the English. Most of the Bhandaris are toddy tappers by profession.[55]

Bhil

They are an indigenous or non-Aryan tribe who have been much in contact with the Hindus and is consequently well known. The name Bhil seems to occur for the first time about A.D. 600. It is supposed to be derived from the Dravidian word for a bow, which is the characteristic weapon of the tribe.[56]

The position of the Bhils as the earliest residents of the country was also recognized by their employment in the capacity of village watchmen. One of the duties of this official is to know the village boundaries and keep watch and ward over them. They are supposed that the oldest class of residents and would know them best. The Bhils worked in the office of Mankar, the superior village watchman in Nimar and also in Berar.[57]

Grant Duff states that the Ramosi or Bhil was employed as village guard by the Marathas and the Ramoshis were a professional caste of village policemen.[58]

When the Marathas began to occupy Central India, they treated the Bhils with great cruelty. A Bhil caught in a disturbed part of the country was without inquiry flogged and hanged.[59] Hundreds were thrown over high cliffs, and large bodies of them assembled under promise of pardon, were beheaded or shot. In Khandesh, during the disturbed period of the wars of Scindia and Holkar, about 1800 Bhils had taken themselves to highway robbery and lived in bands either in mountains or in villages immediately beneath them. The revenue contractors were unable or unwilling to spend money on the maintenance of soldiers to protect the country, and the Bhils in a very short time became so bold as to appear in bands of

---

55 Ketkar: *Maharashtriya Dnyan Kosh*, Vol.VI. Maharashtriya Dnyan Kosh Mandal, Nagpur, 1925, p. The Bhandaris had various surnames. Mahanayak was one name from which the word Maynak comes. Sarang and Tandel were other names. Udaji Padwal and Sawalya Tandel are famous names. The Tandel was the head of the crew. The Sarang observed the direction of the wind and gave warning of storms.

56 Ibid., n. 28, p.278.

57 Ibid., p.282.

58 Grant J. Duff, Ibid., n.37, p.24.

[59] 59Sen Ibid., n.28, p.282.

hundreds and attack towns, carrying either cattle or hostages, for whom they demanded handsome ransoms.

Koli

Koli is the name given to entirely two different groups, the sea-fisher of the West Coast, while the other is a very widespread tribe which is found in the whole of the Sahyadri and Satpura ranges. They are mentioned as 'Kolla' in Sanskrit are described there as 'petty warriors of mountains and jungles. During the Maratha period they were guardians of the middle reaches of the hill forts and as such received land from the rulers.[60]

The Koli community made a substantial contribution to the success of the Swarajya movement. The Kolis were divided into two sections: the hill-dwellers and the coast dwellers. In their mountain haunts, they were always difficult to control. The Bahmanis kept them pacified by mild methods. The Koli chiefs were given the rank of Sardars and helm charge of the hill tracts.[61] The region in which the Kolis are still found in large number is known as Kolvan, in the Nasik district. Around the forts of Sinhgad and Purandar, they had their homes and the Chhatrapati made use of them to guard the approaches to the forts. The Purandar Kolis were roused by their chief to revolt against the Mughals. Aurangzeb put down the revolt mercilessly and made a pile of the heads cut off. The 'Koli Chabutra' in Purandar fort still stands as a monument to the Kolis' love of independence and their excitable temper.

The coast dwelling Kolis were daring mariners. They had full knowledge of the configuration of the coast, its shoals and rocks. The owner of the celebrated Janjira fort was a Koli named Ram Patil. His followers were attacked by the Muslims and lost their stronghold.

The Sindhudurg site was pointed out by a Koli(fishermen). Shivaji's statue at Sindhudurg bears witness to his great love for this community. He is shown wearing therein a Koli headgear. Leva Patil, a Sona Koli, was invited by Subhanji Kharade Sarnobat and Subhanji Mohite, Havildar of Padmadurg, to enter the fleet. Moropant Peshwa had made a plan to scale the Janjira fort with the help of Laya Patil. The enterprising Koli Chief executed his part very well. But the Peshwa failed to turn up in time. Shivaji honoured the by bestowing on him the title of Sar Patil and the

---

60 Iravati Karve, *Group Relations in Village Community*, Deccan College, Pune, 1963, p.38.

61 M.B.Deopujari, *Shivaji and the Maratha Art of War*, Vidarbha Samshodhan Mandal, Nagpur, 1973, p.263.

distinction of riding in a palanquin. As the Koli chief would not accept the present, Shivaji got a new ship built and named it 'Palkhi'.[62]

Hill Kolis

The hill Kolis of the Ghats claim the title of Maratha with more persistence and their neighbours deny it to them. The Mawale swordsmen who laid the foundations of Raja Shivaji's power were mostly of this race, they are non-Aryan and they dislike distant service which they share with most Indian hill and forest tribes. They were prevented from having any part in the subsequent extension of the empire, which was affected chiefly by the horsemen of the plains. [63]

Ramoshi

The Ramoshi caste also come under the untouchable community. Ramoshi act as village watchmen in some parts of Maharashtra. Ramoshis are to be found in Satara around Khatau Mhaguad, Malavadi, the fort of Mahimangad and town of Phaltan. The Ramoshis in their primitive state led a roving unsettled life.

During Shivaji's struggles with the Muhammadans, the Ramoshis flocked in numbers to the high standard. The Ramoshis always favoured Shivaji's interests and on many occasions exerted themselves greatly in his service and caused great annoyance to the Muhammadans.

They plundered the Muhammadans during the night, attacking the houses or tents.[64] Under the guidance of their principal leaders, and carried off much valuable property including horses and camels and sometimes Elephants.[65] Ramoshis were employed under the rule of Shivaji.

After Shivaji captured Purandhar, he sent a detachment from Sinhgad accompanied by a party of Ramoshis to surprise attack the Muhammadan

---

62 S.M. Edwards, The Gazetteer of Bombay City and Island, Times Press, Bombay, 1909, p.216.

63 Indian Antiquery, Vol.II, Swati Publications, reprint, Delhi, 1985, p.154.

64 Arthur Crawford, Ibid., n.40, p.217.

65 A letter without date addressed by a Satara Raja of Vardoji, one of the ancesters of the late Umaji Naik, applauding the dexterity with which Vardoji had plundered the Muhammadans commandant at Shirval. His steady conduct subsequently inviting him to the Raja's presence in order that Vardoji might be rewarded for having discharged his duty. So gallantly was preserved in the house till 1834.

garrison and capture the fort. With much difficulty, they scrambled unobserved up a steep part of the hill and a Ramoshi contrived to ascent the wall and attach to the top the rope ladders which they carried with them. But as the Ramoshis were ascending the wall the sentry in the vicinity described them and cut the ropes and the escalading party was all precipitated to the bottom. Some being killed and the rest desperately wounded.[66]

The Ramoshis were included in Shivaji's list of hereditary servants and defenders of the fort. [67] They worked as Sarnaiks,[68] Naiks[69] during the time of Shivaji and Sambhaji. The Ramoshis of Purandhar were in the habit of collecting part of the revenue of the forty villages that were assigned for defraying the expenses of the fort.

Among other communities like the Ironsmith, Carpenters, Goldsmith, Potterman and Gardeners whose services were also utilized by the rulers. Their services may not have been directly related with the defence, but as a supporting force their services to the military were used extensively by the various rulers.

Theoretical aspect of military culture

In its composition, the army reflected the nation. No caste was excluded from it on adventitious grounds. The liberalizing influence of this reform is easy to see. A certain amount of levelling up in appreciation in the status of the communities, occupying a lower standing in the social scale, resulted from this mix-up. The army served as an effective instrument to the national education and moral upliftment of the State.

Strategy

Military is related with war and wars must have strategy as it has been pointed out by Clause Witz: "*strategy is the art of the employment of battles as a*

---

[66] Among the wounded on this occasion was Malvilpatti, Vardoji's brother, a very active and enterprising man. He crawled away from the spot and concealed himself under some bushes. At night crept to a small neighbouring village where a friend took care of him and dressed his wounds. After two months, restored to health he returned to Sinhgad, where he learnt the melancholy findings of his wife having destroyed herself as a Sati or chaste and virtuous wife under the supposition that her wounded husband was killed by Muhammadans.

67 S.N.Sen, *Military system of Maratha*, K.P. Bagachi and Co., Calcutta, 1979, p.90.

68 Pilaji Jadhav was appointed Sarnaik of the Ramoshis.

69 Five Naiks were Abaji of Gaidara near Ulti, Malli of Alandh, Bhairji of Malsiraj, Janoji of Loni-Kalbhar, and Sakroji of Mudri.

means to gain the object of war." [70] Another German Author Van Molteche points out that: "*Strategy was the practical application of the means placed at a general's disposal to the attainment of the object in view,*"[71] to achieve the final aim in war. The General's use of his power in a given time is a part of strategy and tactics. According to captain Lidelhaurt: "*Strategy is an art of distributing and applying military means to fulfil the end of pity.*"[72]

Strategy is always used to win the war and for the nation's development, in war it is used to disturb the army, make confusion among them, cut sources of arms, ammunition and food.

At the higher-level human resources arms and ammunition should be divided in such a manner that success can be achieved easily while doing so the resources at hand have to be used effectively.[73] The main aim of the strategy should be cleared more and higher-level destruction of the enemy's material and demoralize the enemy's moral strength.

The Chinese grand strategists Sun-Zue says "strategy is that act which can be used to defeat the enemy without war" Mao always say that "war should always be avoided it should be pressurized and defeat enemy's inner power." According to Bidlehaurt,74 "war for war should not be the part of the strategy, war situation can be created but no war should be brought to the surface to fight, creating war situation is good but fighting is a destructive strategy in this situation enemy is always demoralized and he takes back."

This situation was created by disorganizing enemy's deployment and dislocate enemy's plan, disrupt enemy lines of supply in this situation there is no other way of the enemy except your mistress even if he is not coming to the terms he should be defeated by the direct war.

---

70 Von Clause Witz, *On War, Vol.I*, Routledge and Kegan Paul, London, 1968, p.156.

71 B. H., Bidelhaurt, *Strategy in Direct Approach*, Cassell and Co. Ltd., London, 1943, p.334.

72 Ibid,.n.71, p.335.

73 R.C. Johari, *Western Army thought*, Chandraprakash and Bros, Delhi, 1972, p.102.

[74] Bidlehaurt, Ibid., n.71, p.335.

The Basis of Strategy

War material can be divided to achieve success within time. As stated, the policymakers of war must always keep in mind the economy force [75] because the protection of the force is an important aspect within less army success must be brought. Attention of force must be applied to the weakest point of enemy. For this one requires the knowledge of geography, time management and transportation, pre-knowledge of geography, post wartime of cultural war must be kept in mind, the movement of the army must be faster, transportation is an important factor in the war.

The strategy also must have a clear-cut goal sometime without war can be won, strategy must be applied for the self-benefit and more destruction of the enemy. The geography of enemy, supporting factors, and his planning must be kept in mind. In short, thing say the army of the enemy, to be destabilized morally it should be degraded, and all the successes to be brought to the self-support. Sometimes human destruction is also used to defeat the enemies, in the second world war bombs were used to destroy humans and demoralize the enemy. It is called physical dislocation, nowadays, the term in all wars is psychological dislocation, and by using this scheme, the warmongers are always creating confusion in the mind of army, local population and some time for the success of this strategy. They are also adopting the strategy of surprise attack and false propaganda; unexpected attack has also been used as a strategy for example in 1941 war. The British were believing that the Japanese will attack from seacoast area but in reality Japanese crossed the border of Saygon and attacked British. Propaganda is also important factor which was used by all the countries. Under propaganda common man's psychology can be upgraded, defeated nation are always demoralized. Sometimes through propaganda of war, defeat is forced upon the people. The best example can be quoted that, printed pamphlets were distributed during the wartime, and the general population and army psychologically kept away from the war.

Another part logistic disruption communication and support system is also a part of the strategy, if important services like food, oil, is disrupted enemy can be easily defeated. During the period of Chattrapati Shivaji, many a time during wartime shelter has been taken and the permanent support system was available. Sometimes strategy is used to achieve the political goal, political power. For example, if the purpose of the war, is

---

[75] Clause Witz – Ibid., n.70, p.156.

clear, war can be easily won, even the army men also fight to achieve the goal, beginning of the war, and end of the war must be clear.

Surprise Action

Surprise action is a second important strategy. Surprise action is a summary of war, sudden attack on enemy's important place, the enemy becomes surprised. Enemy then never attacks. At this time an enemy has psychologically no confidence and when anybody loses his confidence according to BidleHaurt "*Gun cannot fight that man fight a man can not fight that moral fight.*"[76] Using this strategy and loss of enemy's confidence we won the battle.

According to Stonewel Jackson, "surprised action is a salt which gave battle to become tasty, and to keep". According to General Fuller, "Surprise Action is the soul of the war system and key to win the war."77

Success of surprise action is important to keep secrets of war strategy. Attack on enemy on that point, whereas he will not be able to counter-attack. Surprise action is based on General's views and his aim. Enemy caught in inattention because of surprise action. Because of that enemy lose his "power and he is not able to resist. This way the battle will go on, and the enemy will lose the battle.

Surprise attack was the part of Shivaji's military attack, e.g. Attack on Shahistekhan.[78]

The Captain of Army must have a flexible strategy of war; there should have scope, to change the strategy at an appropriate time and selection of proper method.[79] On the ground, actual tactics also must be kept in mind.

Tactics have always been supported by attack retreat war material uniting force of army transportation, knowledge of enemy and flexibility, cornering the enemy in difficult situation. These techniques has been used

---

76 Bidlehaurt, Ibid., n.71, p.335

77 (Maj. Gen. J.F.C. Fuller, *The conduct of War,* Army Publishers, Delhi, 1978, p. 74.

78 Lt. Col. M.G. Abhyankar, *Marathyanche Yudhashastra*, Maratha Itsihas Vyakhanmala, Shivaji University, Kolhapur, 1983, p.87.

79 *Encyclopedia of the World*, Vol.XIV, p.419.

in modern technology effectively. The tactics and strategy have been always changed and used as per need and time.[80]

Methodology of Military Culture in Maharashtra

The concept of Maratha art of War

Form of war	Principle of strategy	Tactical Mode
The Defensive Form of War	Active defence of fortified points	Raid Ambush
	Economy in application of force aiming at sapping the enemy strength	Individual enterprises Local attacks
The Offensive Form of War	Positive object	Tactical mode
	Mobility and surprise in attack	Invasion in force and combat
	Extension of the Zone of operation to break enemy concentration	Attack in eccentric form. Concentration through dispersion.
	Co-operation and exertion-combined operations of land and naval forces.	

In the offensive stage of warfare from 1669-1679 A.D., the above-mentioned principles of strategy and tactics were modified in two directions. The first was the extension of the 'Front' and the second, the organization of large corps for making attacks from several directions.

Chhatrapati Shivaji's objective and role of founding a strong independent Maratha state capable of defending itself. The state economically viable and set as an example to other Hindu princes was accomplished in several stages in the teeth of the opposition of a host of well-entrenched powers and with many ups and downs. The creation of a strong nucleus of

---

[80] Clause witz, Ibid.n.75, p. 157.

S.T. Das ,*Studies in Defense Strategy,* Sagar Publication, New Delhi, 1978, p.73.

sovereignty was the first step in the process. The military force raised for realizing this objective. The enterprises undertaken and successfully executed by this force showed boldness and resolution, but their success was, not measured due to the absence of effective and sustained opposition. Fateh Khan's expedition, which gave rise to the first battle of Swarajya, fought in the vicinity of Purandar, only exposed the ineptitude of the opponent in expecting the 'Rebels' to surrender by a military demonstration. Chandrarao Morey lived in fancied security, imagining that Shivaji would not dare enter Javli. The conquest of Kalyan-Bhiwandi was affected without encountering serious opposition. But the military situation changed presently. From 1659 to 1679 the problem confronting the Maratha strategists was two-fold: -

1. The enemy (Ghanim), first a Bijapuri noble and then a Mughal generalissimo, was advancing in superior numbers. How was he to be checked?
2. The enemy was holding a strong position. How was he to be forced out of it.

The first called for a defensive and the second, an offensive strategy.[81] The conduct of war became not a little complicated when enemies threatened the State from different directions simultaneously. The methods of defence and offence developed in the course of the prolonged struggle impressed themselves on the art of War. There shall pass in review a few typical transactions of the Marathas in order to elucidate the application of the principles of strategy and tactical modes enumerated above.

Defensive war strategy and tactics

In defence, the object of strategy is to avoid enemy attacks. An aspiring power, however, must strive to create favourable conditions for the pursuit of its positive aim of conquest. A counterstroke is the essence of dynamic defence. The Mughals and the Bijapuris, who left no stone unturned to destroy the Maratha State, commanded vast resources in men and material. The Mughals moved as many as seventy thousand troops under experienced commanders into the Northern Zone of War (Rajgad-Poona area). The Bijapuris were numerically less strong, but they counted on the loyalty of their Maratha Jagirdars like Baji Ghorpade and the Sawants of Wadi. The defenders, on the other hand, though lacking in the

---

[81] Ibid., n.70, p.133, 134.

sinews of war, had the advantage afforded by terrain, the fortresses and the spirit of resistance animating the people.

To oppose a superior opponent like Shaistakhan at the frontier of the kingdom was to invite a disaster. Nor was it feasible to make a long retreat into the interior. A systematic retreat before an advancing foe with a view to attacking him unexpectedly, a manoeuvre practised by skilled commanders, was impracticable in a small-sized country. Initially, concentration on the frontier or a long retreat being ruled out. The only course left was to wait for the enemy, concentrating military forces in the fortresses on the frontier and inside the country. The assailant had to besiege such forts as threatened his rear or blocked the line of advance. The greater resistance offered by the garrison, the greater would be the wear and tear of enemy forces. The defenders would thereby gain valuable time to concert effective countermeasures and prepare a vigorous counterstroke. The principal forts were used to store supplies with war-like material and were able to stand a siege for a considerable length of time. The garrison commanders had orders not to surrender till all the means of defence were exhausted.[82] But, to make the defence positive and fruitful, strong bodies of troops were sent to harass the invader on his line of march. Such bodies made local attacks inflicting losses on the enemy. Since the invader had advantage of initiative and could choose his targets, the defenders vigilantly watched his movements. Spies moved in disguise collecting information about enemy plans. Kartalab Khan's march to Kalyan through Malwadi – Badgaon – Talegaon route across Umberkhind became known to the Marathas through reports brought by their spies. Acting on this information, Shivaji in person led a select force to attack the invader by surprise. The Maratha struck with the enemy like a bolt from the blue. They had also the advantage of the ground. It was a successful counter-stroke that compelled the assailant to suspend other offensive enterprises. The time gained was used to straighten things out in the Southern Zone.

Warding off enemy attacks in the Desh was a costly as well as an uncertain business. The Mughals were in a position to sacrifice men and material to capture Maratha forts and destroy their armed forces. There was a little positive counterstroke could achieve beyond increasing the wear and tear of the invading forces. It was, therefore, imperative for Shivaji to preserve his fighting strength, even if he had to put up with loss of territories and forts. In the campaign against Jai Singh, this very consideration would seem to have weighed with him in surrendering

---

[82] M.B. Deopujari, Ibid., n.61, p.212.

important forts and allow foreign garrisons to be implanted inside the Swarajya(self-government) territory. The defence of Rudramal and Purandar was obstinate enough to raise doubts in the mind of the Mughal commanders about their ability to achieve a quick victory.[83] It was a factor inducing the invaders to come for terms. Shivaji knew about the Mughals would not care to accept him as an ally unless it was going to be profitable for them. The two Mughal invasions under renowned commanders like Shaistakhan and Jai Singh had resulted in the loss of North Konkan and twenty-three forts, but the Marathas retained the military means to recover them. The resistance offered by them in sieges, local attacks, combat in strength and bold enterprises like the night attack on the Mughal camp and the raid on Surat lifted the defensive war from the plane of passive resistance to that of a positive many-sided counterstroke.

The Principle of Security requires a commander not to willfully expose his men to the enemy attacks. Shivaji's constant anxiety was to strengthen the defensive apparatus of the State. The subjugation of Thal-Konkan, the principal objective of his military effort in the southern zone, provided shelter against material injuries inflicted by the enemy in the northern zone and an assured defence in depth. There the Marathas did not have to suffer from constant interference with their sources of subsistence. It was a zone of security and strength.

The battle of Mira Dongar against Namdar Khan was fought to keep South Konkan inviolate. Repeated efforts of the Bijapuris and their loyal chiefs to reconquer South Konkan were defeated. Shivaji returned to the region no sooner did he obtain respite from his commitments in the Northern Zone. He delivered blows in succession in the same area, threw the Bijapuris on the defensive and held tenaciously to his acquisitions. When Shivaji took the offensive to reconquer the forts and territories held by the Mughals since the Treaty of Purandar. He strove hard to extend the zone of operation far ahead of the Rajgad zone. Altogether, a new line of defence was secured in the Madras-Karnatak. In sum, the principle of security of the State and the armed forces ran like a golden `thread binding together the defensive, and offensive operations.

---

[83] Vakaskar, *Sabhasad,* Venus Prakashan, Poona, 1962.p.37, Jaisingh advised Shivaji through Taghunath Pandit that he should come to see him, after he had demonstrated his military strength and not before. The implication was that if Jai Singh consented to start peace talks at once, he might be suspected of being friendly to Shivaji.

According to Clausewitz, "the defensive could be the stronger form of war if the defender did not rest content with merely repelling the enemy attack but delivered a counterblow in retaliation."

The Marathas, even when they yielded to overwhelming pressure, had this idea of retaliation Passive type of defence and the famous Roman general Fabius offered to the Carthaginians was not suited to an aspiring people determined to come into their own.[84] Shivaji's defensive campaigns have peculiarity this that he was on the defensive in a strategical sense, waiting for the enemy attack, but tactically on the offensive, returning the blows of the enemy by counter-attacks.

The Hindu rulers, in opposing the Muslim invaders, made use of only defensive tactics and hardly used the offensive as a fundamental proposition of warfare as the Muslims did. The purely defensive attitude weakened morale and was responsible for the Hindu debacle.[85] The campaign against Shaistakhan illustrates Shivaji's defensive strategy. No opportunity was missed to hurt the enemy by offensive action, and the defensive was made a steppingstone to ultimate success. Shivaji's night attack on Shaistakhan was an offensive act of calculated daring and in the situation, he was placed in, 'facing the greatest danger was the greatest wisdom'.

Offensive war tactics and strategy

This type of strategy is relied upon the principles of the superiority of number, morale, the fighting qualities of troops and weapons. Surprise attacks from several quarters and advantage of ground are important in this form of war. The battles of the period (1669-1679) were essentially offensive and shed light on the twin principles of concentration through mobility and economy through surprise attack. The assembling forces in the greatest possible numbers with equipment for battle at the required point is the essence of concentration. The Marathas effected concentration and economy both by their mobility and method of

---

[84] Clausewitz, *War,* Vol.II, Ibid., n.70, p.136. It is in complete contradiction with the conception of war to suppose the defensive the ultimate object of War, because war begins when one attacks and the other defends, that is, when one wants to acquire and the other tries to preserve. But the enemy's blows should be returned by offensive fighting, absolute passivity miscalled defence would leave the attacker to carry on the War alone. The characteristics of defence are to wait for the enemy in the theatre of war and return his blows.

[85] B.K.Majumdar, *Military System in Ancient India,* 2nd ed., Mukhopadhyay, 1960, Calcutta, p.185, regarding the general Hindu attitude.

subsisting the troops. The effect of launching the offensive at three or four points simultaneously by means of sizeable corps compelled the enemy also to divide his forces. The battles of Dindori, Salhir, Yelburga and Ahiri arose out of the Maratha attacks on enemy bases. The Marathas were fully prepared to make sacrifices when they deliberately led their forces deeply into the enemy territory. It may be recalled how Peshwa Moropant and Pratap Rao Gujar carried the war into Nasik-Baglan and Berar and won marvellously successes. The object in the offensive war was for conquest and expansion. Offensive strategy had a positive aim of acquisition as opposed to preservation and required for its fulfilment a decisive engagement with the enemy. The assailants were out to impose their will on the enemy. They did not decline but sought a decision in battle.

Mobility

Mobility contributed to a certain economy and effected surprises. At Umrani Bahlol Khan's army was encircled and compelled to sue for terms. The Maratha losses were very small. At Yelburga, a numerically inferior Maratha force won the day against the Miana brothers.

The factors that contributed to the mobility of the troopers were: (1) the Method of subsistence (2) Non-employment of heavy field artillery and (3) attention to logistic. The problem of feeding a large number of troops in the field was non-existent for the Marathas. They managed to procure food and fodder in the country they passed through. Mobility was further aided by the fact that the field armies did not carry heavy artillery pieces. A mobile infantry equipped with rockets and muskets, swords and spears, and the lightly equipped cavalry marched rapidly to its destination. The Mughals encumbered with heavy baggage were notoriously slow, taking three days to cover the distance which the Marathas did in one day. The problem of subsistence was acute for the Mughals. The Maratha skirmishers raided their grain convoys. The Mughals retaliated by burning standing crops, capturing herds of cattle and setting fire to homesteads in order to strike terror and to create in the mind of the opponent a dread of their power, but the method produced near-famine conditions and brought war operations to a standstill. The Bijapuris compelled the Mughals to withdraw from the environs of their capital twice (1666-1676) by making it impossible for them to get food, fodder and even drinking water. The reciprocal action in this manner strained the economy of contending powers. But the Mughals were the greater losers.

In Western Maharashtra heavy military equipment, especially heavy artillery pieces could not be conveyed except by built roads. Hence, they deliberately avoided taking with them such heavy material. The Mughal trooper with the weight of arms and armour could not deploy freely. Daud Khan Qureshi was kept running from place to place by mobile Maratha columns and was overwhelmed by them at Dindori. The Marathas took the line of the least expected and confounded the enemy. The effect of Surprise as a principle of offensive strategy was seen in attacks on important places in the enemy territory. This method of producing surprise upset the moral equilibrium of the enemy and disorganized his war effort.

Logistic

The time factor in war is importance of defence importance. One of the leading principles in modern warfare is that an army must advance on parallel columns to reach the objective, as early as possible. The term logistic was coined by Jomin to explain how the movement and supply of troops should be effectively organized. An army, for instance, advancing along two or more roads towards the same objective would arrive there in less time than if it had marched by one road only. The whole Maratha army did not march by one and the same route. It was divided into columns and ordered to march Separately to its destination. Prataprao and Moropant marched towards Salher by separate routes. Shivaji ordered Hambirrao to proceed towards Tanjore-Jinji by the Koppal route. Shivaji himself went straight to Golkonda. The two forces united in time for opening the offensive against Jinji. The Desh and Konkan tracts contained countless routes known only to the Marathas. The Mughal army had to move on a built road and so the Marathas had every opportunity to surprise them bypass road.

Surprise attacks

The Marathas made night marches on several occasions. In 1664 the Marathas attacked Khawas Khan's camp at Kudal in the early hours of the morning after a hard night march. The Muslims were not prepared for such an attack. Shivaji landed at Basnur in the early hours and sacked the place. Moropant had planned to scale the walls of the Siddi's fort at night. Boats were got ready with scaling ladders and equipment by Ram Koli as settled, but the Peshwa ceased to fire. He found that the Siddi's were too vigilant to be taken by surprise. At mid-night attack is seldom successful against a vigilant foe and is not commended by military critics and generals. But Shivaji had studied the character of his foes and his men, being familiar with the Deccan terrain, almost always succeeded in such operations.[86] Escalating a fort from an unguarded point and launching a

---

[86] Phillips, : *Roots of Strategy,* (A collection of military Classics) 4th reprint, The Military Service Publishing Co., Harrisburg, Pennsylvania, 1955, p.332. Such

sudden attack on the garrison may be regarded as a special form of surprise in which the Mavles excelled. The success of such an enterprise depended upon the condition of the enemy's garrison. The state of the weather and proper teamwork among the attackers. A few enterprises failed for one reason or another. The Mughals were deprived of the means of checking Maratha aggression when they lost key forts like Sinhgad and Purandar. Sinhgad could not have been wrested from a veteran like Udai Bhan, had it not been attacked so unexpectedly. To surprise the enemy is to take a long step towards victory. It is only by offensive action that this becomes possible.

Tactics of Invasion

The Maratha mobile spearheads acted as a screen for hiding, from enemy eyes, the point where the Maratha combat forces were concentrating. The assailants showed a front in all directions – right, centre and left – operating in an extended line in separate corps. The raid on enemy centres of wealth and military power was related to the principle of mobile offensive warfare. This is shown by the fact that even a place like Karanja or Dharangaon, remotely connected with the theatre of war, suffered equally with Aurangabad, Ahmadnagar and Surat. The imposition of Chauth on the inhabitants of Karanja for the proper payment of which written promises were taken, was an indirect preparation for the eventual conquest of the area. In the southern theatre, raids on Vengurla, Sampgaon, Athni and Hubli, were a part of the offensive strategy. Sampgaon was in the Jagir of Bahlol Khan, who had befooled Pratap Rao Gujar into allowing him to go away scot-free after his defeat at Umrani.

To his opponents, Shivaji appeared to be an enemy of trade. The army he had raised for the purpose was in their view a predatory force. Such, however, was not the case. But it is not true a fact, is that the Maratha commercial enterprises were extensive at the time of Shivaji's, and his merchant ships visited Basra and Mocha. Plunder was regarded as a legitimate act of war by contemporary military thinkers in Europe. The Marathas so regarded it, but Shivaji did his best to see that it caused as little hardship to non-combatants as possible. Ghanim Shivaji is, therefore, a myth. The Maratha raiders succeeded in exerting such economic and military pressure on the Mughals that the pay of Mughal soldiers fell in arrears, and disaffection spread in their ranks. Shivaji's last

---

generals as Arthur Wellesley in the siege of Sriraugpaton in 1799 failed to gain any advantage by making a night attack on Tipu's outpost.

exploit was to cut off a convoy of treasure going to the Mughal camp at a time when their soldiers were mutinying for pay.

Mulkhgiri

The connection between such raids and *mulkhgiri* seizure or acquisition of enemy territory appears to be intimate. The country of the Hindus was conquered by Muslim invaders and was regarded by them as the land of the faithful. This was a legal fiction since the vast majority of the people living therein were Hindus. But the theological conception was of practical utility in exciting the war ardour of the soldiers of Islan. The Muhammedan *mulkhgiri* aimed at the conquest of non-Muslim kingdoms on religious grounds. No sooner was a Hindu town or a fort conquered than it received a Muslim name. The ultimate object of the *mulkhgiri* of the Marathas also was conquest, but it was not motivated by the desire to glorify or exalt Hinduism to the detriment of other faiths. The fact is that the situation created by incessant warfare of the period gave the Marathas little time for developing the economic resources of the country, or for framing economic policy. Sabhasad uses the expression (mulukh marne) in the sense of raiding enemy territory for plunder; and (kabij karne) to indicate the aim of conquering it. Another expression of Sabhasad is (takhta taraj karne) which meant utterly destroying the base from which the assailant drew his supplies.[87]

The most important single principle of action, either in attack or in defence, is the principle of exertion, fatigue and privation denoted by a compound word *Shrama-Sahasa* . No positive aim in war can be realized without daring and sustained effort.[88] Shivaji and his lieutenants literally wore themselves out in the service of the country. The garrisons entrusted with the defence of forts uncomplainingly bore the brunt of enemy attack. The accounts of the Mughal siege of Chakan and of Purandar testify to the skill, heroism and resourcefulness of the Marathas. The combined operations of the land and sea forces against the Siddi's and the grand offensive in the Karnatak illustrate the Maratha method of conquest through exertion, daring and teamwork. Judged by the results achieved, leaving aside the element of chance or luck, or the influence of passing political happenings on military events, the methods of defence

87 Wakaskar, Sabhasad, Ibid., n.83, p.25.

88 R.C. Hart, *Reflections on the Art of War*, p.73. 'Tradition, esprit-de-corps, hunger and thirst, heat and cold, utter weariness and misery, these are frequently ignored by the theorist; but the success of a military operation may depend upon attention to such details.'

and offence adopted by the Marathas represent adjustment and adaptation of the methods of War of all civilized nations. There is nothing predatory or barbarous in them. The methods proved effective in making the principal enemies of the Marathas *hors de combat.* Bijapur acknowledged the Sovereign status of Shivaji. Qutub Shah felt honoured by his visit and because his ally in the Karnatak War. The European factors vied with one another in seeking his goodwill. Marathas applied the principles of war in their own way. Their choice in the matter was determined by their own genius, geographical conditions and the historical background. The pragmatic approach to the problem of strategy and tactics was characteristic of the area.

The moral impulse that animated the armed forces and the populace in their struggle promoted the cultivation of military virtues. The pragmatic approach freed the Maratha mind from age-old inhibitions. The adoption of the principles of mobile offensive warfare, a legacy of the bargirs of pre-Shivaji period, was efficacious in compelling the enemy to partition his forces. The defence was pivoted on hillforts which enabled the Marathas to make up for their material deficiency by greater exertion and tenacity. The fortresses were used as shields to assail the enemy for hitting while guarding their own. The desire to retaliate and pay the enemy back in his own coin prevented the defensive from degenerating into passivity, morally dangerous to an aspiring power. Individual enterprises of commanders, besides sustaining morale, produced important results. Mobility and surprise, incessant exertion, economy and co-operation formed the web and woof of the Maratha Art of War.

Military culture in Maharashtra

The Marathas fought most of the war in mountain and jungle areas. The Marathas followed military organization in Maharashtra. On the Chalukya policy, that enemy's enemy is your friend. Under the valiant Rashtrakuta Kings, Hiuen-Tsang was

highly impressed with their warlike qualities.[89] After the Chalukyas and the Rashtrakutas came the Yadava and the Silahara dynasties.

---

89 The Chinese pilgrim says of the people of Maharashtra: The inhabitants were proud spirited and warlike, grateful for favours and revengeful for wrongs; self-sacrificing towards supplicants in distress and sanguinary to death with any one who treated them insultingly. Their martial heroes who led the rear of the army in battle went into conflict intoxicated and their war elephants were also made drunk before an engagement.

Thomas Watters, *On Yuan* Chawong, *Travel in India,* Vol.II, Delhi, 1961, p.239.

The last independent Yadava King became a feudatory of the Turkish ruler.[90] His son-in-law made an unsuccessful attempt to reappear on the scene till the fall of the Bahamani kingdom. The Deshmukhs or petty feudal lords have fought a war for months in their impregnable strongholds perched on the summit of inaccessible hills. They were not reluctant to acknowledge the suzerainty of the Muhammadan princes. They were interested only in their hereditary lands and hereditary rights. The Muhammadan conquerors on his side, recognized that the Maratha chiefs continued to exercise their petty sovereignty over their hill girt.

The climate and the physical features of the land engendered courage and endurance in the Maharashtrian people. They became self-centred and crafty.[91] They went in isolation of their daily life led also to certain parochialism in political affairs. The ambition of the average Maharashtrian villager was confined to their own village and the ambition of the average Maharashtrian chief seldom extended beyond the narrow confines of his paternal principality. The watan[92] became more important claimant; it caused continual strife between rival chiefs and rival families.[93] And as the Marathas did not readily forget a loss or forgive an injury, these quarrels inevitably led to blood feuds, which could only be ended by the complete extermination of one of the rival families. Such hostilities kept the Marathas so busily engaged that he had hardly time or inclination to notice the movements and progress of the external world. The habit narrowed his vision but made a good soldier of him and thus when the time came, he was ready to take advantage of the new situation and improve his fortunes.

After the dissolution of the Bahamani kingdom, the Maratha chiefs began to extend their services in civil and military situations to the new courts. They were welcomed by all the Muslim rulers, who had partitioned the

---

[90] Ravindra Kumar, *Western India in the 18th Century,* Routledge & Kegan Paul, London, 1968, p.3.

Kincaid Parasnis, A History of the Maratha People, Vol.l, Oxford University Press, 1918.

91 S.N. Sen, S.N., *Military System of the Marathas*, K.P. Bagachi and Co., Calcutta, 1979, p.3.

92 Watan: is an Arabic word and originally meant home, but in Marathi it has acquired a special significance, and stands for only hereditary right or property.

93 S.N. Sen, *Administrative System of the Marathas*, K.P. Bagachi & Co., Calcutta, 2002, pp.18-19.

old kingdom.[94] The policy of rival houses of Muslim was uncertain and shifting and their alliances were not a long duration and they had no hesitation in joining their Hindu neighbour. After the battle of Talikota, they employed their energy and resources in the conquest of the weakest members of the confederacy, Berar and Bidar. When this was accomplished the survivors found themselves unable to compose their differences, and while in this position, were suddenly confronted by a new menace from the north. These continual wars offered excellent opportunities to Maratha soldiers and Maratha diplomats, who were eager to earn new and retain their old watans.

By the end of the 16th and beginning of the seventeenth century Maratha Sardars achieved were in high position in the military and the civil services of the Ahmednagar, Bijapur and Golconda Government.[95]

Many of the Marathas came to prominence in the army. The art of war was still in its infancy, primitive weapons like sword and spear, bow and arrows, lane and dagger, were used in the war. Such weapons which demanded little or no technical knowledge were still in general use so that every able-bodied man was a potential soldier. He could enlist as a Bargir[96] or if he had means enough to buy a horse and the slender outfit that a soldier needed in those days, he could join as a Silhedar[97] with much better prospects of advancement. A well to do Silehdar was really a condottiere leader with his ownfollowers whose services he could utilize as he chose. He became a very important person. Success added to the Silhedar's reputation and the following, of course, improved his worldly

94 Ashok Rana, *Chhatrapati Shivraj*, Jagatgury Sant Tukobaray Sahitya Prakashan, Nagpur, 2001, p.17.

See Setu Madhavrao Pagadi, *Chhtapati Shivaji*, National Book Trust India, New Delhi, 1920, p.6.

95 P.A. Gavali, P.A., *Marathyancha Itihas*, Kailas Publication, Aurangabad, 1999, p.33.

96 Bargir, literally means a burden taker but in the Mughal as well as in the Maratha Army the term signified a soldier who rode a horse furnished by his employer.

97 Siledar, more properly Silahar literally means equipment holder i.e. a soldier who finds his own horse and arms.

prospects. He was rewarded Jahgir or military fief. It was in this way that some Maratha families raised their status to prominence.[98]

The Maratha families formed the military aristocracy of the land. Maharashtra the profession of arms was not limited to the noble. The social barrier was low. Shelars and the Jadhavas, decedents of ruling kings, had declined their powers.[99] The other princely family had reconciled themselves to their humble lot and no longer hesitated to marry kunbi girls of lowly origin. They still affected the title of 'Raje' after their first name, but that was the only trace of royalty now left to them. This society was naturally democratic. A promising young man rejected the plebian plough for the more aristocratic sword, could aspire to the land of a daughter of the proud Nimbalkars and could demand a matrimonial alliance with the princely family on the Jadhavas. Social intercourse was more intimate and less formal and in an able leader of magnetic personality commanded not only the admiration but also the affection of his following. The common soldier except the few who formed the king's bodyguard, had nothing to do with the state but looked for pay, promotion and preference to the Jahagirdar under whom they immediately served. A loyal Jahagirdar contributed to the strength of the Government, but in those days, it was no discredit to set up as a 'Pund palegar' or lawless chief, as once did a Nimbalkar and a Jedhe.[100] Yet the state continued its policy of multiplying the military fiefs and conferring fresh jahgirs on each enterprising Silhedar. Even a prince like Muhammad Adilshah laid down that while a disloyal Zamindar should be deprived of his fief, the loyal lord should on no account be discouraged or disturbed. The inevitable results of this policy was that the civil Government of the country was subordinated to military needs and the major portion of Maharashtra was held by a number of military leaders serving under three different masters. When Shivaji rose on power, the principality of

---

[98] The most important of them in rank as well as in power were the Mores of Jawali with the twin titles of Raja and Chandrarao, Next came the Servants of Wadi, the Ghorpades of Mudhol,. The Nimbalkar's of Paltan, the Jadhav's of Sindkhed, the Shirkes, the Mahadiks, the Mohites, the Ghatges , Jedhe, Mane, Dafles.

[99] The Shelars claim to be the decendents of the Silahars and Lakhuji Jadhav was a direct decendant of Ramchandra Deva the last independent Yadava ruler of Devgiri.

100 S.N. Sen, *Administrative system of the Marathas*, K.P. Bagachi & Co., Calcutta, 2002, p.19.

Ahmednagar had already been annexed by the Emperor of Delhi and the kingdoms of Bijapur and Golkonda were awaiting a similar fate.

Organising Military

In reality, the military culture was built up Maharashtra with the rise of Chatrapati Shivaji. He had a clear concept of military organization, a definite plan of military reform and specific views and opinions based upon his personal past experience. He believed in personal selection but had no faith in hereditary genius.[101] He approved of the unity of command but would not tolerate military interference in the civil administration of the country. He wanted a strong monarchy as the only antidote to the prevailing discord, dissension and anarchy and could not, therefore, reconcile himself to feudalism. He had some advantage over his antagonists. His hands were not tied by precedents, but at the same time, as the founder of a new kingdom and a new house, he could not ignore the tradition of the land, not could he afford wholly to alliance the vested interests.[102] Chatrapati Shivaji introduced strict discipline in his Army. His success in this direction was far from complete and he had to fight against tradition and environment. His army was employed in Mulukhgiri or foreign expedition for eight months in a year. They returned to cantonment when the monsoon broke and the four months of the rainy season they had to spend in barracks in enforced idleness. Shivaji laid down the rule and made provision to provide medicine for men and fodder for their horses. He made it clear that should be carefully stored in the cantonments. During the active season, the Maratha army subsisted on the spoils of war but here again it was clearly laid down that the prize belonged to the state and not to the army.[103]

The achievements of Shivaji's army was well known. The Maratha chronicles proudly assert that he fought with success against four great powers.[104] The numerical strength of his army has been variously stated. Krishnaji Anant Sabhasad puts it well above 100,000. But the causes of his military success are not far to seek. Superior discipline, superior leadership and the unquestioning confidence of his men, account for the

---

101 Setu Madhavrao Pagadi, *Chhatrapati Shivaji*, National Book Trust of India, Delhi, 1920, pp.152-153.

102 S.N.Sen, *Military System of the Marathas*, K.P. Bagachi & Co., Calcutta, 1979, p.7.

103 Ibid.,, p.13.

104 Adilshahi, Nizamshahi, Kutubshahi, I, Badshahi.

brilliant victories which the great Marathas obtained over the Mughals, the Portuguese, the Bijapurs and Nizam, not to mention the petty polygons who acknowledge his suzerainty.[105]

Chattrapati Shivaji created national feeling in the mind of the Marathas by using religious sentiments among the rude Maratha peasant soldiers. It was this idea Chattrapati Shivaji that appealed to them. The ideal he put forth was a Hindavi Swarajya, a Maharashtra Pudshahi kingdom.[106] Despite this Dharma Rajya on which Shivaji created a kingdom of righteousness. In Chattrapati Shivaji's army Brahman could fight shoulder to shoulder with the Mahar, who is not allowed to live within the village walls, in this situation Shivaji took the strong step and did not exclude any from his army, not even the Mahars.[107]

Economic aspect of Army

The army consisted mainly of cavalry and infantry. He also developed a modest naval force. The strength of his army of, according to Sabhasad was 2,08,260 including his personal guard, at the time of his coronation. There were 60,000 Silhedars under 31 colonels, 45,000 paga under 29 colonels, 100,000 Mavale under 35 colonels and 1260 elephants.[108] The salary of Senapati, who was a member of the council of eight ministers, was 10,000 hons per year and the other military commanders drew a salary varying from 500 to 4000 hons per annum. As regards the lower ranks, he mentioned that their salary varied from 200 hons to 15 hons per annum.[109]

Salary for the Cavalry

The officials were Sarnobat, Panchhazari, Hazari, Jumledar, Havaldar and their assistants such as Majumdar, Karbhari, Jamenis and a number of spies, water carriers and ferries. The paid trooper was called Bargir and

---

105. Ibid., n.102, p.17.

[106] The term Hindvi Swarajya is used by Shivaji in a letter to Dadaji Naras Prabhu. Please see V.K. Rajwade, *Marathyanchya itihasachi Sadhane,* Vol.XV, p.272.

[107] Ibid., n.67, p.17.

108 P.A. Gavali, *Marathyancha Itihas*, Kailas Publication, 1999, p.106.

Kulkarni A.R., *Shivkalin Maharashtra* , Rajhans Prakashan, Pune, 1997, p.153.

109 Kulkarni A.R., *Shivkalin Maharashtra* , Rajhans Prakashan, Pune, 1997, p.153.

the trooper who maintained his own horse and arms was called Siledar. According to Sabhasad, Chitnis and some papers the annual salaries and allowances of the officials are mentioned in as below

Sarnobat5000 to 4000 Hons.
Panchhazari2000 hons.
Hazari 1000 hons.
Jumledar 500 hons.
Havaldar 125 hons.
Bargir 9 hons.[110]

The salaries of the personal staff of the Jumledar, Hazari and Panch hazari were as below

Majumdar of Hazari 500 hons.
Majumdar of Jumledar 100 to 125 hons.
Karbhari of Hazari 500 hons.
Jamenavis of Hazari 500 hons.[111]

There was a watercarrier and Ferrier for every twenty five troops. There were a number of clerks, reporters, couriers and spies attached to the office Hazari, Panch Hazari and Sarnobat.[112]

Some of these officials enjoyed certain privileges; Sabhasad mentions that the Jumledar had a right to use the palanquin.[113] All officers above him must have been enjoying this privilege though Sabhasad has not enumerated them, and many more privileges and the state must have

---

110 V.K. Rajwade, *Marathyanchya Itihasachi Sadhane,* Bharat Itihas Samshodhan Mandal, Vol. VIII, Granthmalaya , Kolhapur p. 33.

It mentions the salary of a Havaldar posted at Utlur. There need not be any difference between the salary of a fort havaldar and that of cavalry havaldar. Ibid., Martin mentions "the horsemen of Shivaji ordinarily receive two pagodas per month as pay", Foreign Biographies of Shivaji, K.P. Bagachi & Co., Calcutta, p.316.

111 A.R. Kulkarni, *Shivkalin Maharashtra,* Rajhansa Prakashna, Pune 1990, p.155.

112 Ibid., p.156.

113 A.R. Kulkarni, *Maharashtra in the Age of Shivaji*, Popular Prakashan, Poona, 1969, p.248.

been bearing the cost of these privileges. Bargirs were supplied with arms, horses and uniform.[114]

Siledars were under the command of the Sarnobat at Paga there was not much difference atleast in the organization of the Siledar troops.

Infantry

The officials of the Mawla infantry were the Sarnobat, Saptahazari, Panchhazari, Hazari, Jumledar, Havaldar, Naik and civil officials like the Sabnic. We do not get the details of the salaries of these officials except that of Hazari and Jumledar who drew 500 hons and 100 hons per year respectively. The salary of the Sabnis of Hazari was 100 to 125 hons whereas that of Jumledar 40 hons only.[115]

From the salary scales of the military officers described above, it appears that the infantry officers were not so well paid as their colleagues in the cavalry. The Jumledar in the cavalry drew salary five times higher than that of the infantry Jumledar and the cavalry Hazari drew double the salary of the infantry Hazari. The difference in the scale may be explained with the help of the law of supply. Besides, it was a costly affair to maintain a large cavalry. Dr. Sen has rightly pointed out that the figures of cavalry (45,000) given by Sabhasad are exaggerated.[116] Sabhasad mentions that the strength of his infantry was one lakh under 36 colonels.[117]

Besides this, there was a select group of 2,000 soldiers acting as the personal guard of the king. According to Sabhasad, they were selected after careful inspection. This regiment was divided into units of twenty, thirty, forty, sixty and hundred men. This force was splendidly equipped. They received richly embroidered turbans and jackets of brocade cloth, gold and silver earrings and wristlets. The weapons used by them were also costly. All the expenditure of arming and equipping this regiment of 2000 men was borne by the state. [118]

---

[114] S.N. Sen, *Administrative System of the Marathas*, K.P. Bagachi & Co., Calcutta, 2002, p.143.

[115] Krishnaji Anant Sabhasad, *Shivchhatrapatiche Charitra*, S.N. Joshi, Pune, 1960, p.24.

116 S.N. Sen, Ibid., no.27, pp.63-4.

117 Sabhasad,Ibid., no. 115, P.99.

118 Sabhasad, Ibid., p.54-6.

Besides these regular forces, Shivaji used to secure military services from his watandars. The Watandars of Bhiruadi, offered their services with their attendants, on six rukas per head per day basis.[119] (Six rukas means two tirukas or two paisa.) At this rate the monthly salary was paid approximately 3 ¼ taka i.e. about ¼ of a hon per month or three hons a year.[120] Thus the salaries of the other members of the infantry was not having much difference. The wages of the lower rank people appear to be considerably low.

Dr. Sen argues that as Shivaji was strictly punctual in his payment,[121] it was not necessary for him to offer very high salaries.[122] One can agree with him when he justifies the low wages on the ground of the high purchasing power of money in those days. As the major necessities of life could be satisfied with minimum means, one can argue that the soldiers of Shivaji had to little to complain of.[123]

Fort administration: A part of military service

The Maratha ruler paid special attention to the maintenance of forts and strongholds. Shivaji spent lavishly on the construction and repairs of forts. Sabhasad estimates that at the time of his death, Shivaji possessed no less than two hundred and forty forts and strongholds.[124]

Every fort was placed under three officers namely Havaldar, Sarnobat and a Sabnis of equal status and they acted in unison. In addition to these officials there was a Karkhanis in charge of the stores of the fort.[125] Our records reveal that there were certain other officials and servants associated with the fort. We find at Fort Utlur, a superintendent of buildings, a Mujumdar, some Sarnobats, Clerks and some personal

---

119 Bharat Itihas Samshodhan Mandal, 3rd Sommelan Vrutta, Pune,p.163.

120 A.R. Kulkarni, Maharashtra in the Age of Shivaji,Popular Prakashan, Pune, 1969, p.25l.

121 S.N. Sen, Foreign Biographies of Shivaji, K.P. Bagachi & Co., Calcuttta 1927, p.17.

122 S.N.Sen, Administrative System of Maratha, K.P. Bagachi & Co.Calcutta, 1925, P.148.

123 Ibid., no.102,p.10.

124 Krishnaji Anant Sabhasad, Krishnaji Anant, *Shivchatrapatinche Charitra*, S.N.Joshi, Pune, pp.100-5.

125 Ibid., p.122.

attendants of the havaldar and superintendent of buildings.[126] Mahars were the Fort Keepers.

The annual salary paid to officials as per records:

Havaldar 125 hons plus 25 hons for two servants.
Sarnobat100 hons.
Tatsarnobat 12 hons.
Superintendent of Buildings: 125 hons plus 10 hons for one servant.
Sabnis:100 hons.
Majumdar of the superintendent of Buildings: 36 hons, clerks 3 hons.[127]

Karkhanis was in charge of the stores. Paiks, Naiks, Gunners, Archers posted on these forts must have been receiving salaries as in the regular army.[128]

Shivaji paid special attention on the construction of new forts and maintenance as well as repair of the old ones. The Marathas and the other powers attached much importance to forts.[129] Many steep hills were used as forts and new forts were constructed at several places in the territory. He constructed several islands or marine forts like Vijaydurg, Sindudurg and Suvarnadurg etc. The spoils of war and plunder were thus fruitfully utilized by Shivaji in building the forts.[130] He had spent a huge amount in building the Raigad Fort which became the capital place of his kingdom.[131] Housing residential quarters were provided to the officials, and many other buildings were provided to for various purposes on the fort. According to the source, in the year 1672, Shivaji had advanced one lakh and seventy-five thousand hons for constructing houses on the forts, out of which fifty thousand hons were reserved for Raigad alone. The rest was to be spent on eighteen forts including some island forts.

---

126 V.K. Rajwade, *Marathyanchya Itihasachi Sadhane*, Vol.VIII, Bharat Itihas Samshodhan Mandal, Pune, pp. 33, 35, 36.

127 A.R. Kulkarni, *Shivkalin Maharashtra*, Rajhansa Prakashan, Pune, 1997, pp.157-8. Ibid., no.130, pp. 28, 31.

128 M.G. Ranade, *Rise of the Maratha Power*, Pundalkar & Co., Bombay, 1900, p.67.

129 Ramchandrapant amatya, *Ramchandrapant* , Adnyapatra (ed), G.H.Khare, Bide, Pune, Chapter VIII, p.

130 Sabhasad, Ibid., no. 115, p.62.

131 Sabhasad , Ibid., p.68.

Expenditure on Navy

Sabhasad tells us that Shivaji had a naval force consisting of four hundred gurabs, tarandes, tarus, galbats, sibads and pagars, organized into two squadrons of 200 vessels.[132] Besides the construction of boats, and their maintenance as well as to organize the naval force have entailed a good deal of expenditure.[133]

Rewards and Grants

Besides the regular pay and allowances for soldiers and officials were given additional allowances for meritorious work. Shivaji conferred pensions, bounties and prizes on those who shed their blood for the state. Sabhasad writes that the sons of soldiers who had fallen on the battlefield were absorbed in the state service. He directed that the widows of those soldiers, who had no sons, should be maintained by a pension equal to half the salary of their deceased husbands. The injured were given rewards of two hundred, to hundred, fifty and twenty-five hons per head according to the nature of their wounds. The Warriors of renown and commanders of brigades were given horses and elephants in reward; some were sumptuously rewarded with ornaments like bracelets, necklaces, crests, medallions, earrings and crests of pearl. Some were rewarded with grants of villages in Mokasa.[134]

When Moropant Peshwa and Prataprao together won the battle of Salher against the Mughals, the army was rewarded for its bravery.[135]

Cosme da Guarda, a foreign biographer of Shivaji tells us that Shivaji paid a good salary punctually to his soldiers with a view to dissuading them from hiding anything of war.[136]

---

132 Sabhasad, Ibid., no. 115, p.65,

Sarkar, pp.252-4.

133 Ibid., p.159.

V.K. Rajwade, *Marathyanchya Itihasachi Sadhane, Vol. VIII*, Bharat Itihas Sanshodhana Mandal, Pune, 1942, p.159.

134 Sabhasad, Ibid., No. 115, pp.18-9

Wilson defines Mokasa as a village or land assigned to an individual either rent-free or at a low quit rent on condition of service.

135 Sabhasad, Ibid, p.72.

The method of payment according to Sabhasad: "The Sarnobat, Majumdar, Karkun, and the officers of Huzur were given assignments on the revenue for their salary. The lands cultivated by them were assessed at the usual rates and the due amount of revenue was deducted from their pay. For the balance payment, they received orders from the treasury of the huzur or the districts. Men employed in the army, or on the fort's administration were not to be given mokasa right over any village in entirely. All payment was made by 'Varats' (assignments) or with cash from the treasury. None but the Karkuns had any authority over the land. All payments to the army were to be made by the Karkuns.[137]

Shivaji departed from the medieval practice of payment in the form of land or estate only with a view to arresting the growth of feudal power. About the economic position of the superior officials of the state, Ranade writes, "none of the great men, who distinguished themselves during Shivaji's times, were able to hand over to their descendant's large landed estates.[138]

Peshwa and Military

According to Sabhasad,[139] Chattarapati Shivaji army consisted of 45,000 cavalry and 10,000 Mawle infantry.[140] A cavalry trooper was chosen necessarily more experienced and expensive. He was given a good horse, better equipment and a higher salary. Shivaji's military operations were often confined to hilly regions where horses are used. He frequently led his men through unfrequented mountain tracks where the sure footed and his man Mawle alone could go, accurately and according to Sabhasad. The contemporary correspondence of the English Factories recorded that Shivaji's period the infantry preponderated over the cavalry. The infantry continued to maintain its majority in the Maratha Army even after Shivaji's death, in 1680. Similarly, Dhanji Jadhav had under his command a strong infantry force of 25,000, while his cavalry numbered 5,000 only.[141]

---

136 S.N.Sen, *Foreign Biographies of Shivaji, Chapter II*, K.P. Bagachi & Co., Calcutta, 1927, p.17.

137 Sabhasad, Ibid., No.115, pp.24-5.

138 Ranade, Ibid., N.128, p.70.

139 Krishnaji Anant Sabhasad, who wrote the Sabhasad Bakhar.

140 S.N.Sen, *Siva Chatrapati*, K.P. Bagachi & Co., Calcutta, 1920, pp.136-9.

141 S.N.Sen, Ibid., no.27, p.64.

During the Peshwa reign, however, the position was reversed. The Marathas were no longer compelled to defend their hearth and home. Secure in their native territories, they were now in a position to carry war into enemy's country and in these distant expeditions, designed mainly for plunder, a cavalry force was far more useful than infantry.[142]

The Peshwa's army consisting of 80,000 to 1,00,000 horse, 10,000, base army men and 40 to 50 pieces of artillery.[143]

Few military Saranjams, who continuously awarded after Peshwa. According to Tone, the Marathas did not care to accommodate any soldier in the infantry who consisted as outsiders. The Maratha army men were employed mainly for the local suppression of disturbances by the Bhils, Kolis and other turbulent tribes.[144]

Expenditure on War

The money spent on arms, ornaments, military equipment, camps whose actual cost and gains of various expeditions cannot be easily estimated. However, it may be argued that Shivaji spent less on war as compared to the Mughals or the Muslim rulers of the Deccan because of the simplicity of his camps.[145]

He supplied arms manufactured in Maharashtra and armaments and dresses to his soldiers. Ammunition, cannon, guns were secretly purchased from the foreigners like the French, the Dutch, the Portuguese and the English. He secured for instance 80 guns and 2000 maunds of lead from French.[146]

According to Sabhasad he had given costly dresses to the Royal Guards. The dresses supplied were, a Mandil (Headdress), Sakaladi Phatu for the body (a cloak), gold or silver bracelets, gold and silver chains, earrings etc.[147] It may be said that the soldiers in the regular army were also receiving a headdress, a cloak and some other clothes. Sabhasad writes

---

142 Ibid., p.64.

143 Ibid., p.64.

144 Ibid., p.65.

145 Balkrishna, *Shivaji the Great*, Modern Publishers & Distributor, Delhi, 1985, p.70.

146 Ibid., pp.104-5.

147 Sabhasad, Ibid., N.115, p.54.

that Shivaji did not permit anybody to take his wife, maidservants or concubine along with them to the battlefield, and if anybody was found violating this rule, he was punished with death.[148] Francois Martin, the French envoy, endorses this statement of Sabhasad. He had spent three days in Shivaji's camp in Karnatak. He gives a graphic description of the arrangements at Shivaji's camp, in his memoirs. He writes: "His camp is without any pomp and encumbered by baggage or women."[149] He further states that there were only two tents[150] in his camp of a thick simple stuff and very small one for himself, and other for his ministers.[151]

Thus, the moderate salaries of the Army, the simplicity in dresses, the limited number of weapons mostly made locally and the Spartan simplicity of the camps must have minimized the cost of war.

Difference in Peshwai

The Peshwa organized trained battalions into their army and this necessitated further employment of non-Marathas in 1753-54.

After Balaji Baji Rao, the next Peshwa, however, we find a deliberate attempt to strengthen the new infantry force by recruiting a large number of Sikhs, Arabs, Abyssinians, Sidis and other non-Marathas.[152]

Of all these foreigners (outsiders) the Arabs enjoyed the highest reputation for valour and intrepidity. According to Blacker, "Every substantive native power had a portion of these troops.[153]

But the foreigners in the Maratha army were not always better soldiers to the Local Country recruits.

The Arab, Abyssinian, Sindhi, Sikh and other non-Maratha recruits in the Peshwa's army were accommodated by their own Jamadars, commissioned on (contract basis)as per the need of the war situation,

---

148 Sabhasad, Ibid., n.115,p.23.

149 S.N. Sen, *Foreign Biographies of Shivaji*, K.P. Bagachi & Co., Calcutta, 1927, p.306.

150 Ibid., n. 127, p.160.

151 Ibid., n. 127, p.306.

152 G.C. Vad, B.B. Parashis, *Selection from the Satara Rajas and the Peshwas Diaries*, Vol.IX, Poona, 1911, p.336.

153 V. Blacker, Memoir: *The operations of the British Army in India during the Maratha War, 1817*, 18, 19. Parbury and Accer, London, 1821, p. 21

and were equipped by giving arms, or they were equipped by their own arms. This clearly explains the difference between the Marathas and non-Marathas. This also helped the ruler, jamadars and soldiers to identify their interests with those of their masters and show their loyalty to the Peshwa.[154]

The Cavalry of the Peshwa consisted of four classes:

1. The Khasgi paga
2. The Silhedars
3. The Ekas or Ekandas
4. The Pendharis.

The Khasgi paga or the Peshwa's private cavalry was best. They formed the best force armed, equipped and paid directly by the state. They were small in numbers. According to Kasiraj Pandit, the Khase paga at Panipat did not number more than 6,000 out of a total of 38,000 Cavalry under different chiefs.[155]

The state had its own grasslands which grow for the fodder for the horses of the cavalry while stationed at various places in the country and compulsorily acquired free labour, from people often employed for the services of the cavalry.

By the above sources, Peshwa had issued the military services rendered only by 323 Mahars, 54 Mangs, 52 Cobblers and 10 Saddlers, from the districts of Pune, Sangamner, Parner, Raluri, Khed, Junnar, Nevas, Karde, Gandapur and Belapur. They were not employed for fighting on the battleground but for such a petty work as making ropes and repairing the sandles and bridles for the private cavalry of the Peshwa.[156]

The horsemen employed by the Peshwa, were single volunteers, known as Ekas or Ekandas. They joined the camp bringing with them their own horse and accoutrements. They were paid Rupees forty to fifty per month, mostly in the proportion of the value of their horse.[157]

The Pendharis joining the military force formed a source of income to the Maratha generals. They predatory hordes accompanied the Maratha army

---

154 S.N.Sen, Ibid, No.27, p. 67.

155 Ibid., p.68.

156 G.C. Vad, Ibid., 152 pp.185-6.

157 Tone, *Illustrarion of some institutions of the Maratha people* (1818) p37.

in its expedition and were employed not for fighting but plundering the country through which they passed. They received no pay from the Peshwa neither from their principal chiefs, but on the contrary, paid to the general, to whose army they were attached, a tax, called Palpalti,[158] in return for the protection and attachment to the chief. Though the Pendharis class emerged numerously by the end of the Maratha period, they did not match the earlier Maratha method of warfare.[159]

During the reign of Balaji Bajirao, the Pendharis induction into army had become a common feature of the Maratha force. In a letter addressed to Dattaji Sindhia in 1753-54 the name of Pendhari leader was mentioned.[160]

The Pendharis were not employed for fighting but exclusively for plundering the villages. Pendharis were aware of the area and were habituated of these plunders. The Pendharis were carrying tents or baggage an unnecessary encumbrance, each person carries his food and other useful provision for few days provision for himself and for his horse.[161] Daily they crossed the distance at the rate of thirty and forty miles by roads and country's impassable roads. They carried the same arms a lance and a sword, which they used with admirable dexterity, their horses, are small, but extremely active and they pillage without distinction, friends as well as foes. In a group of three thousand men, began their direct undeviating course for their destination. In a small party, they get more facility plunder the country and carry off a larger quantity of booty. Fighting was not their object, they were perfect to resist the attack even an interior enemy. They were aware of the technique to disperse and reassemble at an appointed rendezvous or if followed into their country they immediately retire to their respective homes.[162]

---

158 Palpatti means return for the protection which Pendharis received from Peshwa.

159 G.C. Vad, Ibid., n.152, p.178.

160 S.N.Sen, Ibid., n.27, p.75.

161 Ibid., p.75.

162 Ibid., p.76.

Peshwai and Local Administration

Police

The Judicial administration of the Peshwa begins from the village. The Mahars worked as village police under the Patil, and the chief police officer.[163] The district police was under the Mamlatdar.

In the detection of crime the Jaglass or village watchmen consisting generally of Mahars were helped by tribes as the Ramoshis, Bhils and Kolis.[164] Unless the stolen property could be recovered or the offence could be traced, the police and the criminal classes had to compensate the party robbed. All responsibilities, however, ended with the detection of the offenders or tracing the offence to another village. In the latter case, the inhabitants of the place to which the offence had been traced were liable to make compensation. But sufficient proof had to be put forward for such suspicions before the police and the criminal tribes could shake of their responsibilities.

Metropolitan Police

The Metropolitan Administration and Police at Poona became a model of the last of the Peshwas. The efficiency and honesty of this body had extorted the applause of critics like Elphinstone and Tone. Henry Tone served in the army of Bajirao II, and he had direct knowledge of the Peshwa Government.

According to him "It is little remarkable for anything but its excellent Police which alone employs a thousand men. After the firing of the gun, which takes place at ten at night no person can appear in the streets without being taken up by the Patroles and detailed prisoner until dismissed in the morning by Kotwal. So strict is the discipline observed that the Peshwa himself had been kept prisoner a whole night for being out at improper hours."[165]

According to Elphinston Rs.9000, was spent for the force consisting of a large number of peons, horse patrols and Ramoshis.[166]

---

163 S.N.Sen *Administration system of the Marathas*, K.P. Bagachi & Co., Calcutta, Reprint 2002, p.256.

164 Indian Antiquity, Vol. III, 1924, Reprint, Swati Publication, Delhi, 1985, p.76.

165 Ibid., n.27, p. 260.

166 Indian Antiquity, Ibid., No.161, p.186.

Kotwal

In big cities, the police was placed under an officer called Kotwal.[167] His duties included regulation of prices and taking of census. In 1767-68, as per the guidance of Janardan Hari, who was appointed to the Kotwalship of Poona formed rules.

The Marathas followed the Mughals idea and had nothing to do with the rural police. The village headman was in-charge of rural peace with the help of Mahar watchmen. But the Urban policy was maintained by the state, and herein also we find another instance of the Marathas adopting the Muslim practice.

The head of the city police was the Kotwal his principal duties were: (l) To dispose of important disputes within his jurisdiction (2) to fix the prices of goods (3) to supply labourers for government work and to supervise sales and purchase of land (4) to take a census and keep a record of all persons coming and leaving the city. And over and above these he had to maintain peace and order in the city.[168]

The present chapter investigated the Military services in Maharashtra from village level to State. The chapter also deals with Maharashtra's Military culture. Maharashtrian people were having military culture and had qualities of Warrior. With the help of this background and military culture and the next chapter deals with Mahars Military Services and their cultural development in military areas.

---

167 Ibid., N.27, p.258.

168 Ibid., p.395.

MAHAR MILITARY CULTURE

This chapter deals with the Mahar community of Maharashtra and their military culture. As stated in the first chapter the definition and historical background, the community up to Peshwa has been traced out. Their participation in the important military battles. Their services to Europeans and British and their final confrontation with Peshwe have been discussed herein.

Mahars of Maharashtra

The estimated population of Maharashtra in 2001 is 96,878,627, or 2 per cent total population of India which counts 9.42% which ranks second in number.[1] As per the 1991 census of India Maharashtra's Scheduled Castes population, counted, 1,724,191 and 11.09 %.[2]

As per the Final Population Tools S.C. population accounted 9,881,656, or 12.5% of the total population.[3] According to this source in Maharashtra out of 35% Mahar's population available, including the Buddhist, Mahar population was estimated at 4.3 million i.e. 8% of the total population. Out of which 84.36% are rural based whereas only 15.64% are settled in urban base. As per the source 67% were agricultural laborers.[4]

As per Dr. B. R. Ambedkar's analysis, the Mahar community was a powerful and ancient in Maharashtra.[5] According to Dr. B. R. Ambedkar, Mahar community is a distinct community from the rest of the population. Among the Scheduled Caste they are the largest group. In ancient literature including Manusmruti there is no reference of Mahar up to the advent of Muslims, one does not meet with the word 'Mahar'. One finds its mention only in the Dnyaneshwari written by Saint Dnyaneshwar in 1100 A.D. Before him the name Mahar is simply non-existent.

---

1 Final Population Tools, Series – 28, Director of Census Operation Maharashtra, Mumbai,I of 2001, Census of India, 2001.

2 Census Report 1991, Series l4, Part II-B(ii).

3 Census Report, Census of India, 1991.Series II-C

4 Ibid., no.1.

5 Dr. Babasaheb Ambedkar, *Writings and Speeches, Vol. 17*, (ed). Vasant Moon, Education Department, Government of Maharashtra, Mumbai, 2001, p.808.

Traditionally Mahars are called the 'Soma Vansh'[6] which is one of the branches of the Kshatriya, that the Mahars have had these 'gotra', since long.

In his book, Dr. B. R. Ambedkar asserts that Mahars were the 'Broken Men' and as per anthropologists report the Mahars are the original inhabitants of the region, the word Maharashtra is derived from "Mahar".[7]

The Muslim kings of Berar in 15th Century A.D. sanctioned 52 rights[8] in which carrying dead animals were incorporated in the rights.[9] These rights identified

Mahar as Balutedar and legal Village servants.[10]

---

6 Victor Longer, Forefront Forever, *History of Mahar Regiment*, The Mahar Regimental Center, Sagar, M.P. 1981, p.1.

7 Dr. Ambedkar B.R., *The Untouchables*, Amrit Book Co., New Delhi, 1948, pp.31-55.

8 Dr. Ambedkar B.R., n.5, Vol. VII, 1990, p. 280.

9 R. E. Enthoven, *The Tribes and Castes of Bombay*, Inter Documentation Co., Switzerland, 1922, pp.401-418;

R.V. Russel and Hiralal, *The Tribes and Caste of the Central Provinces of India*, Vol. I, London, 1916, Reprint, Cosmos Publication, Delhi, 1915, pp.129-146;

Alexander Robertson; *The Mahar Folk*, Y.M.C.A. Publishing House, Calcutta, 1938, p.27.

10 The account of the Mahar's position is based primarily on the work of Professor N.G. Bhaware, a noted dalit historian. I have benefited greatly from conversations with Dr. Bhaware who has also given me access to his unpublished articles. B.R. Ambedkar, Ibid, n.7, pp. 43-44.

The Balutedars were as follows: (1) Brahmans-joshi (priest-astrologer),Kulkarni (accountant), potdar (money-assayer); (2) non-Brahmans – sutar (carpenter), Lohar (black-smith), Kumbhar (potter), Nhavi (barber), Parit (washerman) and Gurao (shrine-keeper and the priest of the non-Brahmans); (3) Untuchables – Mahar (messenger, watchman, disposer of dead animals and general village servant), Mang (rope maker and general village servant), and Chambhar (shoemaker and leather-worker).

There were three types of balutedars: religious servants and officials of the village (Joshi, Kulkarni and Gurao); Artisans and Craftsmen, who comprised the bulk of the Balutedars, and were largely non-Brahman sudras by caste, yet included one Untouchable caste, the Chambhars; and menial servants of the village, who had

Mahar in village society and services

The Mahar community of Maharashtra was included among the twelve balutedars of the village, their position was not specifically assigned, regarding work to anyone family, but settled on the rotation basis. Thus, each family could expect to enjoy the special perquisites of the office of Balutedar at some point, as and when their turn comes. Hence none are given a permanent opportunity.

As village servants, they were closely related and tied to the village administration,[11] particularly to the Patil or the village headman, who was generally of the Maratha caste, as the hereditary headman of the village. The Patil, was an important personage not only in the village but also in the supra-village sphere. He was responsible for civil administration, as well as apprehension of criminals. He was the chief revenue collector and transmitter of village revenue to the state his administrative superior known as the Mamlatdar. He worked at the taluka and district level, and the Subedar who was the equivalent of a governor of a province. At the apex of the hierarchy stood the Peshwa and his office at Pune.

The Mahar assisted Patil in village on various occasion in administration and more generally, performed whatever tasks were assigned to him, in a private or official capacity.[12] Interestingly this relationship of dominance and subservience between the Patil and the Mahar frequently invoked much resentment and bitterness in Dalit ideology and is used as a symbol in Dalit literature.[13]

One of the major benefits received by the Patil from the Mahars was access to free labour and services. Mahar could be summoned for the sowing or harvesting of the Patil's own lands and could also be required to tend public lands. Mahars also aided the Patil in revenue collection and

---

no fixed occupation or trade as such, but were required to do any and all tasks that the village authorities required – the Mahars and the Mangs. Even the Mangs had a skill -- rope making or basket-weaving. Thus unique among the balutedars, the Mahars had no traditional occupation or trade, which means that they had no independent base in the village.

11 Alexander Robertson, *The Mahar Folk*, Y.M.C.A., Publishing House, Calcutta, 1938, p.17.

12 Ibid., p.17.

13 Pralhad Chendvankar Pralhad, Audit, Popular Prakashan, Bombay, 1976, p.10.

transmittal, which was one of the most important tasks of village administration.[14]

Mahars participated in couriers and were responsible for taking messages from one village to another. They assisted in the reception of official visitors to the village by carrying their luggage looking after their horses.[15]

The Mahars role as boundary arbiter confirms their position as among the most ancient inhabitants of the land and hence the most knowledgeable about the area and scope of a particular village.

Finally, as a village watchman, Mahars also played an important role in the maintenance of law and order in the village and corves labour at the request of state authorities.[16]

Mahar is emphatically called the village eye. He performed his duty as a watchman and guarded the village. His evidence was final in every dispute. Should two cultivators quarrel respecting the boundaries of their fields, the Mahar's evidence sought to decide it, and should a similar quarrel happen between two villages, the Mahars were always the chief actors to solve it, their decision was final.[17] The Mahars duties were numerous that a complete enumeration of them would be tiresome. In short, the Mahar was an important person to the village.[18]

Mahars were responsible for the disposal of dead animals (which formed a staple in their diets). The public notification of all deaths was to be done in the village and the arrangement and clearing away of funeral pyres, and the cleaning of village sewers.[19]

---

14 R.D. Choksey, Ratnagiri Collectorate (1921-1829) *Selected documents from the Ratnagiri Collector's files (Peshwa Daftar)* Poona, 1958, p.168.

15 Alexander Robertson,Ibid, no.11, p.20.

16 Jayshree Gokhale, *From Concession to Confrontation, The Politics of an Indian Untouchable Community*, Popular Prakashan, Bombay, 1993, p.32.

17 Shankarrao Kharat, *Maharashtratil Maharancha Itihas*, Yeshwantrao Chavan, Samajshastra Samshodhan Kendra, Pune, 2003, p.47.

18 Alexander, Robertson, Ibid., no.11, p.17. R.N.Goodne,

"Report on the village communities of the Deccan" Selection from the Records of Bombay Government, No.IV, Bombay, 1852, p.13.

19 Jayshree Gokhale Jayshree, Ibid., n.16, p.33.

The Mahars were the original inhabitants of Maharashtra. Etymological version of the word Mahar is derived from Sanskrit words Maha and Ari which means 'terrifying enemy.'[20] It was because they had to fight ferocious wars for their existence that aggression was committed one after another.

Mahars were cultured and civilized people. "Avarnas" who occupied territories of present Maharashtra, Goa, Northern border areas of Karnataka, western and southern areas of Gujarat, some part of present M.P., Northern parts of Andhra Pradesh, Northern areas of Karnataka state, etc. They had to surrender to the new tribes and clans, because of their defeat some of them retained their territories to suppress the Mahars forever.[21] The Mahars, in spite of their losing power, had retained some of the important positions both in the army and civil administration.

The names of the Mahars were suffixed by Nak, which seems to be the corrupt form of the Nag. According to some scholars, the Mahars were Nagas, hence their names are suffixed by 'Nak'. Nagas were concentrated around Nagpur region after which the town seems to have been named. Even now Nagpur and the surrounding areas are densely populated by the Mahar population.[22]

The Mahars were the Marshall race and original inhabitants of Maharashtra, therefore, they are known as "Bhoomi's Putra".[23] (son of soil). They served mostly in armies and held many important positions in Maratha, Muslim, Moghul, British, and independent Indian armies. They fought wars and conquered territories in the past. In spite of their bright army career, they could not become rulers in Medieval and Modern period because they were put in the categories of Avarnas. According to religious scriptures, Avarnas could not become anything else but servants and serfs. The social restrictions which were imposed on them proved to be detrimental for their military and economic status also.[24]

---

20 R.C. Enthoven, Ibid, n.9, pp.401, 418.

21 N.D. Kamble, *Deprived Castes and their Struggle for Equality*, Ashish Publishing Houe, Delhi, 1983, p.2.

22 Dr.B.R. Ambedkar's Speech delivered at Nagpur on 15.10.1956.

23 BhoomiPutra, which means the son of the soil or nature. Mate, S.M., *Asprushthomcha Prashna,* Loksagraha Chhapkhana, Pune, 1933, p.32.

24 N.D. Kamble, Ibid., n.21, p.3.

The Mahar's were the most oppressed people during medieval period, particularly under the Peshwa rule. Since centuries they were kept away from the mainstream of the society. Mahar followed somewhat different lifestyle and cycle from the rest of the communities of Maharashtra.[25]

The Mahars were out of the Varna system,[26] they did not follow vedic religious customs. The Mahars did not worship gods like Brahma, Mahesh and Vishnu and other incarnations. Many of their gods and goddesses were more non-Aryan origin. Their rituals were simple. Their customs were designed for smooth inter-personal relationships within their communities and with other communities.[27]

Military service was used as a channel for social mobility by the Mahars. They interacted in a military set up where cosmopolitanism was a way of life. This led to a new exposure and also a fresh dimension of experience for them. It was a strong destiny that the Mahars joined the rank of the British Army to bring about the downfall of the Brahmin Peshwas.[28]

Although many different low castes and tribes were part of the military services in the years before the 1857 Mutiny, among them Mahars of Western India were probably the most heavily recruited... They numbered between a quarter of a fifth of those units in which they were recruited and perhaps 1/ 6th of the entire Bombay army.[29]

Keer refers to this aspect of military service by the Mahars as saying that, "they claim they are the most robust, adaptable, intelligent, brave, virile and leading untouchable community in India".[30]

---

25 Dr. Babasaheb Ambedkar, Ibid,n.5, vol. 17, P.807.

26 Varna System: The general proposition that the social organization of the Indo-Aryans was based on the theory of Chaturvarnya and that Chaturvarnya means division of society into four classes:

Brahmins (Priests) Vaishyas (Traders)

Kshatriyas (soldiers)Shudras (Menials)

see Dr. Babasaheb Ambedkar, *Writings and Speeches, Vol.7*, Education Department, Govt. of Maharashtra, Bombay 1990, p.9.

27 Ibid., n.15, p.6.

28 Patwardhan Sunanda, *Change among India's Harijan*, Maharashtra – A Case Study, Orient Longman, New Delhi, 1973, p.21 and p.239.

29 Cohen Stephen P. in 'The Untuchable Soldier. Caste, Politics and the Indian Army" in the *Journal of Asian Studies, Vol.XXVIII*, No.3, May, 1969.

Early military participation of Mahars

Khushru Khan

According to Shankarrao Kharat, "In the 14th century Turk-Sultan Mumbarak ruled Delhi. In his cabinet a commander whose name was Khushru khan was a Mahar (Parwari or Barwar low caste men). He made purely Army of low people and he revolted on 14th April 1320."[31]

Baharnak

According to Alexander Robertson, the story inscribed on a copper plate in the possession of a Mahar family near Purandhar in the Poona district, which amply illustrates the free and fearless qualities of the Mahars. The copper plate was said to have been given by a King of Bidar to a Mahar of Purandhar called Baharnak.[32] The plate is well preserved and zealously guarded. It is shown only to a select few. The story has it that the king was building the battlements of his fort but they kept crumbling. The king was perplexed. Eventually, the goddess of the area appeared to the King in a dream and demanded the sacrifice of an eldest son and an eldest daughter-in-law who had to be buried under the foundations of the bastion walls to enable the base to hold on. Bharnak, sensing the plight of the king, offered to help his ruler and provided the offerings. The miracle took place and the foundations of the wall were firmed up. The fort was completed. The king was pleased with Baharnak and granted him and his heirs in perpetuity some villages in the Purandhar area. It shows that Baharnak was a mighty warrior and a fierce hunter. He took a great hand in assisting the king, together with his companion, Jeaji Naik, in crushing the revolts of Subhan Khan at Pratapgad and of Abdul Shah at Bidar.[33] He helped the king in building a fort at Rajgad. On another occasion, Baharnak brought a Bengal tiger in a cage and presented it to the King. For these deeds of daring he was awarded several pieces of land and

---

30 Keer Dhananjay, *Dr. Ambedkar Life and Mission*, Popular Prakashan, Mumbai, p.8. Please see Shinde V.R., Bharatiya Ashprushatecha Prashur, Koushyaly Prakashan, Reprint 2003, p.162.

31 Hasan Mehadi, Tughlaq Dynasty, Thacker Spink and Company, Calcutta,1933(1963) P.30, Kharat Shankarrao Maharashtratil Maharancha Itihas, Dr. Shakuntala Kharat, Pune, 2003, p.135.

32 Alexander Robertson, *The Mahar Folk,* Y.M.C.A. Publishing House, Calcutta, 1938, p.29.

33 V.K.Rajwade, (ed), *Marathyanchya Itihasahi Sadhane*, Vol.16, Letter No.58, p.66, Vol. 15, Letter No. 290. Bharat Itihas Sanshodhan Mandal, Pune, 1930, p.399.

villages and was accorded high social status and standing.[34] It may be noted that "Nak" among the Mahars means a leader and several Mahar names ended with the suffix "Nak". This became synonymous with "Naik". It is recorded that the Moghuls too trusted the Mahars and, because of their unfailing loyalty, and courage, brought them to Panhala where they were used by Aurangzeb as guards for his daughter who lived in the fortress. For the good services rendered, the Mahars were granted property rights in villages around Panhala. The Mahars were used by the Moghuls as watchmen,[35] especially when they were in Zenana.

Mahars in Shivaji's military service

In the 16th century Mahars played an important role in Chhatrapati Shivaji's Army. Chhatrapati Shivaji, recognized the great fighting qualities of the Mahars. He for the first time admitted this community in the martial mould. Shivaji rose to power in 1647 and till his death in 1680, this military genius who perfected the guerilla system of warfare and welded the Maratha race into a mighty military built-up nation, fought with all around him. He took on the mighty Moghuls, harassed and battered their forces, nibbled at the boundaries of the Moghul empire and ended the powerful forces of Aurangzeb. He fought with the Sultan of Bijapur, raiding his kingdom and ramming his armies. He responded to the Bijapur Government call "bring back the rebel dead or alive". Shivaji matched his steel against this call and fought against Afzal Khan. Similarly, he fought the Portuguese in India as also the Abyssinians of Janjira.

The forts of Shivaji were the nodal points of power, not only did he control the territories around the forts but also used his forts as a powerful and well-provided base for launching forays assaults and lightning campaigns against his enemies. The forces could be withdrawn within the battlements of the forts and remain secure inside the fort walls. The logistics could be provided for the forces as they were trained for further attacks. The forts provided safe havens, strong storage areas, and live focal centres for gathering intelligence and radiating administrative instructions for the territories adjoining the forts.

---

34 Shivcharitya Sahitya, *Bharat Itihas Samshodhan Mandal, Vol.3*, Letter -609, p.197, Letter 673, p.252, Bharat Itihas Samshodhan Mandal, Pune, p. 252.

35 Shankarrao Kharat, Ibid., no.17, p.140.

In this important military administration, the Mahars were used as scouts in sensitive places and for outpost duties around the forts by Shivaji.[36] They watched all movements in the peripheral hills and jungles and reported on all ingress and egress to the forts,[37] it was during that essential period that gathered primary intelligence report to organize the future planning, defensive arrangements and aggressive marches also were depended on this intelligence report. Byherjee Naik, whose reports and discoveries, vaguely attributed to goddess Bhowani, contributed tremendously to the success and achievements of Shivaji.[38] The Mahars were the most important persons of Byherjee's faceless but omniscient legion.

The Mahars kept a watch on all paths, roads, and tracks leading in and out of forts, misled enquirers, threw enemies off scent, and cut off the enemy's stragglers.[39] Shivaji was constantly improving, revising and reviewing his system of intelligence which was useful to him not only for external information but also for internal control over his forces. He could check on the loyalties of his men, keep himself informed of every abuse of authority, frustrate treachery, overawe the disobedient, and prevent embezzlement of funds. His intelligence services penetrated all levels and acquired intimate knowledge of the most private circumstances. Nothing was left to chance, and discipline was draconic.

Shivaji found the Mahars useful in this task, for the wily Maratha chief realized that the best way of obtaining the maximum results was to mix up various castes in his garrison forces. Men of one caste would keep a watch on the other and serve as double checks on sources of information. The animosity between the castes could be harnessed to advantage and one community could be played against another for the common good of the Maratha Kingdom. Thus, the garrisons of Shivaji's forts had separate and complete establishments comprising Brahmins, Marathas, Ramoosees, Mahars, and Mangs. These were collectively known as "Gurkhurees" who were maintained hereditarily by permanent

---

36 James Grant Duff, *History of Marathas*, Vol. I, Reprint, Koran Publication, Delhi, 2000, p.169.

37 C.B. Khairmode, C.B., *Ashprushancha Lashkari Pesha*, Maharashtra Rajya Sahitya Ani Sanskriti Mandal, Mumbai 1992, p.3.

38 Ibid., p.3.

39 Major R..M. Betham, *Marathas and Dekhani Musalmans* (Compiled for the Indian Army Under the Orders of the Government of India, 1908), C.B. Khairmode, Ashprushancha Lashkari Pesha, Ibid. n.37 p.3.

assignments of rent-free lands in the areas surrounding the forts.[40] Naturally, the Gurkhurees looked upon the forts as their mother who fed them and provided lifelong protection for them. They would do anything for the mother and would gladly lay down their lives for the honour of the mother.

Shivaji raised a regular standing army[41] which was always ready for any emergency duty and was provided with pay and quarters for service throughout the year. The warlike qualities of the people of Maharashtra was well known and had been acclaimed during the seventh, to ninth centuries A.D. The Chinese Pilgrim Hiuen-sang, in the seventh century had admired the military daring of these men. The Maratha infantry was well known in the eighth and ninth centuries and the rulers of Bengal obtained soldier from Maharashtra. Shivaji moulded them in a wonderful manner. His force rose to 40,000 cavalries, which was of two kinds – Bargeers and Silhadars, and 10,000 infantry. He maintained an elephant corps of about 1,260 and a camel corps numbering 3000. He had some artillery, for it is reported[42] that he had purchased some eighty pieces of cannon. Shivaji built a considerable naval fleet too. Strict discipline and outstanding leadership, implicit confidence and loyalty of his men, who were held together in pursuit of the noble ideas of "Dharma Rajya" accounted for Shivaji's brilliant victories, magnificent manoeuvres and strategic wizardry. The Brahman could fight shoulder to shoulder with the Mahar in Shivaji's army.[43] Shivaji took not only the Mahars into his Army but also about 700 Pathan deserters from Bijapur and those Muslims who were prepared to fight for him.[44] Shivaji had a catholic mind. He was not troubled with untouchability. For the first time a well-knit army force, embracing all castes, had been raised in the country. The

---

40 G. Duff, G., Ibid, n.36, p.169.

41S.N. Sen, *The Military System of Marathas*, K.P. Bagachi & Company, Calcutta & Delhi, Reprint 1979, p.1.

42 H.S. Sardesai, Shivaji, *The Great Maratha*, Cosmo Publication, New Delhi, 2002, p.438.

43 S.N. Sen, Ibid., n.41, p.17, p.17.

44 S.N. Joshi, (ed), *Shivkalin Patrasar Sangraha Vol. I*, Art.719, Shivcharitra Karyalaya, Pune 1930, p.157.

V.K. Rajwade (ed), *Marathyanchya Itihasachi Sadhane*, Vol.9, Bharat Itihas Samshodhan Mandal, Pune.

morale of the force was tremendously high, and patriotism of the soldiers was unsurpassed.

The Mahars proved their worth as Robinhoods of the forest, with their knives and daggers, They moved secretly with expedition, covering the longest distance at the shortest notice and with the highest speed, hence they found a place in Shivaji's infantry.[45] The high-caste Marathas looked down upon the infantry; they were cavalrymen and rode to battle on swift chargers. The Mahars served as squires to the Maratha knights. For each Maratha mounted warrior, two army soldiers known as Paik were given. They were "Mahar and Mang castes."[46] The Mahar's accepted the arduous life of infantry. Sleeping under the stars, living off the land, marching miles with the nearest necessities, lightly equipped and encumbered by field artillery. These men moved from place to place with incredible speed, attacking and withdrawing, charging and pursuing and finally, melting away in the surroundings. The Mahars got into Shivaji's artillery too.[47] The Mahars found a place as crews in Shivaji's naval fleet, because the high caste Marathas did not gladly accept the sea services. Shivaji had to employ Muslim naval commanders.[48]

Military services of Mahars post Chhatrapati Shivaji

Nagnak Mahar: Patil

The Mahars continued to be respected for their gallantry, honesty, and loyalty to the Maratha Kings after Shivaji.[49] In fact, in some villages of Maharashtra the Mahars enjoyed the honourable positions and title of Patil. The Village Patil's were held in great esteem and occupied positions of prestige which were hereditary and continued from generation to generation. In some places, the Mahars had been dispossessed of their title of Patil, but it was laid down by the Maratha Kings that if any Mahar who had lost his position of Patil performed some deeds of daring act,

---

45 S.N.Sen, *Military system of the Maratha*, Orient Longmans Pvt., Calcutta, 3rd ed. 1958, pp.17-18.

46 Anil Kathare, *Shivkalatil Ani Peshwekalatil Maharancha Itihas*, Kalpana Prakashan, p.179.

47 Patric Cadel Patric, *History of the Bombay Army*, Longman and Green Co., London, 1938, P. 12.

48 S.T. Das, *Indian Military – Its History and Development*, Sagar Publication, New Delhi, 1978, p.55.

49 Journal of Bharat Itihas Samshodhan Mandal, Quarterly, Pune, 1962, p.l,4,14.

the title and rights would be restored to him. In this regard Nagnak Mahar who was once a Patil in the Satara area but had lost his rights showed his courage, he was determined to get back his lost position. He fought for it along with his redoubtable Mahar soldiers' friends and snatched the fort of Vairatgadh from the Muslims and presented it to his ruler who was overjoyed and in turn, rewarded the valiant Nagnak Mahar with the title, position and rights of Patil.[50]

Sidnak Mahar: A warrior

During Rajaram Maharaj, another fearless fighter-Sidnak Mahar emerged, who raised his own army and helped the Maratha Kings. When Shahu Maharaj, son of Rajaram was released from the Moghul prison, Shidnak stood by him with his Mahar soldiers, he was then rewarded with the village Kalambi where he stayed with his family for generations. His grandson, also known as Shidnak Mahar, was another great Sirdar emerged during the Peshwa Army of Sawai Madhavrao. He was held in high respect as an audacious and daring warrior.[51]

The Peshwas regime was considered the apogee of Brahman orthodoxy and political power. The Mahar's position in the social order was recognized, and individual Mahars were given honours and avenues for advancement.[52]

---

[50] Journal of Bharat Itihas Samshodhan Mandal, seventh seminar, Shake 1841, Pune, pp.54-55 see also V.C. Bendre, (ed) Maharashtra Itihasachi Sadhane, Part III, Mumbai Marathi Granth Sangrahalaya, Dadar, Mumbai, 1967, Art. 172, 510, p.11.

51 V.R. Shinde, Bharatiya Ashprushatecha Prashna, Nav Bharat Granthalaya, Nagpur, 1933, pp.192-93, See also, Journal of Bharat Itihas Samshodhan Mandal, Quarterly, 1-4, Pune 1902, p.141.

52 A 1730 letter from the Peshwa Daftar to the Peshwa's brother, Tryambakrao Somavanshi, whose name suggests that he was a Mahar, indicates that he has been asked by the Peshwa to keep an eye and follow the movements of Udaji Chavan, whose rebellion had caused the Peshwa some trouble. Another letter from Peshwa Daftar also shows that some Mahars had risen to high service under the Peshwas. This letter, dated approximately 173, reveals that a patilki (office of patil) had been awarded to a Mahar, though it had been disputed by a man of the Gurao caste. The dispute over the patilki continued for several years, by which time the village in question had fallen to the, Mughals. Thus the persistent Mahar succeeded in doing, and for his pains here gained his watan Peshwa Daftar, V.II, Letter No. 4(28/4/1730) in Shankarrao Joshi, Maratheleatin Samaj darshan, Chitrashala Press, Pune, 1960, pp.122-124.

During early Peshwas, Mahars were employed within the ranks of the regular armies. In addition to having their own fighting units, Mahars also worked as stretcher-bearers on the field of battle.[53] As per the records Kondanar Mahar distinguished himself in the battle of Janjira (1733).[54] Similarly, in the battle of Wasai, Tuknath Mahar fought gloriously and was suitably rewarded by the Peshwa.[55] At the battle of Kharda a noteworthy incident involving Mahar participation in the Peshwa's armies occurred. During this battle, Sidnak Mahar pitched his tent next to the tent of Brahmans and Marathas. The caste-Hindu Sardars objected and sent complaints to the Peshwa. One of the Chief advisors of the Peshwa during this battle was one Hiraji Patankar. A Chitpavan Brahman. Patankar delivered the following judgement regarding the complaint by the caste Hindus." This is not a dinner party, it is a party of warriors.[56] There is no pollution or untouchability here". The Mahar's tent, therefore, was allowed to remain near the tent of the Hindus despite the objections of the caste-Hindus.[57]

Raynak Mahar

The Peshwa, however, was overwhelmed by Raynak's example of courage, valour and loyalty, and in his honour built a Samadhi which continues to be a place for pilgrimage today. In the environs of Pachad Raynak is still remembered and has a powerful hold on people. They take oaths in his name. They sacrifice goats and worship him as a god. And Raynak's decedents, Potnis and the adversary of the Peshwa join in this

---

53 B.S. Murthy, *Depressed and Oppressed: Forever in Agony*, New Delhi, p.82.

54 D.B. Parasnis, (ed), *Brahamendraswamy Dhawadshikar Charitra va Patravyavahar*, Lek, 270, Nirnaysagar Press, Mumbai 1967.

C.B. Kairmode, *Dr. B.R.Ambedkar Charitra, Vol.l,* Sugava Prakashan, Sadashiv Peth, Pune, 5th ed., 2002, p.199.

55 G.S. Sardesai, *New History of the Marathas, Vol.II*, Pheonix Publication, Bombay, 1958, pp.181 to 186.

C.B. Khairmode, *Dr. B.R.Ambedkar Charitra, Vol. I*, Sugava Prakashan, Pune, 5th ed., 2002, p.200.

56 C.B. Khairmode, *Dr. B.R. Ambedkar Charitra, Vol.I*, Sugava Prakashan, Pune, 2002, p.199.

57 C.B. Agarwal, *The Harijans in Rebellion: Case for the Removal of Untouchability*, Bombay, 1934, pp.68-69.

celebration. The most orthodox Brahmin also pay homage to Raynak's Samadhi.[58]

Peshwai and Mahars

In the military, the Mahar forces were in a small number of the total population involved. There were hardly more than three to four regularly constituted Mahar units. The Mahars were enlisted into the armies as per the need of the time hence their numbers in the Peshwa's forces fluctuated with the tide of the battle. Records show that there were some 5,000 Mahars employed in the military forces of the Peshwa.[59]

Despite the Mahar participation in the military services the social condition of the Maratha Empire remained as it is. The benefits individual Mahars derived from the Peshwa's military policies did not necessarily alter the position of Mahars as a community in Maharashtrian society. Individual Mahars who served under the Peshwa obtained a new perspective for themselves and their relation with the society changed. They discovered a new sense of self-worth, which they transmitted to their friends and relatives who remained in villages. Their progress did not serve as a stepping-stone for other Mahars. Individual improvement did not necessarily lead to social progress. Despite the fact that Mahars served in the Peshwa's army on equal footing with caste-Hindus, it did not mean that the Peshwa gave equal justice in the said cultural life.

The Peshwai was mainly based on pre-eminently a Hindu padshahi (empire), and it worked on the base of Manusmuriti Hindu notions of kingship and politics, particularly the *Manava dharmashastra.* According to these ideas, the state was directed to preserve and strengthen the caste order. It was directed to be the regulating mechanism between the various castes, ensuring that each caste performed its particular dharma (duties,

---

58 Zumbarlal Kamble: "Raynak-Thoda Itihas Thodya Damtakatha" A.D. Oct-Dec. 1978. "Raynakchi Samadhi" A.D. May-June 1977, p.4.

59 S.M. Mate, *Ashprushthanche Prashna*, Loksangraha Chhapkhemu, Pune, p. 223 to 227. Also see Appendix the names of Mahar Phatardar in Peshwa's Army.

(1) Apnak; (2) Umnak, (3) Upnak, (4) Kalnak, (5) Kusnak (6) Karunak (7) Kernak (8) Khandnak (9) Gomnak (10) Gondnak (11) Changnak (12) Chimannak (13) Chidnak (14) Jannak (15) Jhuknak (16) Tuknak (17) Damenak (18) Dasnak (19) Dadnak (20) Devnak (21) Dhavnak (22) Dhulnak (23)Dhondnak (24) Nagnak (25) Padnak (26)Pujank (27) Badnak (28) Bagnak (29) Malnak (30) Maynak (31) Meghnak (32) Bhemnak (33) Yesnak (34) Ramnak (35) Rajnak (36) Rannak (37) Lahalnak (38) Vamnak (39) Satvanak (40) Sambhnak (41) Sivnak (42) Suknak (43) Subnak (44) Sidnak.,

tasks as directed by particular Hindu religion). Thus, in matters which did not involve purely military or political considerations, the Peshwai maintained the Varna hierarchy strictly and preserved the distinctions between the various caste, varna and jatis. The Peshwai was the final arbiter in caste disputes, and the decisions of the Peshwa were binding.

In 1776-77, Mahars of Kasbe village charged that many of their rights were being usurped by Mangs. An important area of contention was access to the dead animals in a village, which was

Claimed by the Mangs as well as the Mahars. Another dispute involved the wedding processions of both communities. The Mahars charged that traditionally their bridegrooms were to be paraded on a horse, and that Mang bridegrooms were allotted a bull for their wedding procession. The Peshwa ruled in favour of the Mahars, and though his decision confirmed the distinctions and distances between the two Untouchable jatis. A letter dated before 1795, mentioned that the Peshwa decided on the hierarchy to be observed strictly among the lower non-Brahman balutedars, and to judge which balutedar takes precedence. The Peshwa's judgement was that the Sutar or the carpenter was the highest of the balutedars. Another letter shows that the Peshwai had undertaken an inquiry into the background and marriage connections of two Shimpi (tailor) families. The Peshwa also enforced the law to maintain distances between the varna orders, as per a letter dated 1795 reveals that "a Brahman family had unwillingly employed and housed a maid of the Chambhar caste (they had thought her to be a Kunbin)". This transgression of caste rules brought punishment consisting of fines and purification ceremonies, (*prayascitta*) to all the members of the family. The sources reveal that "the Peshwai was especially careful in maintaining the distinctions between Brahmans and non-Brahmans", and that violation of this principle brought swift punishment.[60] The position of the Brahmins in the social and ritual hierarchy was given top priority. The Peshwai was punctilious, it safeguarded the exclusiveness and privileges of Brahmans as a jati as well as a varna order. Thus, the pre-eminent ritual and social place of the Brahman was guaranteed by the political power of the Peshwa the caste system was not only a spontaneous social order of the people but also a state order controlled and protected by the state.[61]

---

60 Dr. P.A. Gawli *Peshwe Kalin Maharashtra*, Kailash Publication Aurangabad, 2000 p.269.

61 Hiroshi Fukazawa, *The Medieval Deccan,* Oxford University Press, Delhi, 1991, p.93.

Hence conflict of the inter-relationship between the caste hierarchy and political power continued. It may be seen in various cases involving challenges by the Mahars to the established order.

The Peshwa, always decided the benefit in favour of the Brahmans, by referring to the tradition and based on caste relations under previous rulers. It had a significant effect and indicating that precedents on his decision. On this line, the Untouchables also demanded better treatment, but the state power that suppressed such a demand and left them in the lowest position in the society.[62] Along with social status the State power also maintained that the economic position of the Untouchables should remain low and ensured that they did not deviate from their prescribed duties. Prof. N.G. Bhavare cites several cases from the Peshwa Daftar, which reveals that the extent to which the state-supported the prevailing division of labour. Thus, in one case, a Mahar who had started a fish exporting business which sold to caste-Hindus was told to desist under pain of punishment.[63]

Military positions of Mahars

The Mahar's of Maharashtra is having a brilliant military career. They as soldiers were always on the forefront in all the historical military conquest.[64]

During the sixteenth century under the leadership of Shivaji, the scattered forces of Maratha power were united. It was during this period that the Marathas became rulers and succeeded in establishing their rule in Maharashtra, and in other states of India as well. Shivaji took the help of the courageous trained Mahars for organizing all his military conquests. The marshall race of the Mahars was used as a powerful force for establishing the Maratha rule. They played an important role in establishing and stabilizing the rule of Shivaji and his successors in Maharashtra. Many of them emerged to prominence in the Military and civil administration during and after Shivaji.[65]

---

62 Bhavare N.D., *Marathekalin Ashprushyanchi Stithi*, A.D. Ja fe.,Ma.198.

63 R.V.Parulekar, ed. Survey of Indigenous Education in the Province of Bombay (1820-1830) (Bombay, 1951), p.lvi, See document Nos. 3 & 4, pp.21-52 for the 1825 report by J.B. Jervis presented detailed statistical tables for each of the nine taluka in the South Konkan District.

64 C.B. Khairmode, Ibid, n.37, p.3.

65 Ibid., p.3.

After Sambhaji, the Maratha rule declined and was losing to Muslim and Moghul ruler. During this period the Mahar's fought numerous wars and recovered territories after territories which were lost to Muslim and Moghul rulers.[66] Chatrapati Shivaji depended on the Mahars to a large extent, who them helped in establishing and stabilizing the Maratha rule in Maharashtra. They fought many battles on behalf of Shivaji to establish and expand the Maratha rule in Maharashtra.[67]

Along with Patilship, the Mahars were performing military responsibilities and also military services. Those Mahars who were holding military rights were known as Mete Naik. By the privilege, Mete Naik Mahars were permanently allowed to settle on the plain grounds and on the slopes of the mountains, particularly of those having forts. Such Mahars were also called as Metkar and were responsible for the defence of forts. In all difficult hill forts, only the Mahars were posted as killedars (the fort guard keepers). Even today they are known as Metkar or Mete Naik.[68]

Mete Naiki

Kalnak Mahar of village Majkar and Yesnak Mahar Sondkar were given Mete Naiki in the fort of Rohida during Adilshah Nizam's rule.[69] Both of them were residing on the slopes of the fort on two different sides. They collected and shared equally revenue from the neighbouring areas and enjoyed the privileges. In course of time, they entered into conflict with Azamsekhaji, the Muslim Killedar of Rohida, who ordered to slay both the Mete Naik Mahars and threw their children into the forest to be eaten up by the wild tigers. However, this conflict was averted when Kamalnak Mahar of Natamul negotiated on their behalf and settled the dispute by paying regularly a share in their revenue to Azamsekhaji. After the defeat

---

66 V.R. Shinde, *Bharatiya Ashprushatecha Prashna*, Reprint, Kaushalya Prakashan, Aurangabad, 2003, p.153.

67 N.D. Kamble, Ibid, n.21, p.116.

68 Shiv-Charitra Sahitya, Vol.3, Art-609, *Bharat Itihas Samshodhan Mandal*, Pune, p.197.

69 Khondnak Ramnak Mahar of Karanji (Bhor) Tq. Rohilkhor gave in writing in 1946, that Kalnak Mahar of Majkur was the maternal uncle of his father and enjoyed the Mete Naiki.

Shiv Charitra Sahitya Vol.3, Article 609, Bharat Itihas Sanshodhan Mandal, Pune, 1912, p. 197.

of Mughal rule by the Marathas, Kalnak Mahar and Sondkar Mahars signed a treaty with Shivaji III and retained their title of Mete Naiki.[70]

The Mahars of Wadi Dhavadi were in possession of Sarja Buruj (fort) now popularly known as Raigad fort. Shivaji defeated the Mahar's and imprisoned them, got possession of the Raigad fort which originally belonged to the Mahars. Until recently the Mahars were residing inside the Raigad Fort.[71] Even today the Mahars having surnames as Gaikwad, the endogamous group, reside near the foot of their Raigad fort. Many Mahars possessed Mete Naiki before and during Maratha rule in Maharashtra and enjoyed military positions, powers and privileges.

Participation of Mahars in Battle of Raigad

Raigad, the hard-impregnable fort, could be conquered only by the Mahars as they alone knew the skills and technique of defending or conquering it. As mentioned historically the fort belonged to them but later conquered by the Marathas. Rainak Mahar, fort keeper (Killedar) and the Mahar soldiers were in the Raigad fort when it was attacked by the British army. The Mahar soldiers fought British army bitterly and continuously for 15days and defended the Raigad fort by defeating the British army. However, Rainak, the fort keeper and Sardar of the Mahar army was killed in the battle but retained the Raigad Fort.[72]

While attacking this fort, second time, British made deep study of the Raigad fort and changed their strategy to conquer this fort.[73]

Battle of Vairatgad

During the rule of Rajaram the Maratha king, there was a prominent Mahar Sardar named Seti Bin Nagnak Mahar who was the Patil of Nagewadi in Wai taluk of Satara district. He was selected by the King Rajaram Maharaj to conquer the Vairatgad for him from Mughal ruler. Accordingly, Seti Bin Nagnak Mahar, fought bravely with his limited

---

70 After the death of Kalnak Mahar and Yeshnak Mahar Sondkar, Ramnak Mahar, borther of Kalnak Mahar and father of Khandnak received theMete Naiki from Shivaji, similarly, Bhojnak Rajani, Tq. Utroli, the father-in-law of Khandnak Ramnak Mahar was also given a Mete Naiki.

71 Ibid., No.68, p.197.

72 Bahishkrut Bharat (Marathi Weekly), Bombay 20, May 1927, see also Journal of Bharat Itihas Samshodhan Mandal, Quarterly, 1962, 1-4, p.141.

73 Krishnaji Vishnu Acharya Kalagaonkar, "*Junya Itihasik Gosti" in Bharat Varsh, Bombay, 1900, p.36.*

Mahar soldiers, against the huge Moghul army in the battle of Vairatgad and defeated Moghuls. He conquered the Vairatgad fort from Moghuls. Thus, he joined it to the Maratha kingdom.[74]

Sidnak Mahar and Rule of Shahu

After the murder of Sambhaji Maharaj, the Marathas were having nothing but only anarchy and utter chaos in Maratha ruled provinces. Maratha rule was collapsing. The Mahars who helped in building up Maratha rule with their blood and flesh felt very bad so they wanted to revive the Maratha rule. Moreover, Shahu Maharaj was also imprisoned by the Moghul ruler. With the intention of re-establishing Maratha rule, Sidnak Mahar, raised his Mahar army and helped the Maratha rule to re-establish in Maharashtra. When Shahu Maharaj was released from the prison of Moghul in 1707 and returned to demand his share in the kingdom from Queen Tarabai. But he was denied his share in the kingdom. Sidnak Mahar helped him to restore his rule in Satara district, Maharashtra. As a reward, Sidnak Mahar was given Kalambi, as Inam which was bravely retained by him and his heirs for years together.[75]

Battle of Kharda

Grandson of Sidnak Mahar of Kalambi, in Satara district in Maharashtra, named also Sidnak, occupied very high position in the Maratha army. He considered Moghul rule as foreign he wanted to establish native rule, he raised Mahar Army. He was also not happy with the Peshwa but to eradicate the foreign rule, he joined Savai Madhavrao Peshwa to fight the battle against Moghuls. Despite the fact that the Peshwa rule was known for its casteism, orthodoxy and partiality under which the Mahars lost their status and were defeated. Yet Mahars along with, Sidnak Mahar and his Mahar army joined him on the consideration of establishment of native rule. Since Mahars were on the battlefield at Kharda,[76] they did not care for caste distinctions.

During the battle days, on the battlefield, the tent of Sidnak Mahar was set near the tent of Savai Madhavrao Peshwa. Similarly, the Mahar soldiers of Sidnak Mahar also were resting along with the soldiers belonging to high castes. But the high caste soldiers did not like Mahar

74 Seventh Seminar, News, Bharat Itihas Samshodhan Mandal, Pune, 1912, pp.54-55.

75 Ibid., n.73, p. 36.

76 V.R. Shinde, Ibid., n.66, p.158.

soldiers nearby. They complained to Savai Madhavrao Peshwa and asked him to remove the tents of Commander Sidnak Mahar and his Mahar soldiers from their neighbourhood and be installed away from them. Savai Madhavrao Peshwa consulted Hiroji Patankar an old Sardar, who said that "battlefield is not a row of community dinner where caste distinctions are observed, but it is a row of brave warriors, where one who deserve will preserve his dignity and place of honour (Janchi Talwar Khambir To Hambir) irrespective of caste distinctions".[77]

Thus, same commander Sidnak Mahar and his Mahar army fought with the Pathans soldiers of the Nizams in which they showed rare skills of warfare and prowess and defeated the Pathans and Moghuls in the battle of Kharda. It is not only this; even he saved the life of Parshuram Bhau himself, from attack of Pathan soldiers[78] when he was dragged down from his horse by Pathans. Sidnak Mahar put many Pathans to his sword. He was greatly admired by Parashuram Bhau and by others who were against his keeping tent near their tents. Even after the fall of Peshwa rule in 1818, Sidnak Mahar was alive for long period. His descendants are still living in Sangli town in Maharashtra.

After Shivaji, the Maratha empire lost its élan and strength. When there was no unified control, there was no Indian nation. There were only geographical frontiers without any central authority controlling the territories bounded therein. The Indian polity became a loose conglomeration of a number of states, principalities, kingdoms and holding, wrapped up within the boundaries of India. Various ruler and kings, viceroys and Subhedars, army commanders and chieftains, held sway and were holding laws unto themselves, depending on how far how near they were to some superior authority. It was in this context that the actions of individuals or of social groups must be understood. Indeed, no one was in those days thinking of the Indian nation. Considerations of nationalism and national patriotism hardly ever entered the thinking of the people. As the central authorities like the Moghul empire and the Maratha kingdom kept disintegrating a large number of people moved along, floating rudderless, not knowing how to fend for themselves or seek security and comfort. They were prepared to serve any master, working for one master was as good as good as working for another and there was no opprobrium attached to serving any foreign masters; the terms, national and foreign had lost their meaning. The Indian professional soldiers drifted from one master to another and rarely

---

[77] Ibid., n. 66, p.158.

78 Bahishkrut Bharat (Marathi Weekly), Bombay, 20, May 1927.

realized the consequences of their actions they never weighed or comprehended the historical repercussions of their activities.

Europeans and British in India

By 17th century before the death of Aurangzeb, a new class of people gained entry into India, spreading their trade, commerce and religious networks, especially Europeans who had sailed across the seas and obtained a foothold in India. The Portuguese were the first to arrive (1503).[79] The English, the Dutch, the Danes, and the French followed suit in the opening years of the 17th century A.D. They came as traders, but as they stayed on in India, their ambitions grew in direct proportion to the decline of the Moghul Empire and the disruption of the central and regional political controls. Gradually, not always by design, these foreign powers got sucked into the whirlpools of Indian politics. Soon, they learned to play the game with adroit skill and, of course, to their advantage. They became a force to reckon with and the Indian rulers, forever fighting among themselves and intriguing against each other, appealed to them for help. The Europeans exerted the maximum price for the services rendered and eventually, found themselves in the race for power. They changed their policies to suit the altered conditions and raised, primed, and trained armies to carry their flags forward. In the end, it was the English who got the finishing lines; starting as traders they ended up as imperial rulers. More or less coinciding with the death of Aurangzeb, "The United Company of Merchants of England Trading to the East Indies."[80] (Known as the East India Company) was formed in 1708-09 after the amalgamation of two English trading companies which had grown up in India since December 1613 when the first firman was obtained by "The Company of London Trading Unto the East Indies" from the Mougal Emperor Jehangir. The English had built fortified factories for themselves and the three important English Presidencies of Madras, Bombay and Calcutta had been established.[81] The English factories in India were placed under these Presidencies in 1708. Each Presidency had a separate President who was also the commander-in-chief of such military forces, European and Indian, as existed in Presidency.

---

79 Stewart Gorden, *The Maratha*, Cambridge University Press, New Delhi, 1998, p.64.

80 C.B., Khairmode, Ibid., n.37, p.3.

81 Ibid., p.3.

The Anglo-French hostilities in the Carnatic, following the war of the Austrian succession (1740-1748), focused attention on the Indian Sepoys and revealed what they could do, trained properly. The strength of the Europeans lay in their arms and artillery, their superior infantry training, and their drill, discipline, and regimentation. The French realized the importance of this and were convinced that Indian Sepoys, dressed, trained, disciplined and accounted in the western style, could easily outsmart the out much their brethren in the forces of the Indian rulers.

The French Governor of Pondicherry, Francois Martin, had obtained permission from the Indian ruler to maintain a force of 300 native soldiers for the defense of the town. When Martin died in 1706, his successor, Benoit Dumas, formed a force of Indian soldiers in 1740. These soldiers were dressed, drilled, and equipped in the European style. The English had till then done nothing of this type.[82] In 1742, the infantry in the Bombay Presidency was, for the first time, officially spoken of as the Bombay European Regiment and it's strength in seven companies was 1,591.[83] There were also 843 sepoys in thirteen companies but they were without regular arms and uniforms. When it was declared between England and France in1744, hostilities started between the British and the French in India, too. In the fighting with the British, the French used Indian sepoys trained in the Western style.[84] The English swathe advantage and once they had learnt the lesson, they outstripped the French; they never regretted their decision.

British

Major Stringer Lawrence, "the Father of the Indian Army" and the first Commander-in-chief of all the company Armies in India who arrived in Madras in January 1748, raised the first few companies of Indian soldiers, called Native Sepoys who were trained and equipped in the English style and were led by European officers. The pattern was set.

Ten years later in that decade to establish the supremacy of the English vis-à-vis the Indian rulers as also the competing European powers – the "Lal Paltan" – the 1st Regiment of Bengal Native Infantry Comprising

---

82 R. Orme, *A History of the Military Transactions of the British Nation in Indostan,* Vol. I, 4th revised edition, London, 1803, p.21, indicates that the French had raised four or five companies (400-500 of Indian soldiers who were commanded by their own officers.

83 Sir Patrick Cadell, Ibid., n.47, p.249.

84 Khairmode, Ibid., n.37, p.5.

entirely Indian Sepoys was formed by Robert Clive in Calcutta in January 1757.[85] This was after Calcutta had been recaptured by the English and before the Battle of Plassey (June 1757) which gave the British a firm foothold for their empire in India. Similarly, four battalions of this type were raised in Madras in 1758. A year later, Major William Frazer, who commanded the forces in the Bombay Presidency, presented proposals for the "establishment of 1500 sepoys complete, regulated, disciplined and paid in the same manner as they are upon the coast (i.e. Madras) and in Bengal." These men were to be divided into twelve companies with a reserve force for garrison duties. The Board of directors agreed that a corps of 500 best Bombay sepoys be formed with their own officers. Red broadcloth was issued for their uniform rosette pattern. The independent companies so formed were converted into Native (Indian) Battalions in 1767.

Bombay Army and Mahars

During the initial periods of British rule in India, the British army was raised by recruiting only untouchables and low castes like Pariahs of South India, most of whom were from Tamil Nadu and Mahars of Maharashtra. Being a British Army soldier, they had to fight many battles on behalf of British Crown against native rulers. They won most of the battles and helped the expansion of the British empire. The Mahars, as stated above, in spite of their lower social status, gave judgements on various disputes which were respected by one and all irrespective of their social status in caste hierarchy. Even during the British rule the Mahars were called for giving verdicts on various disputes.

Although they were first recruited in the British army, they were employed after settled conditions of the British rule in India, at the instance of majority community whose support was necessary for their rule in India. But in times of emergencies, the Mahars were recruited in armies.[86]

The Bombay Army is proud of its battle honours. "Mangalore", "Sadaseer", "Kirkee", "Koregaon", and "Meeanee" followed Shivaji's example in enlisting infantry of all classes and castes. In the Bombay

---

85 V.R. Shinde, Ibid., n.66, p.171.

Lord Robert Clive, *First Conquests of the East India Co.* The Imperial Gazetteer of India, The Indian Empire, Vol. IV, Secretary of State for India, The Clarendon Press, Oxford, 1909, p.

86 Ibid., n.37, p.6.

Army, "the Brahmin stands shoulder to shoulder in the ranks, nay, sleeps in the same tent with his Parwari fellow soldier, and dreams not of any objection to the arrangement."[87] If the subject was brought to the notice of the Bombay Brahmin Sepoy he would shrug his shoulder and say: "What do I care? Is he not the soldier of the State?" The Mahars or Parwaris,[88] as they were commonly known, were recruited heavily into the Bombay Army especially in the beginning as the English were fighting with the Marathas and could not trust the Maratha Sepoys. The English in Bombay had come in contact with the Mahars and had come to rely on them for household duties as also for military and police services. The loyalty of the Mahars, their dependability, and the qualities of their heart and brilliant mind were recognized by the English. The knowledge of the Mahars of the local area was of great advantage to the English who were new to the land.

Though in course of time, more so after the break-up of the Maratha power, the Marathas formed the central core of the Bombay Army, the Mahars constituted about one-sixth of the entire Bombay Army.[89] They were mixed up with all the units of the Bombay Army and numbered between a quarter and a fifth of those units to which they were recruited.[90] They showed up because of their merit and gallantry, and secured promotions. It was the distinguishing feature of the Bombay Army that promotions in the regiments of the Army were on merit and through selection. They were not based on caste considerations. In this, the Bombay Army differed from the Bengal and Madras Armies. The Mahars were often promoted to the commissioned ranks.[91] In fact, Mahar as a typical Bombay Sepoy and extolled the qualities of the Bombay Sepoys generalizing the qualities of the Mahars their faithfulness, reliability, determination, and devotion to duty. He said that the Parwaris

---

87 Ibid.

88 Parwaris : Perhaps means "hill men" for Mahars this word used by English men. Shankarrao Kharat, Ibid., n.17, p.170.

89 Patrick Cadell, Ibid., n.47, p.249.

90 Stephen P. Cohen, "The Untouchable Soldier : Caste, Politics and the Indian Army", *Journal of the Asian Studies, Volume XXVIII*, No.3, May, 1969.

91 All references to officers and commissioned ranks in the Presidency Armies when relating to Indian soldiers denote the ranks of Jamadars, Subedars, and subsequently, subedar-majors. This should not be confused with the officer ranks which were not open to Indians. (The rank of subedar. Major was introduced in 1818-19).

became Indian Officers through sheer merit and good conduct.[92] The Mahars, especially the Konkani Parwaris, who had originally enlisted freely in the Bombay Army were invariably commended for their courage and steadfastness under all circumstances, however adverse.

As the Bombay Army grew, the Mahars rose in rank and increased in numbers forming part of all the twenty or more infantry regiments of the Army and one Marine Corps.[93] The year 1768 marked the beginning of a new era in the military organization of the Bombay Army. The experiences of the wars in Bengal and Madras (Arcot, Plassey, Wandiwash, and finally Buxar in October 1764) and the expansion of the territories on the West Coast led to the Court of Directors to declare that:

> "as the Company's rich and expansive possessions cannot be secured but by large bodies of well-regulated troops, we have consulted Lord Clive, General Lawrence, Cailiand, Carnac and other military gentlemen on this important subject and have found it necessary to make some alterations in the present military establishments at the several presidencies. It was decided to raise two battalions of sepoys of 1,000 men each with eight European officers and ten European sergeants to each battalion. These two battalions, formed on 4th August 1768 by amalgamating the existing companies of Indian troops, were called the 1st and 2nd Battalions of Bombay Sepoys (later known as the 108th Infantry and the 103rd Maratha light Infantry). The former survived till 1930 and the latter continued to exist as the 1/5th Maratha Light Infantry. The Mahars formed part of the original 1st and 2nd Battalions of Bombay Sepoys."[94]

The Marine Battalion of the Bombay Army was raised in 1777 to take over the military duties on the companies armed vessels.[95] It furnished detachments for the cruisers of the Bombay Marine. The Marine sepoys were engaged in a number of naval conflicts with the pirates of the Indian coast and in the Persian Gulf as also with the French men-of-war. The fighting of the Marine Battalion ranged as the far East as Macassar and it was in the straits of Sunda that the company's ship, Nantilus, with a detachment of the Marine Battalion on board, engaged the U.S. Ship,

---

92 Victor Longer ,Ibid.,n.6, p.10.

93 Sir Patrick Cadell, Ibid., n.47, p.147.

94 Longer, Victor, Ibid., p.11.

95 Sir Patrick Cadell, Ibid., n.47, p.146.

Peacock – this was the solitary occasion when the soldiers of the Indian Army fought against the Americans. In December 1819, there was an expedition to the Persian Gulf against the Joasmi Pirates who had been harassing the British. In 1820-21, Companies of the Marine Battalion took part in the siege of Mocha in the Red Sea. The soldiers of the Bombay Marine fought gallantly, and the fort fell of them eventually after some initial reverse and serious fighting.[96]

The Mahars, who had already acquired their sea knowledge under Shivaji and later under Kanhoji Angre, formed a large part of the Marine Battalion and played a notable role. The Mahars had no inhibitions unlike the high-caste Marathas and Brahmins in serving on the seas or crossing the waves to get to foreign lands. Not surprisingly, the Mahars made their mark, won a number of awards, and established high principles of excellent decorum and military conduct. A detachment of the Marine Battalion was captured on the company's cruiser, Aurara, by two French frigates during the second Maratha war. The French tried their best to induce, cajole, compel the Bombay Sepoys to defeat of Bengal and Madras had already deserted their armies and was working for the French. They were shown to the Bombay sepoys. The deserters were in French uniform and were enjoying a number of privileges and luxuries. But the Bombay detachment would not relent and the Bombay sepoys, when they shamelessly forgot their oath of loyalty to their colours. They were not true to their salt; they had let down their army, their regiment, and the honour of their arms. The French gave up and the Bombay sepoys were severely punished, roughly treated and seriously wounded. To the seventeen survivors who reached Bombay with honour, a special medal was given by the Company. Twelve of those brave and loyal men were Mahars.[97] On another occasion, a small party of eight men of the Marine Battalion was serving on the Indus river steamers at Multan. This party was acting as a treasury guard when the 26th Regiment of Bengal Infantry mutinied and attacked the Bombay Sepoys. The guard of eight protected their charge dauntlessly and killed twenty-six of their assailants. All these eight men of the Marine Battalion were Parwaris, Mahar's.

There were a number of Mahars of the Marine Battalion who won awards and promotions for acts of heroism. Havaldar Madnak Esnak of the Marine Battalion earned distinction in an encounter (1797) on the west coast of Bombay and was promoted Jemadar.[98] In the same encounter,

[96] Shankarrao Kharat, Ibid. n.17, p.173.

97 C.B. Khairmode, Ibid. n.37, p.10.

Subannak Wahnak of the same battalion also earned distinction for his valour and bravery and was awarded a silver badge and chain; he was promoted to the rank of Havaldar. Dhondnak Pundnak of the Marine Battalion was awarded a silver medal and appointed Lt. Havaldar for dauntless daring in an encounter with the French (1810).[99]

The Bombay Presidency saw a good deal of fighting and the sepoys of the Bombay Army together with the sepoys of the other Presidency Armies who joined in the fray were engaged in a number of military campaigns. The Presidency Armies, including the Bombay Army, had come in for a general reorganization in 1796. Unfortunately, this reorganization, which reduced the importance of Indian Officers and accommodated an influx of young and inexperienced British officers who came flooding into the Presidency Armies after the Napoleonic wars, was greatly resented and led to some ugly incidents and violent protest including the mutiny at Vellore in 1806. But the Bombay Army remained firm and there were some remarkable incidents which mirrored the unflinching loyalty of the Bombay sepoys under adverse conditions. Some Bombay Sepoys had been taken prisoner by Tipu. In spite of all the temptations offered to them and the pressure put on them, those sepoys, braving privations, refused to be disloyal to their army. It did not worry them that 2,500 sepoys of the Madras Army, under similar circumstances, had joined Tipu's forces. On the conclusion of peace, the Bombay Sepoys who had remained firm and had suffered as prisoners were marched across the Madras coast and it is recorded by Gen. John Malcolm that even while they were marching, weak and bedraggled, they never lost heart and were on their best behaviour sharing their small savings and scanty food with their officers and their brother soldiers.

Gen. Malcolm praised the Bombay officers and Sepoys for their fidelity. Writing to the Secretary of the Board of Directors in 1818, Gen. Malcolm confirmed that the Bombay Army was composed of all classes and all religions like Hindu, Muslims, Jews and Christians. Among the Hindus of Maharashtra, the Parwaris (Mahars) were more numerous than the Rajputs and some other higher castes. These Parwaris hailed from the South Coast of Bombay. Much praise was showered on the Mahar Sepoys of the Bombay Army who endured the rigours of difficult marches when rations were low and diseases was high among men and animals. Whether they were charging ahead or were besieged or taken prisoner-of-war, whether they were storming fortresses or making tactical withdrawals,

---

98 Shankarrao Kharat, Ibid. n.17, p.173.

99 Ibid., p.173.

they always stood steadfast by their officers and comrades, never letting down the honour of their Regiment.

Mahars delistment from British Army

Despite the Mahars' long martial history, the British ceased recruiting them in 1893.[100] The Bombay and the other Presidency Armies were reevaluated following the 1857 mutiny. The Peel Commission first examined class composition of the armies in 1858. A report to the Commission "emphasized that:

> "we cannot practically ignore it (the caste system), so long as the natives socially maintain it."

This led to the discrimination against the Mahars and other low-caste groups as well as some Brahman castes which were considered unreliable.[101]

General Lord Roberts, while not originating the concept of martial races, was instrumental in implementing a strategy of building "class regiments." Recruiting policies were rewritten, and the Bombay Army was notified that the Mahars, together with a number of other classes of the Bombay Army, would no longer be recruited to the Army. Lord Roberts writes:

> "I have no doubt whatever of the fighting powers of our best Indian troops; I have a thorough belief in, and admiration for, Gurkhas, Sikhs, Dogras, Rajputs, Jats and selected Mahomadans; I thoroughly appreciate their soldierly qualities; brigaded with British troops, I would be proud to lead them against any European enemy."[102]

Roberts thought that the first step to making the Indian Army was "to substitute men of the more warlike and hardy races for the Hindustani sepoys of Bengal, the Tamils and Telagus (sic) of Madras, and the so-called Mahrattas (sic) of Bombay." He was convinced that:

> "In the British Army the superiority of one regiment over another is mainly a matter of training; the same courage and military instinct are inherent in English, Scotch, and Irish alike,

---

100 Military Department, Peel Commission, Vol.13/1891, p.122-23. Maharashtra State Archives, Mumbai.

101 C.B. Khairmode, Ibid. n.37, p. 19.

102 Fredrick Robert, Fredrick, *Fort-one years in India, From Subaltern to Commander in Chief*, Longman & Green Co., New York, 1898, p.14.

> but no comparison can be made between the martial value of a regiment recruited amongst the Gurkhas of Nepal or the warlike races of Northern India, and of one recruited from the effeminate peoples of the south."[103]

The Mahars believed that their martial history demonstrated their abilities as warriors, but the British had made their decision. Mahars could only enlist as bandsmen or clerks. This would not provide the same opportunities for promotion and allow little change in their social status. As expected, the Mahars felt the British had betrayed them after over 100 years of loyal service to the British Raj.

Throughout India, there was controversy about which groups should remain in the Army. The Mahars had support from some British soldiers, including commanders who recommended their continued service: the Parwari (Mahar) is of far better fighting material than the Deccani Mussulman, and suggested that the Marine Battalion might be made a class regiment of Parwaries. The commanding officer of the 9th Bombay Infantry thought that a regiment of Parwaries, especially from the Deccan, would give a very good account of itself. They are possessed of as much soldierly quality as many castes of whom much higher opinions are entertained.

However, their assistance was not enough to overcome the sentiments of Lord Roberts and other senior officers of the British Indian Army.[104]

Longer provides an excellent commentary on the impact of the decision of the Mahars. He writes:

> The excellent system with its cosmopolitan composition, which had worked out over the years, was dismantled and destroyed. The Mahars, who had proudly carried the colours of various Regiments of the Bombay Army, were crestfallen and heartbroken. For years they had provided abundant evidence of their farewell to arms there were eight Subedar-Majors, 62 Subedars, 34 Jamadars, and a host of Non-Commissioned Officers and Sepoys of the Mahar community who had served with distinction in the Bombay Army.[105]

---

103 Fredrick S. Roberts., *Forty-one Years in India, From Subaltern to Commander-in-Chief,* Longman Green & Co., New York, 1898, p.15.

104 Letter of Shivram Jamba Kamble to the Secretary of State for India, London, Khairmude Collection, University o Mumbai Fort Library.

105 Victor Longer, Ibid., n.6, p.18.

The Mahars would continue to fight for the right to re-enlist in the Indian Army. They were loath to lose the benefits that the military provided. Furthermore, the education provided to the soldiers had created an educated cadre that would transfer their skills into political action. However, there were few Mahars left in the Army by the beginning of World War I.[106]

The Mahars' ability to work among the British exposed them to Western ways, and helped them to realize that their status as Untouchables did not keep them from working in successful and satisfying occupations. They aggressively used the advantages provided by their relationship with the British.

Military service provided important benefits to its soldiers. The benefits include "pay and pensions, access to education and/or specialized training, preferential access to employment, enhanced social status, and personal satisfaction." For the Mahars, the access to education and increased social status was the most important benefits. The best example of their results was Dr. B. R. Ambedkar. Eleanor Zelliot writes that

> "Ambedkar's experiences were free from the traditional village role, his early life was spent among educated ex-army men, imbued with the pride of soldiers and acquainted with a more sophisticated Hinduism than that found in the village."

In fact, Dr. B. R. Ambedkar extends much of the credit for the start of the movement to improve the Untouchables' place in society to contact with the British Army. He maintained until the advent of the British, the Untouchables were content to remain Untouchables… In the army of the East India Company there prevailed the system of compulsory education for Indian Soldiers and their children, both male and female. The education received by the Untouchables in the army… gave them a new vision and a new value. They became conscious that the low esteem in which they had been held was not an inescapable destiny but was a stigma imposed on their personality by the cunning contrivances of the priest. They felt the shame of it as they ever did before and were determined to get rid of it.[107]

---

106 Eleanor Zelliot, *Caste in Indian Politics*, ed. By Rajani Kothari, Orient Longmans Ltd., New Delhi, 1970, p.35.

107 Dr.B.R. Ambedkar, *What Congress and Gandhi Have Done for the Untouchables,* Thacker and Co. Ltd., Bombay, 1946, p.189.

Mahars joined the military with the intent of improving their social status. They were successful in this regard. This was within the closed circle of the regiment, caste prejudice was, if not actually absent, at least officially discouraged. According to army regulations no distinction was made between soldiers on the basis of their caste or community. Mahar officers were able to command men of other castes apparently without difficulty.

After growing up in this environment of equality it was a shock for the Untouchables to travel and live in situations away from the military cantonments.

After retirement, there was a period of adjustment for Mahars who lived outside the cantonment, this was as nearly as can be deduced from rather limited information, it would seem that while actually in the army, or after retired or taking other employment, while in contact with British employers and officials, the Mahar soldier was not treated in any way differently from a soldier of higher caste. Once retired and living in his native village, a Mahar soldier, although he might have a relatively high status among the Mahar community and even among caste Hindus, would nevertheless once again have to accept his untouchable status.

The important point is, even after retirement, Mahars with a military background still had access to the British government. The retired military officers were an effective lobby for Mahar rights.

Retired officers also created a group of political leaders with access to the Indian government. This was especially true near military cantonments in Poona, Satara and Ahmednagar. Basham relates an incident where Mahar children were not being offered equal educational opportunities. Local caste Hindus and low-level British education officials refused the Mahar demands for Mahar boys to be integrated into classes with caste-Hindu boys. The dispute was resolved in favour of the Mahars.

Mahars were seeking not just education for their sons, although this was obviously important, but also an improvement in their social status. The fact that many of these parents were retired officers, and therefore could legitimately make a claim on the attention to government officials, indicates the value of military service in this respect.

Clearly, the type of access available to the soldiers, active or retired, was unavailable to most Untouchables.

All the benefits the Mahars received were the result of their ability to develop a link with the British. His helped them overcome the obstacles erected by the Hindu social system.

It was their entry into the British army which proved significant for the subsequent history of the Mahar movement. It is important to gauge this significance. It consists not in any automatic elevation in the social hierarchy through military service, which indeed is ruled out in a hierarchical system governed by considerations of ascriptive status and ritual purity. It rather consists in the fact that military service at such an early date exposed them to British institutions much before the dissemination of western culture took place on a large scale.

Such an exposure socialized them sufficiently early to the new political order so that when new opportunities and alternatives became available, they were found prepared to use them more effectively than those groups which did not have this opportunity. Following the delistment of 1893, the Mahars would need all the access and knowledge they had gained to overcome the impact of being refused service in the army.

Reactions of Mahars

The Mahar's did not accept defeat. They resented the Government orders of 1892 and raised their voice of protest. They saw no reason why they should be excluded from the Army. The Mahar leaders picked up courage and gradually gathered strength to agitate against the Government decision. Representations were sent on their behalf to the British Government. These were submitted deferentially and, in the beginning, hesitatingly.

Gopal Baba Walangkar,[108] a Konkani Mahar, who had been in service in the Army, drew up a petition in Marathi in 1894. He entreated the Government[109] to take back the Mahars, as also the other classes, into the ranks of the Army. He illustrated his representation with a number of examples of the intrepidity, courage and gallantry of the Mahar soldiers who had served with great credit both in the Army and in the other services. He pleaded that the Mahars should be allowed to reenter the Army, the Police, and the Civil Administration. He drew attention to the

108 Eleanor Zelliot , Caste in Indian Politics, Orient Longman Ltd., New Delhi, 1970, p.34.

109 Letter of Gopalbaba Walankar, Khairmode Collection, University of Mumbai Library, Fort Campus.

promise held out by Queen Victoria in the Royal Proclamation of November, 1858.[110]

Unfortunately, Walangkar could not muster enough support for his representation. This was understandable for, to start with, some members of his community were apprehensive of the worth of the Government, especially as a number of ex-Army Mahars depended on their pensions from the Government and did not want to provoke or annoy the Government. They wanted to be cautious in their approach and would not go head long into the fray. The challenge had to be accepted, but it was wise to take careful steps with deliberation and at the appropriate time.

Another Mahar leader who found the Government order irksome and stood up for his people was Sub-Maj. Ramji Maloji Sakpal, the father of the illustrious Dr. B. R. Ambedkar, who rose to stellar heights and won immortal fame as the chief architect of the constitution of the Republic India. Ramji, hailing from the Ratnagiri district, came from a military background as his father Maloji Sakpal had also served in the Army and belonged to a good Mahar family. In fact, Ramji's wife too came from a family of Army men, for her father and six of her uncles had been Subedar-majors and subdedar's in the Army. Ramji, well known as a strict military disciplinarian, had served as Headmaster in a Military School and had attained the rank of Sub-Maj. In the 2nd Grenadiers.[111]

It hurt Ramji that the Mahars, who were recognized as "the most robust, adaptable, intelligent, fighting, brave, virile and leading community,[112] were being denied the opportunity of serving the Army. He had decided to launch a protest against the Government order of 1892 and approached the noted social reformer and Justice M. G. Ranade, to help

---

110 Eleanor Zelliot, "Learning the use of political Means: The Mahars of Maharashtra" in Rajani Kothari (ed), Caste in Indian Politics, Orient Longman Ltd., 1970, p.34.

111 Dhananjay Keer, Dr. Ambedkar: Life and Mission, (in Marathi), Popular Prakashan, Bombay, 1989, p.10-11.

W.N. Kuber, A Critical Study of Dr. Ambedkar, Peoples Publishing House, Bombay.

112 Dhananjay Keer Ibid., p.9.

him draft a memorandum petitioning the Government to revoke the discriminatory order.[113]

It took another decade for the Mahars to organize themselves and gather sufficient strength: 1,500 Mahars of Deccan and Konkan held a conference at Poona in 1904 and their very active, able, and eloquent spokesman, Shivram Janba Kamble,[114] who was fluent in English,[115] drafted a memorandum which was sent to the Governor of Bombay. Once again, in 1905, the Mahar's appealed to the British authorities to remedy the injustice done to their community and accord them their rightful place in the defence and security services of the country. The collector of Pune replied on behalf of the Governor regretting his inability to accede to the request of the Mahars. There was little that he could do to ensure the admission of the Mahars to the Army, the Police, and the Public services. The Mahars had turned into a blind alley, but they were still looking for an opening. Shivram Janba Kamble organized a mission in 1906 with branches all over Maharashtra to advocate their cause. Vithal Ramji Shinde was the President of this mission.

After four years Mahars were again up and about kicking at the administration. The Mahars of Deccan met at Poona under the Chairmanship of Sub. Bahadur Gangaram Krishnajee. Shivram Janba Kamble was the Secretary of the Conference. A petition was this time addressed to the Secretary of State for India urging the Government to permit the employment of the Mahars in the Army and other services. It requested

> "we may be reemployed in the Indian Army as soldiers. We have been declared by the highest Government authorities in the Bombay Presidency as competent both physically and morally, for employment in the capacity of soldiers. Separate regiments might be made of us… or separate companies of our people might be annexed to existing regiments with the privilege for our people, as before, of rising to the position of native officers."

---

113 It is not known what ultimately became of this petition. Dr. Ambedkar, Ramji's son, said that he found this petition in his father's papers after his death.

114 H.S. Nawalkar, H.S., *The Life of Shivram Janba Kamble and Brief History of the Poona Parvati Satyagraha,* Sugava Prakashan, 1997, p.45.

115 Letter of Shivram Janba kamble to the Secretary of State for India, London, Khairmode Collection, University of Mumbai, Fort Library.

The petitioners appealed to British justice and stressed the fact that their requests were perfectly legitimate, based as they were, on the excellent record of service of the Mahars in the Army. The memorandum said: "We are making no new demands; we do not claim employment in services in which we have not been engaged before. Indeed, some few of our people do still hold positions in the Police force and have acquitted themselves most honourably. So also have our people been employed in the Indian Army from the very commencement of the British Raj in our country, and they have risen to the highest position by their valour and good conduct." A list of 104 Mahar officers of the Army (Jamadars, Subedars, and Subedar-major) who had served in the infantry and Rifle Regiments of the Bombay Army and in the Bombay 21st Marine Battalion was appended to the representation. There is no record of any answer to this petition of the Mahars submitted in 1910.[116]

In the two decades between 1892 and 1914 the Mahars had taken to working in the docks and railways, and on the roads. They were employed in diverse capacities, particularly as workers in textile mills and government industries. A sizeable number of Mahars had been taken on by the Government in the Ammunition factory at Kirkee. Thus, when the war started it was easy for the Mahars to get into the labour units of the army which comprised a variety of classes and were formed for various theatres of war, especially France and Mesopotamia. Many thousands of Mahars were so enlisted in the early years of the Great War.[117]

The Mahars were "anxious to enlist" in the Army but the Army Headquarters stood in their way. When, at last, the approval of the Army Headquarters

> "was obtained after much local pressure", the Mahar recruits were "first ordered to join tow Madras Battalions at St. Thomas Moun."[118]

The Mahar leaders had been badgering the Government to set up a regular Mahar battalion for service during the war. These persistent pressures and particularly the influence and exertions of Rao Bahadur. R.G. Naik, MBE, and Sri Gampat Govind, made the Adjutant-General, Army Headquarters, write on 23 January 1917 to the chief Secretary of

---

116 *Khairmode Collection,* Petition in University of Mumbai Library, Fort.

117 Victor Longer, Ibid., n.6, p.23.

118 S.P.P. Thorat, *The Mahar Machine Gun Regiment*, Army Press, Dehra Dun, 1954, p.10.

Bombay that it had been decided to make an attempt to raise two special companies of Mahar of 218 men each to be attached to the 3rd and 88th Infantry at Secundrabad and Madras respectively. By 23 April 1917, 412 Mahar recruits were obtained. It was reported that the response of the recruiting officers to the Government orders was slow and it was mainly the Konkani Mahar's who were enlisted.[119]

The Mahar leaders were not content. They did not stop at this and continued pushing the Government to raise a regular battalion of the Mahars. They succeeded, though towards the tail end of the war. In June 1917, a battalion, the 111th Mahar was raised.[120] The war had already dragged on over the years and the nations and their armies were weary. There was not much that the Mahar battalion was required to do. The nature of their duties was such that there was no way in which the Mahar soldiers could have expressed themselves or made their presence felt on the battlefields of the Great War.

In any case, by the time the 111th Mahar was primed and prepared, the war was over. In 1920, the 111th Mahar was moved to the then North-West Frontier Province where it stayed only for six months. Thereafter the battalion shifted to Aden after its amalgamation with the 71st Punjabis. Finally, as a measure of economy, it was decided to disband the battalion and orders to this effect were passed in March 1921.[121] Seven Mahar leaders – Papana Jalliat, Kalesh Yeshwant Dhale, Gundo Sattaji Pale, Gunoo Tulasiram, Hav (Retd.) Bhikaji Gangaji, Hav. Bhujang Sakharam of 110th MLI, and Jem (retd). Ramji Ratujee of 111th Mahar – sent a memorandum to the Governor of Bombay on 24th December 1921 protesting against the intended disbandment of the Mahar Battalion as also its amalgamation with the 71st Punjabis.[122] They wanted "to preserve the full Mahar Battalion" and "treat the Mahar Battalions as a separate unit". The appeal was forwarded through Rao Bahadur, R.G. Naik who sympathized with the Mahars and had assisted in raising the Mahar Battalion. The Commissioner of Southern Division, P.R. Cadell, supported the appeal saying,

---

119 Ibid., p.10.

120 Kesari, News Paper, Dated 5.3.1918.

121 S.P.P. Thorat, S.P.P., Ibid, n.118, p.10.

122 Maharashtra State Government Archives, Home Department, 'E' Branch, File No. 1114 of 1922 (first series).

> "It is well known to Government that Mahars used to be freely enlisted in the Bombay Army and that they formed one of its most loyal and useful constituents."

He recalled the fighting qualities of the Mahars in the battle at Koregaon and the fact that they had risen to the rank of "Commissioned Indian Officers" which indicated "their intelligence and the high esteem in which they were held by their officers". The Commissioner, Central Division, L.J. Mountford, who together with Rao Bahadur R.G. Naik and Raosaheb Papoma Jalliat, was "chiefly instrumental" in raising the 111th Mahar battalion, too, backed the Mahar petition.[123] But the Government of India, Army Department, eventually turned down the appeal. The battalion returned to India in 1922 for disbandment. No place could be found in the post-war Army for a single class battalion of the Mahars. It was said that the battalion was too young and had not been tried under modern war conditions. This reluctance with which the battalion had been raised and the prejudices under which it operated were too obviously reflected in the haste with which the battalion was disbanded.

Dr. B. R. Ambedkar's efforts

Dr. Babasaheb Ambedkar, coming from a military background, spoke of the advantages which his community had secured through its contact with the Army in the days of the East India Company and after. He explained "In the Army of the East India Company there prevailed the system of compulsory education for Indian soldiers and their children both male and female. The education received by the Mahars in the Army gave them a new vision and a new value". Dr. B. R. Ambedkar pleaded for the renewed association of the Mahars with the Army and hoped that the Government would let the Mahars re-enter the Army. He was unhappy with the disbandment of the 111th Mahar Battalion and voiced his feelings which were in consonance with the general protests that were raised in Maharashtra.[124] In his efforts in 1927 to obtain the recruitment of the Mahars into the Army.

Dr. B. R. Ambedkar was making concerted efforts to obtain the recruitment of the Mahars into the fighting arms of the Indian armed forces. He met the Governor of Bombay and drew his attention to the well-known and highly commended fighting qualities of the Mahars who

---

123 Khairmode, C.B., *Ashprushyancha Lashkari Pesha*, Maharashtra Rajya sahitya Ani Sanskriti Mandal, Mumbai, 1992, p.55.

124 The Kesari 5th Sept. 1922. Criticizing the Government decision and urging the Government to retake the Mahars into the Army.

had been dealt a raw deal continuously since 1892. The short interregnum of World War I was too brief and reluctant to have served any purpose. The discrimination remained and the Mahars, in spite of their excellent performance, had suffered because of the ill-conceived "martial class" concept. Dr. B. R. Ambedkar recounted the daring deed of the Mahars and their long history of soldiering. He appealed to the Government to raise a regular battalion of the Mahars.[125]

Towards the end of July 1941, the Viceroy expanded his Executive Council and set up a Defence Advisory Committee. Dr. B. R. Ambedkar, who had always taken keen interest in defence affairs and as a young man had joined the Baroda State Forces as a Lieutenant, was appointed on the Defence Advisory Committee. Dr. B. R. Ambedkar could then exert pressure from inside. He spoke to the commander-in-chief on behalf of the Mahars and his perseverance succeeded. Government sanction was accorded in September 1941 to raise a Mahar Battalion.[126]

Dr. B. R. Ambedkar appealed to the Mahars to join the Armed forces in large numbers. He was opposed to the Hitler-Mussollini-Tojo combine and wanted the Mahars to take up arms for the defence of democracy. He advised the Mahar youth to suspend their studies and qualify for military service to preserve and enhance their age-old martial traditions.[127] Addressing the All India Depressed Classes Conference at Nagpur in July 1942, Dr. B. R. Ambedkar reiterated that the war was between democracy and dictatorship based on racial arrogance. He exhorted the Mahar youth to fight for the just cause and make sacrifices willingly.

A large number of Mahars came forward to join the Army. Some of them had already served, prior to the war, in the Territorial Army Battalion of the Maratha Light Infantry. Several thousands of them had also enrolled themselves in the logistical units of the Army. Two troops of Mahars had been raised in 1940 and allowed to join some ambulance units. They had achieved notable successes. In 1941, there was renewed activity and a Mahar leader of Nagpur, G.M. Thaware, said that the Mahars "formerly belonged to a class of warriors and rose to a high position in Shivaji's Raj". Some men of these Mahar community were appointed recruiting officers. One of them, in particular Dr. B. R. Ambedkar's trusted worker, Jadhav alias Madakebuva, who had a genius for organization and did

---

125 C.B. Khairmode, Ibid., n.37, p.69,

126 C.B. Khairmode, Ibid.

127 The Times of India dated 31.1.1940 and 18.6.1941.

much to draw in the best Mahars into the Army. Also helping the Mahars was the Southern Area Recruiting staff and particularly the Assistant Director of Recruiting (South), Col. K.E. Franks, DSO. They had the full support of Dr. Ambedkar who continued to take active interest in the militarization programme in the country and attended the various sessions of the National Defence Council in 1941 and 1942.

Noticing the success which Dr. B. R. Ambedkar's efforts had obtained. Mahar Battalion had formed an important resolution which was introduced in the Legislative Assembly by Piare Lall Kureel Talib of U.P. in 1943. It recommended to the Governor-General-in Council that "the key service of the Army" should be thrown open to the members of all castes and that "the military service should not be the monopoly of a few privileged classes". The mover of the resolution emphasized. "The Military status gives people an important place in the body politic, no greater injustice can be done to a community than if that community is deprived of its due share in the military services."[128] The Secretary of Defence Department, Sir Chandulal Trivedi, accepting the resolution of Kureel Talib, affirmed that there would not be any discrimination against any classes if they possessed the requisite educational and physical qualifications.

Establishment of Mahar Regiment

The Mahars had won their battle. They had got their Regiment, the I Battalion of the Mahar Regiment was raised at Nanawadi Belgaum on 1st October 1941 by Lt. Col. H.J.R. Jackson of 13th Frontier Force Rifles with the help of Sub. Maj. Sheikh Hassnuddin, a seasonal soldier of twenty-five years' service. Two companies were formed initially. They were trained by the Maratha Light Infantry Regimental Training Centre at Belgaum and most of the Viceroy's commissioned officers were drawn from the 11th and 12th Battalions of the 5th MLI (Indian Territorial Force). The biggest problem was to train the VCO and NCO or to obtain such trained personnel. Some rapid promotions took place initially to fill the gaps in the training staff. Batches of VCO and NCO were sent on special training courses. But there was an acute shortage of specialists. The composition of the battalion was entirely Mahars except a few VCOs who were Deccani Musalams. The battalion moved to Kamptee, near Nagpur in February 1942 where it was brought up to the authorized strength by the end of September. Col. K .E. Franks, DSO, was of great help in building up the Regiment. Some of the British officers of the Regiment had attended battle school courses in the United Kingdom and employed

128 M.S.A. Rao, "*Caste and the Indian Army*", Economic Weekly, 29 August 1964.

the latest training methods in training the Mahars who, according to a British officer who joined the 1st Battalion in early 1942 said "they made very good progress and were becoming very smart in appearance and very keen to establish themselves as efficient soldiers."[129] Political movement is the best example of this. Therefore, even after military service was taken away from the Mahars, the traditions and accrued benefits continued to be an advantage to this untouchable community.

A Mahar Regiment was reformed in 1941 and has existed ever since. The ceremonial Colonel of the Regiment is K.V. Krishna Rao, former Chief-of-Staff of the Indian Amy and former Governor. The preface of the Regimental History states:

> "Militarily, the Mahars faced the vicissitudes of fortune, but once the Mahar Regiment was reborn in 1945, it came into its own after India became free… A three-battalion (one class) Regiment blossomed into a eighteen-battalion Regiment with men from all classes and communities of the country fused together to form a rich and radiant amalgam."

The Regiment has taken part in all of India's major military operations since 1947. Just as the Mahars have survived and prospered so has the Mahar's Military legacy.

The 2nd Battalion of the Mahar Regiment was raised in the Outram Lines at Kamptee on 1 June 1942 by Lt. Col. J.W.K. Kirwan, assisted by Sub.-Maj. Bholaji Ranjane. Similar to the 1st Battalion, most of the VCOs for the 2nd Battalion were drawn from the 11th and 12th Battalions of the 5th MLI (Indian Territorial Force) and the composition was all Mahars. This battalion was initially raised from the "E" Training Company of the 1st Mahar Battalion which had a strength of 500 and had been formed on 1 January 1942.[130] The Company Commander of the "E" Company, Maj. C.B. Ponnappa, was appointed second-in-command of the battalion. The battalion was fortunate to possess an artist-officer, Lt. E.E.L. Mortlemans, who designed the first cap badge for the Mahar Regiment. This badge, which was used by the Regiment from 1942 to 1946, till it

---

129 Major E. Stanley-Jones, who was with the 1st Battalion from 1942 to 1945 sent an account of his experiences to the author through the Mahar Association in the U.K. Ibid., n.6, p.

130 The raising day of the 2nd Battalion is accepted as June 1. The date on which the "E" Training Company of the 1st Battalion was formed, January 1, has not been considered as the raising day of the battalion. Ibid., n.6, p.January 1, has not been considered as the raising day of the battalion. Ibid., n.6, p.

remained an Infantry regiment, had the replica of the Koregaon obelisk rising above the letters "MAHARS" and bearing the letters "KORE" and "GOAN" on two side banners dropping down, left and right, from the top of the 1821 Koregaon monument.

Another battalion of the Regiment – the 25th Battalion – was raised in the lines of the 10th Battalion of 5th MLI at Argan Tank, Belgaum, on 1 August 1942 by Lt. Col. V. Chambier of 10/5th MLI and Sub.-Maj. Ladkojirao Bhonsle, Sardar Bahadur, OBI. This battalion was formed mainly as a garrison battalion for the protection of the defence installations and important communication centres during the war. The instrumental staff of the battalion was drawn from the 10/5th MLI and the composition of the battalion was 75 per cent Mahars and 25 percent Maharashtrians. The battalion was brought to full strength by the end of 1942.

A Training Company, to act as a reinforcing unit for the newly raised battalions of the Regiment, was raised at Kamptee on 1 October 1942 by Capt. F.D. Marshall and Sub.-Maj. Dattu Jadhav. The instructors for the Company were taken from the 1st and 2nd Mahar Battalions and the 5th MLI Regimental Centre. The recruits – mostly Mahars – came originally from the surpluses of the 2nd Mahar Battalion. The Training company was expanded to form the Mahar Training Battalion on 1 June 1943. Maj. F.D. Marshall took over the command of the battalion and Sub.-Maj. Dattu Jadhav of the 5th MLI Regimental Centre stayed on with the battalion. On 1 February 1944, Lt. Col. G.A. Crawford of the 5th MLI assumed the command of the Training Battalion.

The 3rd Battalion of the Mahar Regiment was raised in the Ambala Lines at Nowshera in the then NWFP on 1 November 1943 by Lt. Col. R.N.D. Frier, MC,[131] and Sub.-Maj. Bholaji Ranjane. The battalion which was placed in reserve to allow it to train and organize itself came up to its full strength by the end of November 1943. The recruits for the battalion were trained by the 11th Sikh and the 2nd Punjab Regimental Centres. The NCOs were trained by the 8th and 16th Battalions of the Punjab Regiment. The VCOs continued to be attached from the 11th Sikh Regimental Centre.

Soon after their formation the 1st and 2nd Mahar Battalions were placed on escort and internal security duties: Two Companies of the 1st Battalion were sent to Ranchi in May 1942 to escort two special trains which were

131 He took over command on 14 November 1943 from Maj. J.B. Dobbyn, who became second-in-command. Victor Longer, Ibid., n.6, p.

transporting Italian prisoners-of-war to Bangalore. The battalion was then moved to Nagpur in aid of civil power during the "Quit India" disturbances in August 1942. From there the battalion proceeded in 1943 to NWFP for frontier defence duties. A Company of the battalion, commanded by Capt. G.K. Karandikar, had gone to Kabul in December 1942 as a demonstration company at the Military School of Frontier Warfare. The Company remained there for six months, rejoining the battalion by the middle of 1943 with a flattering report from the Commandant of the School.

Likewise, the 2nd Battalion was trained and employed on internal security duties at Nagpur in August 1942. Thereafter, in December 1942 the battalion went by rail to Jamshedpur and, as part of the Eastern Army, was located, three miles away from the town, at Golmuri, a virgin forest full of snakes and mosquitoes. The battalion had to protect the Tata Steel Factory, the rail communications, vital bridges, and the operational aerodromes at Chakuliya, Chakardharpur, Chaibassa, Kharagpur, and Cuttack which were being used by long-range bombers to hammer the Japanese-occupied areas.

About the same time, on the western coast, the 25th Battalion too was protecting defence installations and vital communication centres. The battalion was placed in Santa Cruz inside Greater Bombay to guard the dockyards and the coastal islands of Mankhurd and Butcher. When an explosion took place in an ammunition-laden ship in the Bombay dockyard in April 1944, causing serious damage to the yard and other installations, the battalion was put to a severe test. Working day and night to save public property and prevent the spread of damage, the battalion gave proof of its vigilance, steadfastness, and devotion to duty.

The 1st and 3rd Battalions remained in the NWFP for frontier defence duties. The 1st Battalion was stationed at Nowshera, Malakand, Risalpur, and finally at Gardai in Waziristan. It was training intensively during the whole of 1943. In Nowshera the troops went on several long marches and combined battalion exercises. Inter-Company sports competitions were also organized and the Koregaon shield was introduced. The battalion did well in the Peshawar District Hockey Tournament. In March 1943, the battalion moved to Malakand, bewitching in its scenic beauty and exciting for all its free fishing in the river Swat. After a few months the battalion moved to Risalpur to join the 155th Infantry Brigade and then to Gardai, one of the worst camps in Waziristan. On the very day that the battalion moved there, one of its picquets was attacked by a band of tribesmen in the evening. The Mahars stood up to the occasion and beat back the attack. Thereafter, they defended their camp and picquets as also carried out road openings with great courage and alacrity. Two of its men – Sep. Mallappa Waghmare and Sep. Balwant More – fell to the bullets of Pathar snipers. The Mahars saw snow for the first time at Gardai but they faced the bitter cold, incisive winds, sleet and snow for nine months - three months more than the normal tenure. They astonished everyone with the speed and ease with which they could ascend and descend the snow-covered mountains on road-opening days. As soon as orders were received to leave a picquet, the men had to run down fast. The Mahars were exceptionally swift footed. Starting from scratch, in just three years, the 1st Battalion had reached an excellence which was the envy of many. From Gardai the battalion was taken to Budni near Bhopal in Madhya Pradesh where it carried out intensive jungle warfare training. In October 1945, the battalion became part of the renewed 8th Indian Division.

The 3rd Battalion which had moved to Risalpur in February 1944 to complete its individual training, got to Nowshera four months later and was trained for frontier defence duties. Towards the end of 1944, the battalion was participating in the Nowshera Brigade Training Columns. The training continued throughout the bitterly cold winter months when the wind-swept rocks and bald hills o the NWFP were most inhospitable. The Mahars matched their strength against the inclemencies of nature and were so well toughened, physically and mentally, that the speed with which they scampered up rugged, steep hills, establishing posts and picquets, astonished their commanders. The excellent performance of the battalion won the commendation of the Brigade Commander, Big. R.G. Ekins, who gave the unit an outstanding report. The battalion reached Malakand on 1 November 1944 and was required to guard the forts of Dargai, Malakand, Chakdara, and a post known as "Guides Picquet". Besides these duties, the battalion continued to train itself with vigour taking part in some very tough exercises. In one such exercise all the twelve platoons of the battalion were set out independently, each with three days' man-pack rations, on different routes, covering about 54 miles of rugged terrain. They were required to conduct aggressive patrolling and ambushing; any rival platoon which was encountered on the route was to be considered "an enemy". These exercises gave realistic training in actual terrain to the VCOs, NCOs, and Other Ranks of the battalion who evinced initiative and fortitude. The battalion came back to Nowshera on 19 April 1945 and then proceeded to Fort Sandeman in Baluchistan on 23 September 1945 to become part of the "Zhob Brigade". The battalion continued to train itself with diligence and determination.

The 2nd Battalion saw active service during the war in Burma. Detachments of this battalion served on the muddy and misty roads and in the thick jungles clustering the hillsides of Burma. In August 1943, the first detachment of the Company under the command of Capt. Bolton was sent to the precipitous Tiddim area in the Chin hills, south of Imphal. Throughout the years 1943 and 1944, detachments of this battalion, each comprising one officer, one VCO, and 20 Other Ranks, replaced every three months, were attached to the 4th and 6th Battalions of the Maratha Light Infantry which were operating in Burma as part of the 23rd Indian Division – the "Fighting Cook".[132] The Fourteenth Army was preparing to push the Japanese out of Burma. It was training itself intensively in jungle warfare and building up the morale of the troops who had suffered defeat in Burma but had to overpower and beat back the Japanese. The Commander of the Fourteenth Army, Gen. W.J. Slim, said that he was in the beginning confronted with "three major anxieties – supply, health and morale". But these formidable difficulties were surmounted and Gen. Slim said: "My Indian Divisions after 1943 were among the best in the world. They would go anywhere, do anything, go on doing it, and do it on very little."[133] Gen. Slim had decided "that for the first time we should fight the Japanese when the precarious line of communication was behind them and not behind us."

Detachments of platoon strength of the 2nd Mahar Battalion went into action with 6th Battalion MLI in the malaria-infested, treacherous Kabaw Valley making long-range excursions through some scarcely passable mountain tracks and over the jungle-clad hills, held by the Japanese. These detachments also took part in the fighting in Ukhrul, Imphal, and Bishanpur where the Japanese made determined efforts to push through and capture Imphal and its airfield. There were other detachments of the battalion which saw action in the Arkan (1944) and participated in the operations leading to the capture of Akyab (1945).

In the fighting in Burma, Maj. C.J.Biggs was Mentioned-in-Despatches and the 2nd Battalion suffered two casualties. Three persons were wounded.[134]

In April 1945, the 2nd Battalion moved to Ranchi and stayed there till the end of the war. One company of the battalion took part in the Victory Parade march past. Immediately after the war the battalion proceeded to Iraq to join the Paiforce. It sailed from Karachi on September 9, in

---

132 The Twenty Third Indian Division – A History of the Division brought out by the Director of Public Relations, War Department, Government of India.

133 F.M. Sir William Slim, *Defeat Into Victory*, Cassell, London, 1956, p.167.

134 Maj. D.W.A. Barr and Sep. Sampat Bhise were killed. Jem. (later Sub.) Raghunath More, Nk. Sagan Sonaone, and Nk. Sakharam Chaure were wounded.

Jaldurga and landed at Basra with its mascot, Banda, the goat. From Basra it proceeded to Qurumshahr on the river Tigris and with the 14th MLI and the Royal Fusiliers it formed part of the 27th Infantry Brigade. At Qurumshahr the battalion had the responsibility of protecting the harbour area and the telephone and telegraph lines connecting Qurumshahr with Baghdad. This involved patrolling from Qurumshahr to Baghdad as also providing men for static duties. The battalion was sent to Shahiba where it was employed on guarding the Base Ammunition Depot spread over seventeen miles. The work was important as a number of thefts of ammunition had taken place and it was necessary to put an end to this. Strict vigilance had to be exercised. The battalion did excellent work, living in parched sandy wastelands facing extremes of climate. Sub. Baswant Bansode and two Sepoys were awarded the Commendation Cards for risking their lives and recovering some loaded ammunition trucks from a gang of armed robber who had come in sufficient strength and could be apprehended only after some stiff fighting. The gangsters were overpowered, and the ammunition was retrieved. The battalion did well in sports too. Ably guided by Maj. Ramaraje Bhonsale, it won the Brigade Athletics Championship and stood second in the Divisional athletics as also in the Paiforce rifle shooting matches.

Finally, the battalion was alerted to remain ready to move to Palestine where some serious disturbances had erupted. The battalion was to be airlifted to Palestine, but the move did not eventually take place.

The 25th Battalion was moved out of Bombay where it had done well during the war and had discharged its onerous duties with credit. It left for Deolali by road on 15 September 1945 to relieve the unit which had been placed there for the protection of the important defence installations and communication centres. But the battalion was no longer required. The war was over and the purpose for which the battalion had been raised had been served. Therefore, the new Commanding Officer of the battalion, Lt.-Col. R.H. Lowe, who had come from the Jat Regiment,[135]had to bread the sad news of the disbandment of the battalion. The special Battalion Order of 1 March 1946 said: "It is with deep regret that I have to announce that orders have been received from the GHQ India for the battalion to move to Kamptee for disbandment. I

135 The First Commanding Officer, Lt.-Col.V. Chambier, handedover command to Lt.-Col. H.S.I. Pearson, who, in turn, handed over command to Lt.-Col. C.B.Ponappa in June 1943. Lt.-Col. C.B. Ponappa left the battalion on 26 January 1946 and Lt.-Col. R.H. Lowe took over on 24 February, 1946.

want all ranks to realize that this is inevitable now that the war is over and that other garrison battalions are also being disbanded. It is no reflection on officers, nor men nor on the battalion or the Mahar Regiment. The Mahar Regiment of which this battalion is an important part, has rendered loyal and meritorious service during the War and has done so well that a part of it is to be retained after the War. It is still the duty of all ranks to keep the name and reputation of the Mahar Regiment in the high place it now occupies, and I look to all ranks to maintain the present high standard of discipline and turnout. Much will fall on the shoulders of British Officers and Viceroy Commissioned Officers and I want them to do all in their power for the welfare and contentment of the men."

The battalion went to Kemptee where its disbandment was completed by 15 May 1946. Most of the officers, VCOs, and ORS were absorbed in the Mahar Regiment.

About the same time the Commander-in-Chief, India, Field Marshal Sir Claude Auchinleck, visited the 1st Battalion at Gardai in Waziristan in March 1946 and the 2nd Battalion at Shahiba. Addressing the officers and men of these battalions he lauded the commendable achievements of the Mahar soldiers and announced that it had been decided to retain the Mahar Regiment as part of the post-war Indian Army. It had also been decided to convert two Regiments of the Army into Medium Machine Gun Regiments and the Mahar Regiment had the signal distinction of being one of these two Regiments.[136] The change was to take place on 1 October 1946.

The Training Battalion of the Mahar Regiment was now named as the Mahar Machine Gun Regimental Centre from 1 October 1946. Lt.-Col. R.H. Lowe was the first Commandant of the newly formed Regimental Centre and was mainly responsible for reorganizing the Centre and the new training programme.[137] Sub.-Maj. Ramji Gopal Jadhav was the first Sub.-Maj. Of the Centre. On October 15, the Regimental Centre moved from Kamptee to Arangaon near Ahmednagar to stay near its recruiting areas. The conversion into the Medium Machine Gun Regiment started and the switching-over of the Infantry battalions to their new role demanded considerable reorganization, training and redistribution of stores. This was done.

---

136 The other Regiment, 15th Punjab, went to Pakistan.

137 Lt.-Col. R.H. Lowe, after the disbandment of the 25th Battalion, had taken over command of the Training Battalion in June 1946. Likewise, Sub.-Maj. Ramji Gopal Jadhav had been with the Training Battalion since May 1946.

The three battalions of the Regiment got down to intensive MMG training with the help of instructors from the Madras Regiment. The 1st Battalion which had completed the jungle warfare training took to its new conversion training. But the training was adversely affected by the release of men, the repatriation of British officers, and the frequent moves of the battalion. The battalion moved to Jhansi in September 1946 and continued its training. But the battalion moved again, this time to Gaya in Bihar where it joined the 123rd Infantry Brigade of the 5th Indian Division. The 2nd Battalion, at the end of October 1946, returned to India from Shahiba and concentrated at Dhond for leave and reorganization. Its reorganization and training too were hampered by the movements of the battalion. The 3rd Battalion, becoming the 3rd Battalion. The Mahar Machine Gun Regiment left Fort Sandeman on 13 November 1946. It reached Poona on November 21 and became part of the famous 4th Indian Division – "Red Eagles".

The Allied victory in Europe was celebrated on 8 May 1945. Japan surrendered on 14 August 1945. World War II was over. It was estimated that between 3 September 1939 and 31 August 1945, 10,059 Mahars had served in the Army.[138]

The tide of the war had turned in favour of the Allies about the middle of 1942. General Montgomery's at El Alamein, Benghazi, El Agheila, and Tripoli had driven Rommel out of the Western Desert in North Africa. Stalingrad had stood up like a rock shattering the waves of the Nazi armies and blunting much of their power and strength. Sicily and Italy were invaded by the Allies. Italy signed an Armistice and was out of the ring (8 September 1943). Benito Mussolini had resigned and was subsequently killed. The Germans fought alone in Italy. The Anglo-American armies entered Rome (4 June 1944). Two days later the Allied forces landed on the Normandy beaches and by the end of August 1944 Hitler's Wehrmacht was crumbling on all sides. Gen. Eisenhower's forces were advancing from the west and the Russians were pushing from the east. The Germans surrendered in Italy (2 May 1945). Two days later they gave up in Berlin; Adolf Hitler was dead.

In the east, a separate South-East Asia Command with Admiral Lord Louis Mountbatten as the Supreme Commander was created in August 1943. The Fourteenth Army of Gen. W.J. Slim had been forging the shield, befriending the jungle, and preparing to convert defeat into victory. Early in March 1944, Indian troops started chasing the Japanese

---

138 Official History of the Indian Armed Forces in the Second World War, 1939-45.

and by the end of June the "Invade-India" Army of Japan was in pieces. The re-conquest of Burma commenced. The Irrawaddy was crossed in January/February 1945 and Meiktila was taken (March 3). Mandalay fell to the Allies (March 20) and Rangoon was reoccupied (May 3). Russia declared war on Japan (August 8) and the American atom-bombed Hiroshima (August 6), and Nagasaki (August 9). Japan fell and sued for peace (10 August 1945).

After the war in Europe general elections were held in Britain and it was known on July 26 that the Labour Party would get into the saddle. The British Labour Party was committed to closing down the India Office. General elections for Provincial Assemblies were held in India in December 1945. The British Labour Government announced in February 1946 that it would dispatch a Cabinet Mission to India. This Mission led by Lord Pethick-Lawrence, Secretary of State for India, reached Delhi on 24 March 1946 and left on June 29 without much success.

Nevertheless, it was decided to reconstitute the Governor-General's Executive Council with Jawaharlal Nehru as the Vice-President and eleven other Indian members. Sardar Baldev Singh was the Defence Member in the Council. This Interim Government took over on 2 September 1946. The Muslim League, which had abstained from joining the Interim Government in the beginning, changed its mind on October 15 and the Council was reconstituted on October 26 with five representatives of the Muslim League headed by Liaquat Ali Khan.

Within ten days of assuming office, Nehru sent a memorandum to the Commander-in-Chief, Field Marshal Sir Claude Auchinleck, on India's defence policies and regretted that the Army was not fully "National" or "in accord with public sentiment. It was necessary to make it so. On 22 November 1946, Nehru and Baldev Singh jointly appealed to the people "to make the armed forces their own". They said: "The Army must be treated like, and must become, a real national Army and all barriers between the armed forces and the civil population must disappear."

The first Battalion Commanders' Conference was held at the newly formed Mahar Machine Gun Regimental Centre at Arangaon on 28 January 1947. Lt.-Col. R.H.Lowe, Commandant of the Centre, presided and the Conference was attended by the Commanding Officers of the three Battalions of the Regiment: Lt.-Col. E. Johnson (1st Battalion); Lt.-Col. G.H. Nash, OBE (2nd Battalion), and Lt.-Col. R.N.D. Frier, MC (3rd Battalion). A number of subjects were discussed at the Conference, the most important being the changing of the cap badge of the Regiment to conform to the new role and the designation of the Mahar Machine Gun (M.G.) Regiment. The design of a cap badge prepared by the 1st Battalion was approved unanimously by all the Commanding Officers. This badge now had the central Koregaon obelisk crossed by two Medium Machine Guns with the semi-circular scroll bearing the lettering "KORE" and "GAON" on top of the lettering "THE MAHAR M.G. REGIMENT" in a wavy band forming the scroll at the base. (See Appendix No. XIII).

Thus here in order to show the Military History of Mahar's from period of various rulers of Muslims, Marathas and British to independent India. This way Mahars established a large and cultural military activity now there 6th generation of military background who survived in Maharashtra and India. Next chapter deals with the Battle of Koregaon which was fought on 1st January 1818. Mahars participated in this battle and why they fought besides with British, and how the generation of 21st century viewed that battle in detail with the help of primary and oral history.

KOREGAON BATTLE AND ITS AFTERMATH

This chapter deals with the Koregaon Battle and focuses on the battle which was fought on 1st January 1818 on the bank of Bhima river. No battle take place unless two parties disagree with each other it is a hypothesis.

The specific emphasis is laid upon the internal social situation under the Peshwa tyranny. The chapter further deals with the authentic analysis of war, taking into account the geographical location of the Koregaon village where the actual battle took place and the causes leading to the war. Further, it also deals with why Peshwe were defeated and the British succeeded and it was built the Koregaon Monument in the memory of warriors after the war.

It is, therefore, pay attention to know how the 21st century Koregaon battle is viewed. The final analysis of this chapter it consists on the oral sources in the form of questionnaire from people those who were directly related with the area where this battle actually took place and note the various reactions, revealed the true history at the final conclusion. In the final analysis, issues emerging out of this chapter and its impact on the present generation also has been analyzed in short.

Historical background

Conflict in Maratha Polity

After the death of Aurangzeb in 1707[1], Maratha polity arose with many problems like conflict; confrontation, suspicion, mistrust, treachery, and the destruction of law and order situation.[2] The immediate confrontation among Maratha was created by Shahu and Tarabai.[3] There were many prominent Maratha Sardars who were working under several rulers at different places in Maharashtra. Raghuji Bhosle, Nagpur Dabhade from Talegaon. Fatesingh Bhosle from Akkalkote, Nemaji Shinde from

---

[1] Aurangzeb died on 20th Feb. 1707 at Ahmednagar in Maharashtra.

[2] P.A. Gavali, *Peshwekalin Gulamgiri va Ashprushyata,* Prachar Prakashan, Kolhapur, 1990, p.153.

3 A.R. Kulkarni, Thc Marathas, Books and Book, New Delhi, 1996, p.70.

Gwalior, Tukoji Holkar, Ahilyabai Holkar of Indore, Gaikwad of Baroda.[4]

After the entry of Shahu, the Desastha Brahmin from Kurhad Purushottam Pant also joined Shahu.[5] At the same time Chitpavan Brahmin from Sreevardhan Konkan, Balaji Vishwanath Bhat was also closely related to the events.[6]

Balaji helps Shahu by bringing important people in the mainstream such as Kanhoji Angre, a supporter of Tarabai also was brought along with Dhanaji Jadhav to the services of Shahu.[7] Balaji Vishwanath died in 1720.[8] Two groups emerged in the court of Shahu like Chitpavan Kokanastha and Desastha Brahmin. The policy of Balaji Vishwanath continued till 1740. After death, Balaji Vishwanath of son Balaji Bajirao, (19 years old) was appointed as Peshwa. Shahu died in 1749. The kingdom and the polity of Shahu came under Balaji Bajirao. His first son Vishwasrao died in Panipat War (1761).[9] Nanasaheb died immediately after the war, his other son (17th Years old), Madhavrao became the Peshwa and Raghunathrao his uncle (Raghoba) was appointed as caretaker,[10] at this time Chitpavan Brahmin, Peshwe opposed by Nagpurkar Bhosle, Nimbalkar of Phaltan and Gopalrao Patwardhan.[11] At this time conflict between Madhavrao Peshwa and Uncle Raghoba (Caretaker) began. According to Gordon: "*this event marks the beginning of a shift in power between the Centre and the periphery which was to become much more serious in a decade.*"[12]

---

4 Stewart Gordon, *The Marathas*, Cambridge University Press, New Delhi, reprint 2000, p.108.

5 Ibid., p.105.

6 Ibid., p.107.

7 Ibid., p.109.

8 Maharashtra State Gazetteers. *History Part III, Maratha Period.* Maharashtra State Publication, Bombay, 1967, p.238.

9 Ibid., n.4, p.114.

10 Ibid.,n.3, p.126.

11 Ibid., p.145.

12 Ibid., p. 156.

However, in 1773, Madhadrao Peshwa also died,[13] his younger brother Narayanrao Peshwa became the Peshwa of Poona. After nine months Narayanrao Peshwa was also murdered. Raghunathrao was held responsible[14] who ultimately took shelter of the British and thus, the British intervention in Maratha State began.For a short period Madhavrao, Savai Peshwa ruled Pune and finally, Bajirao II continued till 1795-1818.[15]

Social Conflict

The social conflict is one of the significant factors in Indian Social context which paved the way towards war situation. Koregaon Battle is viewed in this direction. During the Peshwe period as mentioned earlier, there were deadly fight among the Brahmins, Chitpavan between the Desastha and Karhade to the other side.[16] Among the minority communities there was conflict and revolt at the end of Peshwai. Along with this the Pendhari communities also revolted[17] the other community Vanjara, Berad. Among the Berad there are Berad, Durga Bhirgi, Halage, Jas or Myas. Naik, Bhil and Ramoshi these communities were known for their destructive activities. Sometimes the military officer of Peshwe also participated in destructive activities.[18]

On this issue, the Brahmin and Maratha conflict also began. Chitpavan became important and rest of the Brahmins communities joined the opposition group. Sardars were divided by so many reasons on the basis of caste, hatred, jealousy, plot, killing, suspicious behaviour, communal riot, revolt, loot, robbery, theft, murders, arrest, punishment and killing without trial began which brought down the trust in society. Socio-economic, political and cultural devaluation of the society began. The low caste people especially Mahars were targeted everywhere by the upper

---

13 Ibid., p.156.

14 Ibid., p.154.

15 P.M. Joshi, (ed), *Selection from Peshwa Daftar*, Letters 1-6, Part III, New Series, Bombay, 1962, Duff, James Grant, History of the Marathas, reprinted, Vol. II, Karan Publication, New Delhi, 2000, pp. 119-20.

16 P.A. Gavali, *Peshwekalin Gulamgiri Va Ashprushyala*, Prachar Prakashan, Kolhapur, 1990, p.154.

17 Ibid., p.153.

18 Ibid.

caste and the social policies based on religion was applied strictly by the Peshwe.[19]

British East India Company's intervention

The conflict between Chitpavan and Desastha,[20] continued Peshwai became weak and almost came to the breaking point. The other Maratha Sardar like Shinde, Bhonsle could not bring peace to the Maratha policy. Nizam[21] acquired political rights began to acquire the area Berar, Bidar and Adoni. The Marathas defeated Nizam in Kharda Battle in April 1795.[22] After the Battle of Kharda, the Maratha Sardars like Daulatrao Shinde (Malwa), Parshuram Bhau Patwardhan (Tasgaon) Southern Maharashtra, Raghuji Bhosle of Nagpur, returned to their respective areas, Tuloji Holkar remained in Pune.[23]

Still the conflict continued between Nana Phadnavis[24] and Raghunathrao's son. Out of these two camps emerged Shinde and Nana Phadnavis in Maharashtra and Nizam and Tipu Sultan in South, thus the conflict continued.[25]

The British emerged into area April 1789. They adopted the policy of engagement and subsidiary alliance[26] with remaining power. Their aim was to isolate from the French, Nizam, Tipu and Marathas. Nizam was very anxious to join the British against the Marathas. He signed the treaty

---

19 Ibid., p.93.

20 Ibid., p.156.

21 Nizam – Nizam-ul-mulk, the founder of the Nizam Dynasty at Hyderabad, See Maharashtra State Gazetteers, History Part III, Maratha Period, Directorate of Printing & Publication, Govt. of Maharashtra, Bombay, 1967, p.188.

22 Ibid., p.260, Sidnak Mahar was one of the commanders of Maratha in this battle.

23 Stewart Gordon, Ibid., n.4, p.169.

24 Nana Phadnavis, A Chitpavan Brahmin and extraordinarily able administrator and Negotiator, he had served in the administration of Madhavrao for ten years.

25 Stewart Gordon, Ibid., n.4, pp.169-171.

26 Subsidiary alliance, - In 1798, Lord Wellesly came to India as the Governor General. His objective was to bring the Indian states under 'Subordinate Isolation' by his most potent weapon of subsidiary system. Mysore was the first of the Indian States to be forced to accept the subsidiary alliance.

with British in 1798.[27] Nana Phadanavis opposed British and joined Tipu Sultan. By 1800 only two independent powers remained on the field, the British and the Marathas, all other groups entered into the subsidiary alliance with the British.[28]

In 1800 Nana Phadanavis died along with him other important leaders Tukoji Holkar, Mahadji Shinde, Ahilyabai Holkar also died. (1795 to 1800).[29]

The conflict between Shinde and Holkar continued in Malwa state. Shinde defeated Holkar, October 25th, 1802. Holkar defeated the forces of Peshwa and Shinde in Pune. Peshwa took shelter under the British at Basein where he signed the subsidiary alliance treaty with British in 1802.[30]

In 1813, Lord Hastings became the Governor General of India and a major portion of India by that time came under the control of the East India Company. Raghuji Bhosale, Daulatrao Scindia and Yeshwantrao Holkar had retained a semblance of independence by not signing the subsidiary alliance but the treaties signed by them after the second Anglo Maratha War were crippling enough. They would have formed a powerful opposition possibility they had come together but chances of this eventually were remote. In those time Deccan, Maratha Power in Kolhapur, Satara, Sawantwadi emerged as political centres but they were weak.

The Company's position was strong enough to start a major war. Hasting aimed to complete subjugation of the Maratha power through diplomacy and war were ever possible. Thus, the stage was set for the third Maratha War. The Governor General didn't take time to think that the British had a good opportunity to become a paramount power in India, as the so-called local powers could either be destroyed or formed into confederacy.

---

27 The Imperial Gazetteers of India, The Indian Empire, Vol. IV, Secretary of State for India, The Clarendon Press, Oxford, 1909, p.10.

28 Ibid., n.4, p.172.

29 Ibid., n.4, p.172.

29 Kincaid Parasnis, Comprehensive History of the Maratha Empire, Vol.III, Anmol Publication, Delhi, 1986, p.200, Ibid., n.27, p.76. also see Appendix no. 16.

30 Kincaid Parasnis, *Comprehensive History of the Maratha Empire,* Vol.III, Anmol Publication, Delhi, 1986, p.200, Ibid., n.27, p.76. also see Appendix no. 16.

The British resident appointed in Pune, British wanted to acquire territory of Surat and Maharashtra on this date onwards Peshwa lost their independence. British appointed Lord Cornwallis[31] who directly tied the Maratha houses to the British power. Peshwa rule became powerless could not control the Deshmukh neither able to collect taxes. The troops Shinde and Holkar best known as the Pendharis destroyed the State economy and law and order situation. The major shift taken place in the Peshwai by June 1817 when a new treaty was signed with helpless Peshwa by this treaty all his powers were stripped.[32]

Treaty of Poona

The East India Company signed a treaty with the Peshwa in 1817.[33] The terms and conditions of the treaty were very severe. It reimposed the conditions of the treaty of Vasai and renounced the Peshwaship. The Peshwa wanted to give up his claims of supremacy over the Rajas of Kolhapur, Sawantwadi, Berar and Holkar, Scindia and Gaikwad.

Because of this treaty by taking away the powers of the Peshwa, the English position became stronger. The Peshwa was to raise a contingent of 5000 horse and 3000 infantries to furnish to the British Government. The force was to be commanded by British officers but was to be paid by the Peshwa.

The Peshwa's revenue was considerably reduced and this brought their his economic power to an end. The Treaty completely subjugated by the Peshwa. The situation in Pune court deteriorated and Bapu Gokhale a Maratha Sardar became powerful, his influence was disseminated. The Peshwa left Poona trying to recruit men in the Army.

The Peshwa reconciliated with the Jagirdars in the south, but most of them were trying to safeguard their jagirs. Out of the two brothers of the Peshwa, Amritrao was not at all in favour of opening hostilities against the British and maintain peace at all cost.

Elphinstone discovered that a large-scale anti-British correspondence was going on between the Maratha Sardars. There was frantic activity in

---

31 Ibid., n.4, p.176. Lord Cornwallis succeeded to the Governor Generalship in 1786. He came out with the instruction and the desire to pursue a pacific and moderate policy.

32 Ibid.

33 The Imperial Gazetteer of India, The Indian Empire, Vol.IV, Secretary of State for India, The Clarendon Press, Oxford, 1909, p.76.

Maharashtra and elsewhere. The British imposed a new treaty on Scindia on 5th November 1817. The Governor General also concluded a treaty with Holkar.

The war between the Marathas and the East India Company broke out in November 1817. The first battle was fought at Khadaki, in this war Marathas were defeated. The Battle of Khadki decided the fate of the Peshwa. Brig. General Smith came down with his division from the north and Peshwa ran away.

After the battle political changes took place the last act organized from the Peshwa camp in Pune. The British residencies was attacked and burnt simultaneously in Pune and Nagpur.[34] The British quickly took majors by sending Army to Pune and Nagpur wipe out the revolt. By the end of 1817, the Pendhari Army was completely routed out.[35] The British totally destroyed Peshwa in the final battle of Koregaon.[36]

Mahars of Maharashtra

In India, the caste system was established as hereditary by the Indians, based on birth. Once born as Mahar always remains a Mahar. The caste conflict became sharp during the orthodox rule of Peshwa.[37] Veda, Priesthood and Yajna were applied as code of conduct, manners, custom, behaviours, rules and regulations were governed as per religious direction.[38]

Profession or occupation was one of the main causes of the multiplication of castes.[39] The professions and occupations were not based on the peculiar tastes and aptitudes of the individuals but on sheer accident of birth. Violation of hereditary profession or occupation

---

34 Ibid., n.4, p.177.

35 Ibid., p.177.

36 V. Blacker, *Memoir Operations of the British Army in India, Mahratta War, 1817-18-19,* Black Kingsbury Parbury and Accer, London, 1821, p.179.

37 Jayshree Gokhale, *From Concession to Confrontation, The Politics of an Indian Untouchable Community*, Popular Prakashan, Bombay, 1993, p.34. See also,

P.A. Gavali, *Peshwekalin Maharashtra*, Kailas Publication, Aurangabad, 2000, p.88.

38 Gavali, P.A.,Ibid., p.108.

39 Ibid., p.148.

especially by the lower castes was considered as a crime by the Hindu. The status of the lower caste people degraded under Peshwas.

The social precedence of the different castes was not dependent upon differences of intellect or the best and moral character of the individual but on his birth. Caste graduations and the notion of superiority attached to each higher caste and it was the real cause of conflict. The jealousy and hatred among different caste groups developed so deep superiority or inferiority led always to conflict. The conflicts sometimes led within the castes and also outside. Every caste had sub-castes even among the Brahmins there were several sub-castes, (See Appendix No.V) that differed in rank and reputation. Some of them were reputed to be so holy and held in such high veneration that if another section of their caste tried to degrade their social precedence with encroachment upon their rights and perquisites, clashes inevitable arose between them.

Apart from the distinctions of rank fostered by the institution of caste we find that every caste expropriated to themselves certain privileges (man-pan) from which others were excluded.

Sometimes caste men behaved against the established rules and regulations in case of marriage and they were ex-communicated.[40] Thus caste rules strictly followed which prevented the inter mixture of blood.[41]

---

40 Please refer

B.R.Ambedkar, Who were the Shudras? How they came to be the fourth varna in the Indo-Aryan Society, Thacker & Co., Bombay,1946.

B.R.Ambedkar, The Untouchables who were they and why they became Untouchables, Amrit Book Co., New Delhi, 1948.

B.R. Ambedkar, Annihilation of caste: with reply to Mahatma Gandhi, Bharat Bhushan Press, Bombay, 1936.

Dr.Babasaheb Ambedkar, Writings and Speeches, Vol. VII, Vol. XVII, Education Department, Government of Maharashtra, Mumbai, 2001.

G,S, Ghurye, Caste and Race in India, Popular Prakashan, Pune, 1932.

J.H. Hutton, Caste in India, Oxford University Press, Bombay, 1977.

G.C. Vad , (ed), Selection from the Satara Raja and Peshwa Diaries, Vol.II, Poona, p.317.

41Abbie Dubois, Hindu Manners, customs and ceremonies, Reprinted in India by Shree Publishing House, New Delhi, 1991, p.34.

The various types of social conventions influenced sub-groups of different castes including marriages. The impact of social maxims and conventions upon different castes and sub-castes led to conflicts among themselves. For instance, a sanad, which was given to Mahars stated that 20 castes were permitted to take brides on horse-back, 16 on oxen, 5 on foot, and 2 castes were permitted to take brides on a male buffalo.[42]

Food cooked or touched by inferior castes was not to be accepted. If anybody among them took a meal along with another caste's person was ordered to undertake penance or purify himself and then seek re-admission into the original caste. Sometimes they were excommunicated.[43]

Watan was the only source to preserve the position, status, rights and perquisites in the society. Sometimes one caste tried to adapt itself to others watan and clashes inevitably arose between them.

The caste conflicts mainly arose on the following categories: (i) conflicts between Brahmin castes, (ii) conflicts between Brahmin and non-Brahmin castes. (iii) conflicts between non-Brahmin castes (shudra) (iv) conflict between untouchables[44] (Atishudra).

As per historical survey and records indicates the disputes among the untouchable (Atishudra) castes viz. the Mahars, the Mangs and the Charmakars. The disputes arose between the untouchables on the issue of man-pan (privileges, rights and perquisites). For example, in 1776-77, 9 disputes arose between the Mahars, the Mangs and Kunbis. When the Mahars of the Nagar and Parner complained. Inquiry was made of the Mahars at Poona and at Paithan. The allegation of the Mahars was proved to be correct, and orders were issued to the Kamavisdars of the various provinces to remove their grievances.[45]

Mahars versus Chambhars: A dispute arose between the Mahars and chambhars. The Chambhars, on certain occasions, complained that they

---

42 Bharat Itihas Samshodhan Mandal, Fourth Sammelan Report, Pune, 1916, 17, pp. 56-57.

43 P.A. Gavali, Ibid., n.37, p.219.

44 Ibid., p.220.

45 Ibid., p.244.

were obstructed by the Mahars in taking the offerings of food prepared for the bullock on the Pola Day.[46]

Untouchability under Peshwa reign

Untouchability a Hindu's age-old social discriminatory institution[47] which condemned the fourth varna shudra untouchables to sub-human social standard, existed in the worst form under the rule of the Peshwas in Maharashtra.[48]

Manu mentioned the untouchables as Antya, Antyaja and the Antyavasin and put their abode outside the village.[49] The Antyaja's were also Avarnas those not belonging to any of the four varnas or castes. So the Shudra is a Savarna while the untouchable is an Avarna, i.e. outside the Chaturvarnya or the system of four castes. According to Dr. B. R. Ambedkar, "*the word Antya in Manusmriti means not end of creation but end of the village.*"[50] Hence they were called Antyajas or Antyavasins. These two castes would not live along with the Savarnas, not even with the Shudras, as they were the Atishudras.

The Maratha Hindu society with its peculiar untouchability practices and beliefs developed in itself a more serious form. In the course of time, it has become hereditary. In India, the practice of untouchability became a permanent character of the Hindu communities. The caste Hindus became pure by adopting a purificatory prescription. But the untouchables could never be made pure. Because "*they were born impure, they are impure while they live, they die the death of the impure, and give birth to children who are born with the stigma of untouchability affixed to them. It is a case of permanent hereditary stain in which nothing can cleanse.*"[51]

---

46 R.V. Oturkar, Peshwekalin Samjik Va Arthik Patravyahar (1723-1856), Bharat Itihas Samshodhan Mandal, Poona, 1950, p.70.

47 Dr. Babasaheb Ambedkar, *Writings and Speeches, Vol.V,* Education Department, Govt. of Maharashtra, Mumbai, 1989, p.19.

48 Dr. Babasaheb Ambedkar's *Letter to Editor of Newspaper, Kesari*, 10.7.1936.

49 F. Maxmuller, (ed), *Sacred Books of the East, Laws of Manu,* Motilal Banarasidas, Delhi, 1975, p. 51.

Also see, Gopalshastri Nene, (ed), *The Manusmriti, The Chowkhamba*, Sanskrit Series Office, Varanasi, 1970.

50 Dr. B.R. Ambedkar, *The Untouchables*, Thakersey & Co., Mumbai, 1946, p.33.

51 Ibid., p.21.

Thus, the untouchability practised by the Hindus, for centuries, had led to the virtual 'isolation' and 'segregation' of a large section of society and people of their own religion. The places where the untouchables lived were cordoned off. They lived, not in the same places where the Hindus lived, but in those places meant for impure people like the untouchables. Gradually it led to the creation of a 'ghetto' in each village. When the castes in Hindus lived in village, then untouchables lived in the ghetto. This meant that the untouchables carried the badge of inferior status forever, without any remission or redemption either in this world or in the next.[52]

Manu and Untouchability

Manusmriti the code of conduct professed by Manu states the following on the Untouchables"

> (51) But the dwellings of the Candalas (Chandalas) and the shvapakas shall be outside the village, they must be made Apapatras and their wealth (shall be) dogs and donkeys.
>
> (52) Their dress (shall be) the garments of the dead (they shall eat) their food from broken dishes, black iron (shall be) their ornaments and they must always wander from place to place.
>
> (53) A man who fulfils a religious duty shall not seek intercourse with them; their transactions (shall be) among themselves and their marriages with their equals.
>
> (54) Their food shall be given to them by others (than an Aryan giver) in a broken dish; at night they shall not walk about in the village and in towns.
>
> (55) By day they may go about the purpose of their work, distinguished by mark at king's command, and they shall carry out corpses (of persons) who have no relatives; that is a settled rule.
>
> (56) By the king's order they shall always execute the criminals in accordance with the law, and they shall take for themselves the clothes, the beds and the ornaments of (such criminals)."[53]

In Manusmriti caste privileges and disabilities are reflected in criminal law. Different punishments are laid down for the same offences for members

---

52 Ibid., p.22.

53 Ibid, n.48, pp.414-15.

of different castes. As per the rule of Manu, Brahmins were to be exempted from capital punishments. "No greater crime is known on earth than slaying a Brahman; a king, therefore, must not even conceive in his mind even the slightest idea of killing a Brahmana."[54] A severest punishment for the Brahmin was that he should be banished with permission to take all his property with him.[55]

Normally, a distinction in the status of the varnas is made everywhere as per the code of Manu giving legal sanction to the status of each caste and the violation of caste rule should result into punishment. For instance, Manu says: "With whatever limb, a man of a low caste does or hurt to (a man of the three) highest (castes), even that limb shall be cut off.[56] Thus the untouchables had no right to perform religious rituals sanskaras(rites), and even the legal rights to redress their grievances.

Untouchables under Peshwas

In all the literature of the Peshwa period, the Mahars, the Mangs and the Chambars were mentioned as untouchables.[57] The Mahar sometimes was called as Dher "Bhoomia" or guide, Yeshkar or Watchman, "Taral" or gatekeeper.[58] The Mangs were also known as Vajantri or musician. Records also refer to the Mangavargant snake-charmers.[59] The Charmakars were known as Mochis (shoemaker) Jingar (Saddle makers), etc.,[60] in all this Mahars are the principal untouchable community in Maharashtra. It is the single largest untouchable community found in Maharashtra.

---

54 Ibid., p. 381.

55 Ibid., p. 380.

56 Ibid, p.279.

57 Dr. Babasaheb Ambedkar, *Writings & Speeches, Vol.XVII*, Education Department, Government of Maharashtra, Mumbai, 2000, p.807.

58 Arthur Crawford, *Our Troubles in Poona and the Deccan*, West-Minister Archibald Constable & Co., London, 1897, pp.214-15.

59 R.V. Russell and Hiralal, *The Tribes and Caste of the Central Provinces of India*, Vol.IV, Reprint, Cosmo Publication, Delhi, 1975, pp.184-185, See also, Ghurye G.S., Caste and Race in India, Popular Prakashan, Pune, 1932, p.39.

60 R.V. Russell & Hiralal, *The Tribes and Caste of the Central Provinces of India*, Vol.II, Reprint, Cosmo Publication, Delhi, 1975, pp.407-8, G.S. Ghurye, Caste and Race in India, Popular Prakashan, Pune, 1932, pp.36-37.

In Maharashtra Mahar community are to be found in every village. Every village has constructed a wall and the Mahars have their quarters outside the wall. The Mahars were performing their duties of watch and ward on behalf of the villagers; and they claimed 52 rights[61] against the Hindu villagers."[62]

Socio-Religious position of Mahars in Peshwai

The Peshwas followed a traditional pattern of socio-religious rules and regulations formulated in the laws of Manu. The Manusmruti denied the religious Sanskaras[63] to the Shudras, in consequence of this denial the Shudras were degraded, and other negative results followed. Thus, the basic distinction was made between the men with the right of Samskaras and those without it. Thus socio-religious conduct of the society was formulated on pure religious guidelines in the days of the Peshwas. Peshwa also suggested and formulated certain codes of behaviour for the society. If castes or individuals tried to adapt themselves against the established code of conduct, they were punished by various methods. For instance, in the Bassein region, the Brahmins belong to (Samavedi race) were ordered by the Government in 1750 that they should recite holy words after performing ablution, and conduct themselves according to the Dharma of Brahmins, otherwise they would be punished.[64]

Though the Government had thus suggested and formulated certain codes of behaviour for Brahmins, it had also assured them the highest social status by expressing forbidding lower castes to initiate usages and customs practised by the former. For instance, lower castes were prohibited to wear the sacred thread (Janeu) or to perform certain specific ritual[65] both of which were allowed only to Brahmins.

Thus, the discriminatory caste laws were imposed on untouchables strictly and they were the worst sufferers among the Hindus. In 1783-84, the Government formulated seven rules of worship at the holy places of

61 52 rights sanad, Given by Badshah of Bidar to Mahar's.

62B.R. Ambedkar, *The Untouchables*, Thakersey & Co., Bombay, 1946, pp.33-34.

63 Samskar, Hindu Ceremony Custom practiced by Brahmin, Khastriya, Vaishya which is very necessary to a Hindu.

64 P.A. Gavali, *Society and Social Disability under the Peshwa*, National Publishing House, New Delhi, 1988, p.143.

65 Sacred thread – means Janeu which is worn only by Brahmins after the ceremony of Munj.

Pandharpur and ordered the administration to carry out strictly. The seven rules were: 'That the stone-image of Chokhamela,[66] be kept at the north of the main temple for untouchables (Atishudra) who can worship. The place is so narrow and crowded that the visitors bound to touch one another to this situation Brahmins opposed. Therefore, the untouchables should perform worship from a distance from the stone-lamp in front of the image of Chokhamela or from a nearby untouchable hamlet (Maharwada).[67]

In 1786, the Mahars in the Konkan region demanded some Brahman priests were nominated as for their marriage ceremony, and their demand was initially supported by the local bureaucrat. But the priests refused to perform the ceremony by saying that according to ancient usage to the marriages of the untouchables were not officiated by the Brahmins but by untouchable priests themselves and that a new practice should not be started. Then the local bureaucrats who were supporting the demand of the untouchables forcibly attached the office of the Brahmin priests, who then appealed to the Poona Government. The Government summoned the hereditary officers and priest of the place for enquiry who gave evidence that there was no usage that Brahmin priests of Junnar region had officiated. On hearing this matter when they wrote to the Poona Government they were given information that the region was under the Mughals, some untouchables had made a similar demand and appealed for its execution to Emperor Aurangzeb, who made an enquiry into the custom and decided against their demand and since then no Brahmin priest officiates at the marriage of the Untouchables. Accordingly, the Poona Government decided that "whereas this ancient usage was not violated nor improvised even under the former Mughal rule, it is quite improper to threaten (the priests) and enforce a new usage in our Maratha Kingdom."

The Government reprimanded the local bureaucrat and ordered him to restore and attach office to the priests on the one hand and commanded on the other. The untouchables must perform their marriage officially by their own priests threatening "if they trouble the Brahmin priests in future, they will meet with bad consequences.[68]

---

66 Chokhamela – a 14th century saint belonging to Mahar caste, lived Mangalvedha, Solapur, Maharashtra.

67 Maharwada – Areas where Mahar lives in, outside the village of Maharashtra. In some villages of Maharashtra called Maharwada a Rajwada.

68 Ibid., n.64, p.145.

The Mahars were denied the right of military services they were also subjected to many restrictions and prohibitions. The concept of untouchability was rigorously imposed on them by the Peshwa rule.[69] They were prohibited strictly from using good clothes as well as walking on roads in daylight because it was believed that it would cast a long shadow, touching from them was believed to pollute higher castes. They were compelled to spit in earthen the pot which hanged in the neck and not on the ground as it would pollute the street. They had to tie a hanging broom to the waist to sweep their footprint automatically on the roads even by the touch of which[70] the higher castes people were believed to get polluted.

Suppression of the Mahars did not over here, but they were even slained by both caste people and rulers on the pretext of their shadow falling. There are examples of such killing of the Mahars for example, once Bajirao Peshwa was passing through Kopargaon, presently in Ahmednagar district of Maharashtra, during this time by a innocent mistake, a shadow of Mang (a caste below the Mahar) fell upon him, in a fit of anger he butchered him into pieces. While on their way Ramachandra Bhide, Wamanrao Apte, Triambak Dengle, etc., high caste *Sardars* looted the Mahars and the Mangs and tortured them.[71]

After Chhatrapati Shivaji's rule, the Marathas became weak. But After the death of Aurangzeb, the Marathas became powerful. Now the Peshwe took overall power. They made divisions in the society on the basis of caste and suppressed the low caste people. The Mahar caste went out through many difficulties and they were targeted. The Mahars had no other way but to join the Military services.

When Europeans came to India, they recruited many Maratha Sardars including Brahmin to military services as well as Mahars also joined their military services.

The British in Bombay had come in contact with the Mahars and had come to rely on them for household duties as also for military and police services. The loyalty of the Mahars, their dependability, and the qualities of their heart and head were recognized by the English. The knowledge

---

69 G.S. Ghurye, *Caste and Class in India,* Popular Prakashan, Bombay, 1957, pp.166-67.

70 Ibid.

71 Ibid.

of the Mahars of the local areas was of great advantage to the English because they were unknown to the land.

The Mahars were often promoted to the commissioned ranks. British officers and historians confirmed the Mahar as a typical Bombay sepoy and extolled the qualities of Bombay Sepoys generalizing the qualities of the Mahars – their faithfulness, reliability, determination and devotion to duty.

Recruitment of Mahars in British Army

The main strength of the Europeans army was their arms and artillery, their superior infantry training and their daily drill, discipline, and regimentation. The French realized the importance of this and were convinced that Indian sepoys, dressed, trained, disciplined, and accoutered in the western style, could easily outsmart and outmatch their brethren in the forces of the Indian rulers.[72] The French Governor of Pondicherry, Francois Martin, had obtained permission from the Indian ruler to maintain a force of 300 native soldiers for the defence of the town. When Martin died in 1706, his successor, Benoit Dumas, formed a force of Indian soldiers in 1740. These soldiers were dressed, drilled, and equipped on the European style.[73] The English had, till then done nothing of this type. In 1742, the infantry in the Bombay Presidency was, for the first time, officially formed as the Bombay European Regiment and its strength in seven Companies was 1,591.[74] There was also 843 Sepoys in thirteen Companies but they were without regular arms and uniform. When the war was declared between England and France in 1744, hostilities started between the British and the French in India, too. In the fighting with the British, the French used Indian Sepoys trained in the western style. Major Stringer Lawrence,[75] arrived in Madras in January

---

72 Channa, Wickremesekera, *Best Black Troops in the World*, Manohar Publisher, Delhi, 2002, p.66.

73 H.H. Dodwell, *Sepoy Recruitment in the old Madras Army*, Superintendent Govt. Printing, Calcutta, 1922, pp.3-5.

74 Sir Patrick Cadell, *History of the Bombay Army,* Green and Co., London, 1938, p.

75 Major Stinger Lawrence, The Father of the Indian Army and the first Commander in Chief of all the Indian Armies in India.

Charles *Floyer to the Court of Directors,* Fort St. David, 13 Feb. 1748 Dodwell, Calender, p.50.

H.H. Dodwell, *Sepoy Recruitment in the Old Madras Army*, Superintendent, Government Printing, Calcutta, 1922, p.50.

1748, raised the first few Companies of Indian soldiers, called Native Sepoys, who were trained and equipped in the English style and were led by European Officers.

Ten years later the supremacy of the English vis-à-vis the Indian rulers increased as also the competing European powers. The "Lal Paltan" the 1st Regiment of Bengal Native Infantry comprising entirely Indian Sepoys was formed by Robert Clive, in

Calcutta in January 1757.[76] Major. William Fraser, who commanded the forces in the Bombay Presidency, presented proposals for the "establishment of 1,500 sepoys complete, regulated, disciplined and paid. This was done in the same manner as they were dealt at the Coast (i.e. Madras) and in Bengal". These men were divided into twelve Companies with a reserve force for garrison duties. The Board of Directors agreed that a corps of 500 best Bombay Sepoys be formed with their own officers. Red broadcloth was issued to them as their uniform and set pattern. The independent Companies later converted into Native (Indian) Battalions in 1767.[77]

Mahar`s bravery in British Army

British those who came nearly five to six thousand miles away from India and conquered the land and ruled over India for quite a long time due to social disorder of the Indian society were given jobs and equal opportunities in social field. This was done only when they understood fully well the water-tight compartments of Indian Society which were divided into castes and sub-castes. The British East India Company recruited these so-called low caste men in a large number of oppressed castes particularly the untouchables. It was because they were the most oppressed and worst affected and neglected section of the Indian society, they served their masters as per their guidance.

The Mahars of Maharashtra in spite of their decisive role in establishing and protecting the Maratha ruler, they were given inferior social status on the basis of their caste grounds during the late periods of Maratha rule.

---

76 Amiya Bharat, *The Bengal Native Infantry: Its Organisation and Discipline*, Firma K.L. Mukhopadhyay, 1962, p.48.

When clive raised the 3rd Bengal Sepoy Battalion in January 1758, the men were drawn from the Bhojpur district in Bihar, Clive of Bengal 30 June 1758, Bengal Secret Consultation, Oriental and India Office Collection P/A/2,p.28.

77 An unpublished account of the Bombay Army by Edward Sambrooke John Anderson; 2 vol. Oriental and India Office Collection, Cadell, n.78, p.67.

Moreover, they were continuously discriminated even in the army during the Peshwa rule. Various taboos were imposed on them. Regressive laws were made for them detrimental to the interest of the low castes as well as the Mahars. Consequently, the Mahars were not happy and discontented with the native rule due to social oppression. Therefore, in many places, they revolted against the Indian but failed. When the British came here, they willingly joined with society but they mainly wanted to get rid of the torturous rule of the native kings. As soldiers, they performed their duties well and participated in various battles against native rulers and by the side of the British. In fact, they were used beyond military requirements.

Battle of Arcot, 1751

Confidence of East India Company increased when Lord Clive[78] won the battle of Arcot (presently in Tamil Nadu) with the help of Pariya, Mahars and Untouchable Tailiar castes. Socially they were the worst affected people. They were recruited on cheap labour as battle soldiers. The Pariyas,[79] the Mahars and the Untouchable castes also happy to join the British force for self-existence because of the regular income. They also felt free and happy through meagre and day to day tortures furiously from the high castes. Even if the low payments is given to them in the army it was high for them than the payments received from the locals for their day to day jobs in their villages. In those days, getting wages at all in the villages were rare and difficult. In fact, they fought the battle of Arcot in 1751 as if it was a battle against local high castes rather than the battle between the East India Company and Native rulers. For them, it was the war for their liberation from their own torturous native masters.[80]

Battle of Plassy, 1757

The ambitions and passion of the British had grown due to their success in various battles against the native rulers. They took advantage of the desperate and unhappy untouchable castes and fought the battle of

---

78 Lord Clive worked as a clerk in East India Company's branch at Madras. Then he rose in the Army of East India Company.

See also, V.R. Shinde, Bharatiya Ashprusatecha Prashna, Govt. of Maharashtra Publication, Bombay 1972, p.165.

79 Pariyas – An untouchable community of Tamil Nadu (Madras) which was in British Military Services.

80 Oriental and India Office Collections, Orme India II, p.284.

Plassy.[81] In this battle, the help of the Pariya and the Mahar and untouchable caste soldiers were taken.

War with Maratha (1802-1803)

During the third battle between the Marathas and the British in 1802-1803[82] untouchable soldiers from Madras (present Tamil Nadu) and Maharashtra were used under the command of Arthur

Wellesley to defeat the Marathas.[83] The Mahar soldiers of Maharashtra were in the Maratha armies for centuries together. They were knowing the war techniques; hence they could easily defeat the Maratha army without any difficulty.

Battle of Khadki in 1817

Bajirao Peshwa and British developed a strained relationship which leads to the battle of Khadki.[84] The Battle of Khadki (1817) was fought by the British in the help of the Mahar soldiers by the side of the British. It is striking event in the Indian history, for following reasons; (a) the Mahars helped in establishing, protecting and continuing the Maratha rule in Maharashtra, (b) the Mahars not only disliked the Peshwa rule, (the offspring of Maratha rule) because the Mahars were discriminated with inhuman treatment. (c) The British gave them an opportunity in the Battle of Khadki in 1817, (d) in the Battle of Khadki only a few suppressed and discriminated caste wise Mahar soldiers fought the battle with Bajiraorao Peshwa II with a large organized and trained army at Khadki and badly defeated.

---

81 Channa Wickremesekera, *Best Black Troops in the World, British Perception and the Machinery of the Sepoy 1746 to 1805*, Manohar Publishers Delhi, 2002, p.89.

82 John Pemble, "*Techniques and Resources in the Second Maratha War*" Historical Journal, Vol. 19, no.2, 1976, pp. 393-4.

83 Ibid n.81, p.75.

Sydney J. Owen, (ed), *A Selection from the Despatches, Treaties and other Papers of the Marques* K.G. Wellesley, during his Governorship of India, Clarendon, Oxford, 1877, pp.299-309.

T.E. Colebrook, *The Life of the Honourable Mountstuart Elphinstone*, Vol.I, John Murray and Co., London, 1884, pp.47-85.

84 P.C. Gupta, Bajirao IInd and East India Co., Oxford University Press, London, 1939, pp.167-68.

Conflict between British and Peshwa

When Peshwa Bajirao II treated Mahar people at a low level. The Leader from Peshwa Sarsenapati Bapu Gokhale and Peshwa joined together ill-treatment to the Mahars with insults and disrespect. Whereas British allowed the Mahars to join the British army, on equal and resected rights. Bapu Gokhale acted wrongly and forced Peshwa to sign the war agreement with British, 19th October 1817 and 28th October 1817.[85] On these two dates, the time of attack was decided by the Peshwa. Peshwa also wrote a letter to Holkar, Shinde, Bhosale and Gaikwad asking them to fight with British. The Marathas such as Nipankar, Akkalkotwale, Bhosale, Nimbalkar, Ghorpade, Jadhav, Vinchurkar, Patwardhan, Bapu Gokhale, Raje Bahadur, Bhoite, Purandare and other Saranjamdar joined together, with their strength becoming more than a lakh with this infantry Arabs, Rohila, Pathan, Sindhi, Gosavi, Rajput also joined together 50,000 extra men.[86]

On 29th October 1817, Bapu Gokhale attacked British along with Dixit, Chindamani, Patwardhan, Tasgaonkar, Mirajkar, Patwardhan, Appaji, Patankar, Ghorpade, Purandare, Rao Bahadur, joined him in this attack Akkalkotwale attack on Ganeshkhind where the British resided. Once again the war took place on 6th November 1817 and British defeated Bapu Gokhale in the war of Kirkee.[87] By seeing this defeat Bajirao Peshwa left Pune on 6th November 1817. Union Jack was put on Shaniwarwada.[88] After this again they got ready to take retribution the Maratha Army and the British Army met on the Battleground of Koregaon on 1st January 1818, was known as Historical war.

Koregaon Battle: The final act

After the battle of Kirkee, Maratha Commander Bapu Gokhale and his army was consisted on largely of new levis, lost all spirit and the English advanced the Marathas fell back on Poona. Colonel Burr, in turn, fell

---

85 R. Temple, *Oriental Experience*, John Murray Albemarle Street, London, p.80.

86 P.C. Gupta, *Bajirao II and East India Co.,* Humphrey Millford, Oxford University Press, London, 1939, pp.167-168.

87 Ibid., p.178.

88 Union Jack was put on Shaniwarwada Brahmin himself named Balasaheb Natu from Pune.

N.V. Gadgil, *Devachiya Dwari,* Venus Prakashan, Shaniwar Peth, Pune, 1966, pp.32-33.

back on Kirkee and awaited reinforcements. After evening the light battalion and the light horse from Sirur joined him. On 17th November 1817, the English entered Poona without opposition, for Bajirao Peshwa II had fled to Satara, where he seized.

On the 22nd November, General Smith began the pursuit to the Peshwa. Then unhappily prince now doubled back to join Trimbakaji Dengale north of Junnar. General, Mr. Smith followed him but learning that the Maratha army might slip past him into the Konkan and overwhelm the small English detachment there under Colonel Protter, he directed Colonel Burr to send reinforcements to Colonel. Protter and to call in from Sirur the 2nd Battalion of the 1st Regiment. Colonel Mr. Burr acted on these instructions and on receiving their orders, the 2nd Battallion of the 1st regiment, which was composed with Mahar soldiers, set out for Poona at 8 p.m. on the 31st December 1817. Their commander was Captain Francis Staunton.

The final battle was fought between the British and Marathas with the help of the Mahars against the Peshwa Rule at Koregaon on 1st January 1818.[89] Mahar soldiers were given the opportunity to set their age-old suppression by the British, they fought besides with the British. The II'nd Native Infantry of Mahar's 1st Bombay Regiment.[90] In this battle at Koregaon, only 500 Mahar Soldiers took part and defeated the huge trained and organized army of the Peshwa counted 25,000.[91]

Geography of Koregaon

Koregaon Village is located in the Sirur Taluka,[92] twenty-five miles South-west of Sirur district, Pune. Geographically, it is situated in 18° 39'N and 74° 4'E on the right side of the Bhima river,[93] 16 miles north-east of Poona city.[94]

---

89 Poona Residency correspondence, English Records of Maratha History, Vol.13, Poona Affairs, Elphinstone's Embassy Part II, 1816, 1818, p.281.

90 Lt. Col. V. Blacker, See footnote, Memoir operations of the British Army in India. Maratha war of 1817, 1818. 1819, Nlack Kingsbury Purbury and Accer, Leader Hall Street, London, 1821, p.178.

91 Ibid., n.80, p.168.

92 Bombay Gazetteers, Poona District, p.244.

93 Ibid., n.90 , p.179.

94 See map of Pune, Maharashtra.

IInd Native Infantry arrives in Koregaon

Towards the end of December 1817, in the pursuit of Bajirao Peshwa which followed the battle of Kirkee (5th November 1817),[95] news reached to Colonel Burr, who was in charge of Poona, that Bajirao was passing south from Junnar and meant to attack Poona.[96] Colonel Burr was sent to Sirur for help. Report of Col. Burr (See Appendix). At this time, Bajirao was having 25000 to 30,000 army men in Pune.[97] At Chakan, 16 miles away, General Smith wrote a letter to Fitzsimon requesting to send Bombay 1st Regiment division in which most of them were Mahars.[98] Captain Staunton directed 5 officers and 500 Mahars, 270 horsemen 25 gunpowder. Captain Staunton left Seroor on 3lst December 1817, at 8.00 p.m. towards Pune.[99]

These regiment soldiers were well trained and were full of confidence. After the journey of 25 miles, Captain Staunton reached Koregaon at 10 a.m. on 1st January 1818.[100]

Peshwe were having 30,000 soldiers, 20,000 horse, and 8000 Infantry, 2000 Arab, 5000 cavalry, 2500 horsemen and were ready for war on the East side of Bhima River.[101]

Finally, on the early morning of January l, 1818 the war began. British Machine Gun did not allow Peshwe soldiers to enter Koregaon.

---

95 Maharashtra State Gazetteers, History Part II, Maratha Period, Directorate of Government Printing and Publications, Maharashtra State, 1967, p.122.

96 J.G. Duff, *History of the Mahrattas*, Reprint, Karna Publication, New Delhi, 2000, p.307. P.R.C., See Appendix, Letter No.93, p.286.

97 See Appendix No. Letter No.88, p.279.

98 N.D. Kamble, N.D., *Deprived Castes and their Struggle for equality*, Ashish Publishing House, New Delhi, 1983, p.127

C.B. Khairmode, *Dr. Bhimrao Ramji Ambedkar, Charitra*, Granth Vol.9, Maharashtra Rajya Sahitya Anisamskriti Mandal, Bombay, 1987, p.215.

99 Ibid., n.96, letter no 91

100 J.G.Duff, Ibid., n.96, p.307.

101 P.C. Gupta, Ibid, n, 84, p.184.

Geography of battle ground

Koregaon is very irregular, and composed having terraced buildings, substantial and surrounded with a wall. It also contains a small choultry, of which the British gained possession; but the most commanding situation was left to the enemy.[102] The war positions were obtained by the English for the two guns, but even this advantage was greatly reduced, by their being exposed to a snipping fire from neighbouring walls.[103] The village became extremely crowded; both horsemen and footmen, as well as baggage cattle and followers, being obliged to take shelter in it, and a multitude of the enemy pressing on them with daring impetuosity.[104] Situated in this the two parties were pressing each other, the British had every reason to expect, that even a desperate resistance must soon be overcome. Captain Staunton failing in his endeavours to drive the enemy from their strong positions, was reduced to the measure of defending his own.[105]

The Battle

Captain Staunton was able to cross the river took the village. Koregaon was surrounded by a weak mud wall.[106] Captain Staunton then secured a strong position for his guns and awaited the enemy's attack. As soon as the Maratha infantry saw the British army they recalled a body of 5000 infantry which was some distance ahead. When the infantry arrived three parties, each of 600 – choice Arabs, Gosavis and regular infantry, under cover of the river bank and supported by two guns advanced to storm the village on three points.[107] A continued shower of rockets set on fire of many houses. The village was surrounded by the horses and footmen and the storming party broke down the wall in several places and forced their way in and secured a strong square enclosure from which they could not be dislodged. Though the village situated on the bank of river the besiegers cut them off from water. Wearied with their night's march, under a burning sun, without food and without water, handful men held

---

102 C.B. Khairmode, Ibid., n.98, p.281.

103 Ibid., n.90, p.179.

104 Ibid., p.179.

105 Ibid., p.180.

106 J.G. Duff, Ibid., n.96, p.308.

107 Ibid., p.308.

the village against an army.[108] Every foot was disputed several streets and houses were taken and retaken, but more than half of the European officers were wounded. The Arabs made themselves masters of a small temple, where three of the officers were lying wounded.[109] Assistant Surgeon Wingate, one of their numbers got up and went out, but was immediately stabbed by Arabs and his body mangled. Lieutenant Staunton had two severe wounds, he advised his remaining companions to suffer the Arabs to rifle them, which they did but without further violence. In the meantime, a party of the battalion under Lieutenant Jones and Assistant Surgeon Wyllie came to their rescue, retook the temple and carried their companions to a place of greater safety. Thirst drove the besieged nearly frantic and some of the gunners, all of whom fought with glorious bravery, thinking resistance hopeless, begged for surrender. Captain Staunton would not hear of yielding. The gunners were still dissatisfied when their officer, Lieutenant Chisholm happened to be killed[110] and the enemy encouraged by his death rushed on one of the guns and took it. Lieutenant Pattinson, Adjutant of the Second Battalion, a man six feet seven inches in height of giant strength and heroic courage was lying mortally wounded shot through the body. Hearing that the gun was taken he called on the Grenadiers once more to follow him, and seizing a musket by the muzzle, rushed into the thick of the Arabs and felled them right and left till a second ball through the body disabled him. He was nobly seconded, the gun was retaken, and dragged out of a heap of dead Arabs. Lieutenant Chishlom's body was found with the head cut off.[111] It's part of the destiny Captain Staunton, became emotional sheds the tears, all of who dead or alive into Maratha hands. The gunners took the lesson to heart and fought on with unflinching courage, and the defence did not slacken though only three officers, Captain Staunton, Lieutenant Jones and Assistant Surgeon Wyllie, remained fit for duty. At the evening their case seemed hopeless. As night fell the attack lightened and they got water. By nine the firing ceased and the Marathas left. For 834 defenders of Koregaon and 273 were killed wounded and missing, of whom were twenty of the twenty-six gunners.[112] The Marathas lost about

---

108 Ibid., p.309.

109 Ibid.

110 Ibid.

111 Ibid., p.310.

112 Ibid., p.311.

500 to 600 killed and wounded. In reward for the defence of Koregaon which General Sir. T. Hislop described as 'one of the most heroic and brilliant achievements ever recorded on the annals of the Army'.

In reality, the battle of Koregaon was fought by natives themselves on one side of the warring camp. There were upper caste soldiers and on the other side of the warring camp were the Mahar soldiers and other soldiers of different castes who discriminated.[113]

In the battle of Koregaon and even in the other battles, foreigners gained without sacrifice mainly due to the infighting's bravery of the natives. The natives fought against each other because of the insult they received through the existing social system which was maintained and glorified for centuries for depriving large sections of society. The social, economic and political benefits and powers.[114] The defeat of mighty Peshwa rule met out on 1st January 1818, at Koregaon by the very few Mahar soldiers was in a way the defeat of native rule due to the divisions of natives into castes, sub-castes and tortures thereof. The Mahars during the later period of Maratha rule, particularly during the Peshwa rule were suppressed and inhuman treatment was given to them, they were humiliated to the maximum possible extent.[115] They were denied even the right to enter into army which was their right for generations. Therefore, they were annoyed waiting for revolt. They revolted through this war to teach a lesson to Peshwas. After 70 years of the oppressions of the Mahars, they fought and defeated Peshwa rule. They felt that the Peshwa rule destroyed their life it was the rule of elite class as well as rich caste-men where they had no place at all.

The defeat of huge Peshwa army of 25000 trained soldiers by only 500 Mahar soldiers in battle, it is a milestone victory of Mahars, traditional and higher caste historians pushed back the sources of this battle, and did not made available and even they did not write single word about this battle in their writings of Maratha history , some wrote but they write it be difficult to form opinion on the Koregaon battle, they said this was only inflexible defence of Koregaon.

---

113 C.B. Khairmode, *Ashprushyancha Lashkari Pesha*, Maharashtra Rajya Sahitya Ani Aanskriti Mandal, Mumbai, 1992, p.69

114 N.D. Kamble, *Deprived Castes and their Struggle for equality*, Ashish Publishing House, New Delhi, 1983, p. 125

115 Shreenivas Bhalerao, *Nagvanshiyano Tumdi Asmita Geli Kuthe*, Siddharth Prakashan, Pune, 2002, p.9.

Saga of the Mahar soldiers

It would be difficult to form any opinion but one, respecting, the inflexible defence of Koregaon. Thus the public, as well as every constituted authority, though differing in the expression of their sentiments on many occasions, concurred in bestowing their unqualified and enthusiastic commendation of their behaviour both of officers and men.[116] In the general alacrity to acknowledge their services, the hackneyed expressions of applause appeared insufficient and unsatisfactory. In order to strain the imagination to the utmost, this brave detachment is represented as having defeated by without fearing attacks on the Peshwa's entire army. Such exaggeration, probably, arises from a common quality of the human mind, which renders it incapable of forming a distinct idea, when under the influence of admiration; for there can be no greater mistake than to imagine the attack of Koregaon by all the Peshwa forces.[117] The infantry of Peshwai amounting to four times more in numbers of the British force was assailed from all sides. It does not even appear that this division of the enemy was ever relieved or reinforced. The twenty thousand cavalries were distributed over the plain, on both sides of the river; but none of this army could be brought into action. (Please see Appendix No. XVI).[118] The utmost effect which could have been produced by this development of the whole army was to appal, through the eyes, a handful of men, with whose numbers there was no parity. But this handful was composed of soldiers who required to be addressed through other senses and despised a display which could only impose on the ignorant and untried. The embellished report (please see Appendix No.XVII.),[119] of the commanding officer, clear as it is modest will always command from the intelligent, higher admiration than any figurative exhibition. The facts were such, that their unadorned exposure presents the most forcible appeal for well-earned applause.[120] If a similar defence occurred in European warfare and proposed for its object the detention of the enemy from some other point of great importance, it would be justly appreciated on that account, but in the absence of that, or some other object of equal moment, it is a question if such determination

---

116 V. Blacker, Ibid., n.90, p.182.

117 V. Blacker Ibid.

118 See Map of Koregaon Battle

119 See Poona Residency, letter no 92, 93

120 V. Blacker, Ibid., n.90, p.183.

would be held excusable. The apparent hopelessness of the situation would afford sufficient arguments for the necessity of surrender, and the detachment might, or might not, according to circumstances, be permitted to march out with the honours of war. But this reasoning applies to civilized warfare, where prisoners of war are treated with respect; whereas, with a native enemy, no dependence can be placed on their promises of security. Whenever they had been trusted, immediate slaughter, or cruel treatment, has been the invariable consequence.

The faith on a British officer is so well established, and native garrisons will surrender to a British force, but perhaps, there is no example of a body of troops, in the field, laying down their arms.[121] When defeated, they expect no quarter and the irregularity of their flight is such, as to afford no opportunity of offering their chief is generally, on such an occasion, the first to fly, and there remains no one to be answerable for the rest, or to whom the victors can offer terms.

Mr. Elphinstone,[122] visited Koregaon after two days the fight (3rd January 1818) found every sign of violence and havoc.[123] The houses were burnt and scattered with accoutrements and broken arms, and the streets were filled with the bodies of dead men and horses. The men were mostly Arabs and must have attacked most resolutely to have fallen in such numbers.[124] Some wounded were treated with the same care as the British wounded. About fifty bodies within the village and a half a dozen without, with the wounded and the dead, made not less than 300.[125] Nearly fifty bodies of Sepoys and eleven European besides the officers were found imperfectly buried.[126]

Victory Pillar

On the bank of river Bhima, a round stone tomb has been built where the artillerymen were killed in the action and buried. At this point, the river is crossed, and 300 yards to the left of the Poona Road on the opposite

---

121 Ibid.

122 Mr. Mountstuart Elphinstone, Resident Ambassador of East India Co. at Pune.

123 Ibid., n.90, p.183.

124 Ibid.

125 See Appendix No.XVI.

126 Ibid., n.90, p.184

bank is an obelisk[127] 65 feet high of which 25 feet is pediment 12'8" square. It stands on a stone platform 32'4" square. The obelisk of polished hard stone and is enclosed with a stone wall six feet high on three sides, and an iron railing with a handsome iron gate and two lamps on the west side. The inscription on the north and south sides is in Marathi and the inscription on the west side is given below in English. The inscription on the north and east sides mentions the names of the English killed and wounded and of four natives attached to the artillery who were killed, from which it appears that of the eight officers engaged three were killed and two wounded, and of the twenty English artillerymen eleven were killed. The English inscription on the west side is:[128] (see Appendix n.XVIII).

This column is erected to commemorate the defence of Koregaum by a detachment Commanded by Captain Staunton of the Bombay establishment which was surrounded on the 1st January 1818 by the Peshwa's whole army under his personal command and withstood throughout the day a series of the most obstinate and sanguinary assaults of his best troops. Captain Staunton under the most appalling circumstances, preserved in his desperate resistance and, seconded by the unconquerable spirit of his detachment, at length achieved the signal discomfiture of the enemy and accomplished one of the proudest triumphs of the British Army in the East.

To perpetuate the memory of the brave troops to whose heroic firmness and devotion it owes the glory of that day the British Government has directed the names of their corps and of the killed and wounded to be inscribed on this monument. MDCCCXXII.[129]

Honour for Mahar soldiers

The pillar is standing in the memory of the gallantry of the Mahar Soldiers, a memorial pillar was curved at Koregaon which still stands on the right bank of Bhima river in Pune district of Maharashtara State. (Please see appendix No.XIX). The names of 23 Mahar soldiers were

127 a tapering stone pillar, typically having a square or rectangular cross section, set up as a monument or landmark.

128 Inscription on obelisk at Bhima Koregaon

129 Ibid.

written on it. Out of them first twenty were killed and the last three were injured. Their names are as given below, dated 1818.[130]

1. Somnak Kamalnak Naik.
2. Ramnak Yemnak Naik
3. Godhnak Kotnenak
4. Ramnak Yesnak
5. Bhagnak Narnak
6. Ambanak Kannak.
7. Gannak Balnak
8. Balnak Kondnak
9. Rupnak Lakhnak
10. Vapnak Ramnak.
11. Vitnak Dhemnak
12. Rajnak Gannak
13. Vapnak Harnak
14. Rainak Vannak
15. Gannak Dharmnak
16. Devnak Aannak
17. Gopalnak Balnak
18. Harnak Hirnak
19. Jetnak Dainak
20. Gannak Kakhnak
21. Jannak Hirnak
22. Bhiknak Ratannak
23. Ratannak Dhannak.

Victory Pillar at Koregaon is called "Vijaystambha" by the Maharashtrian people.

The memory of the brave Mahar Soldiers who fought in the Battle of Koregaon on 1st January 1818 is still kept alive by the Mahar regiment, whose soldiers wear the badge bearing the emblem of Koregaon pillar before 1947.[131]

Koregaon battle viewed in 21st Century

Collection of oral sources of history is very useful for form an opinion on available sources of incident. I collected information through

---

130 Ibid.

131 Poona Residency Correspondence letters no 89, 90. Elphinstone Embassy Part II available at Maharashtra State Archives, Mumbai

questionnaire i.e. oral history, for this purpose I collected some 500 interviews. Information collected from those people who have retired form military services, or members of military background family of Pune, Satara, Solapur, Sangli, Kolhapur, Mumbai and different parts of Maharashtra.

Here I put some selected interviews and their views on Koregaon Battle and Why the section of Maratha society participated in this battle against the Peshwa? This account gives us the peoples view and right direction to arrive on conclusion.

Persons from military background were interview to know what do they feel about military culture of Mahars ? What kind of information do they have about their forefathers? What are their perceptions about Koregaon battle and what is their opinion about the same in today's scenario?

There are two age group has been formed to understand their opinion first is 32-50 and another age group is from 51-85 years of the age. The people from fist age group having education from 7th to M. Sc. And the second age group is of the people from illiterate to SSC passed.

On the question why the Mahars entered in British military forces on large scale? all the respondents told that people from Mahar Community joined British military service because the Untouchability, social and economic discrimination, harassment, and denial of human rights by the Hindu Upper Caste was prevailed in Indian society the Mahars didn't have any profession by caste and also not allowed to take any job due to suppression of Peshawa rule which denied recruiting them in the army and they made social restrictions and atrocities on them and to take revenge on Peshawas suppression they joined the British Military services.

Some people who were interview said that To show resistance against all type of suppression including that of untouchability, Mahars entered in British Military all the respondents said that Britishers acquired knowledge, that Mahars were warrior and were faithful and honest, that is why the British gave them entry into their army and respect, education and employment in their military services. The entry of Mahars in British service helped to change every aspect of Mahars social life which gave education, which changed the socio-economic and cultural life of people.

Their family members joined military services as hereditary duties to serve the nation. Also, under the influence of Dr. Babasaheb Ambedkar's ideas on military services and his urge to join military services.

Mahar Battalion

Mahar battalion raised on 1st October 1941 at Nanawadi Belgaum and then in Komptee at Nagur and then Mahar Regiment established center at Saugar in Madhya Pradesh After independence all the schedule caste people were put in this regiment they were named in Mahar Regiment.

Before this Mahar soldiers were recruited in other battalions like Army Transport Co., Bombay Syprus, Native Infantry, Maratha Battalion etc. After 1941 Mahars fought many battles and after independence they fought in 1948, 1962, 1965, 1971 and other operation of Military always fought in the forefront... He gives information about after independence the Mahar Battalion fought 1st war in 1965, 1971 with Pakistan and also on the front of Kutch and Bhuj. Mahar Battalion is officially known as Machine gun Regiment.

They did good work and got many gallantry awards, further this Battalion established due to the efforts of Dr. Babasaheb Ambedkar's, has the 19th Regiment with them. The Mahar regiment is the only regiment which gives entry to men of all caste and religion. Mohan Arjun Pawar (75) According to him, the Mahar Battalion was formed with Army Transport Company (A.T.C.) and the Maratha Infantry after Independence is known as Mahar Regiment.

Mahar Regiment is only Machine Gun Regiment in Indian Army. He adds that the This was the only Regiment which fought on the forefront in all the wars. The establishment of this battalion or Regiment was the efforts of Dr. B.R. Ambedkar. Subhedar, Ganpat Baburao Gaikwad (77), 7th Pass. said that the information about Mahar battalion was formed in Nagpur in 1941-42. This Battalion's flag colour is Maroon. Mahar Battalion fought the war of 1948, 1962, 1965 and 1971. After independence this battalion was known as Mahar Machine cum Regiment. This Battalion always put to fight on the forefront in all the wars with enemy. According to him the Mahar Battalion was and is the 1st and only battalion working with light Machine gun. After independence this battalion was renamed and placed as Mahar Regiment and H.Q. at Sagar, M.P.

Gangadhar Dattaji Sonawane (60) provided the Information about the This battle took place on 1st Jan. 1818, in this Battle Britishers conquered Peshwa Army which was known as Guerilla Maratha Army. British Army had handful of soldiers, majority of them belonging to the Mahars. This Mahar Battalion marched from Shirur to Koregaon throughout the night and reached early in the morning on the Battlefield at Koregaon on the Bank of Bhima River. The battle was fought throughout the day. In this battle Britishers side Commandant is Capt. Staunton and Peshwa side Peshwa Bajirao II himself and this battle was won by the Britishers.

He also told that in this battle Commander Capt. Staunton was ready to surrender but Mahar Soldiers refused to lay down arms and preferred to die in battle with dignity. So, fighting continued till 8 or 9 p.m. and finally Peshwa's army started fleeing. Mahar soldiers drove them out. The glorious victory over enemy with their determination and outstanding courage and iron will. After driving out the enemy they drank water in the Bhima River this war continued nearly 12 to 14 hours. This is a golden page of Mahar soldier's bravery. They carved their victory and they raised a pillar at Koregaon known as Vijaystambha.

Britishers raised this pillar in memory of the soldiers who fought this great battle of Koregaon. Size of pillar shows the greatness of the events and importance of battle in history. Koregaon pillar is 50' x 150'bare plinth and height is 25 feet. Grade of black stone and all four sides of the pillar information is carved and details are given in English and Marathi, names of soldiers and officers those who are killed or wounded in this battle. Now in Mahar Battalion shoulder batch is this pillars image. This Pillar was honoured and saluted by Guard of honour platoon from Satara every year on 1st January at 11 o'clock. Another respondant Subhedar, Ganpat Baburao Gaikwad (77), 7th Pass. Retired from Mahar Regiment. Informed that from his family, Subhedar Gangadhar Jadhav Dabholkar worked in 101 Maratha Light Infantry. Among 7 brothers 5 served in Maratha Light Infantry and Mahar Battalion. He added that his family members joined military services as hereditary duties to serve the nation and also under the influence of Dr. Babasaheb Ambedkar's ideas on military services and his urge to join military services. He added that the pillar built by Britishers in memory of those Martyers. From 1923 Mahar Pensioners began to visit Koregaon on every 1st January. During the British period they provided vehicles to those pensioners who wanted to go there. In this battle Peshwa had thousands of soldiers and Britishers had only a few 500 Mahar soldiers to fight with them. The Peshwa Army had a lot of ammunition but no unity they were divided on caste basis hence lost the battle.

Ordinary-Naib Subedar, Shreerang Dashrath Owhal aged 69 years and passed the 7th Standard, Said that his forefathers served in Military services in the 17th and 18th century. He saw some ammunition in his house. He joined military service under the influence of Dr. Babasaheb Ambedkar. And gives information about the Battle of Koregaon, that the battle was fought on 1st January 1818 on the Bank of Bhima River near Koregaon village. This battle was part of the third Maratha-Anglo war. In this battle Mahars fought besides the Britishers. Mahars showed their gallant in this battle and won this battle in favour of the British thus making an end of communal orthodox Peshwai. He gives information about the triumph pillar which was built by Britishers in the memory of soldiers who died in this battle. He adds important information that people of the surrounding area of Koregaon village identify this pillar as "Mahar Stambha".

Further he gives information that Dr. B.R. Ambedkar visited this place on 1st January whenever he was in Pune. Even today many ex-untouchables (Mahars) Buddhists visit this place on 1st January to pay their homage to the brave soldiers. As for the triumph pillar built by Britishers in memory of Martyrs who died in the Koregaon battle. On this pillar the carving reads names and an inscription - *"the proudest triumph in the East for the British Army."*

Mahars joined the military with the intent of improving their social status. They were successful in this regard. This was within the closed circle of the regiment; caste prejudice was, if not actually absent, at least officially discouraged. According to army regulations no distinction was made between soldiers on the basis of their caste or community. Mahar officers were able to command men of other castes apparently without difficulty.

Thus, this chapter gives an idea about the Koregaon Battle. It is an oral source on which we are able to link the events and sequence in building of this book.

With the help of this oral history collection some information is same and authentic on the historical methods people added their information on Koregaon Battle they think this battle was the victory over the Caste system and Orthodox Peshwai. Mahar people now they converted themselves into Buddhism and they remember this battle as a source of inspiration for fighting with the unequality and demorality which prevailing in contemporary society.

In the 17th century Mahars were recruited in the Peshwas Army, when Peshwas acquired full authority over the state they adopted the policy of Varna system which created by Manu in Manusmriti and upper caste people did so many atrocities on the lower caste which we discuss in previous chapter. This was the main cause of Mahar's joining the British Military service and fight for their human rights.

Military service gives education and discipline to Mahar people and because of this they are socially, economically and educationally modern among the other untouchable communities in Maharashtra and India.

The Mahar Machine Gun Regiment remember their Martial history and they served for Nation which is stand on Dr. Babasaheb Ambedkar's Vision, i.e. Constitution of India which written by him for Modern India.

Today people join military service for employment, Mahar also join the military services for employment in 16th century and even now. They served for various rulers of Maharashtra and they created their history in military culture.

CONCLUSION

Under the discipline of history, no definite study has been undertaken so far to highlight the Military Culture in Maharashtra.

The present book tries to fulfill the need, hence the title has been suggested "The battle of Bhima Koregaon, History of Military culture in Maharashtra." Maharashtra has been a unique place in the Asian Sub-continent and has played a vital role in the making of Modern India. It is located in the western part of India, and Marathi speaking people reside in this state. The state has been surrounded by four Indian states and occupies a centre stage in India. As Iravati Karve mentions that "Aryans from the Northern India and Dravidians from Southern India joined together in Maharashtra" and it seems that since ages the Brahmin and non-Brahmin conflict of co-operation and continuation is going on.

According to census report the setting for the Mahar in Maharashtra (as formed in 1960), which today has a population of over fifty million. Out of this figure, Buddhists (almost exclusively Mahars) and Scheduled Castes account for roughly 6.3 million, this is 12.5% of the total population. Of the 3 million Scheduled Castes in Maharashtra, Mahars represent some 35% of the population, or roughly 1 million. Hence, Mahars are the most populous Scheduled Caste in Maharashtra, followed by the Mangs and the Charmakars. Counting the Buddhists, Mahar's number roughly 4.3 million or 8% of the total population. The overwhelming majority of the Scheduled Castes are rural-dwellers (84.36% rural, 15.64% urban for the Mahars; 81.81% rural, 18.19% urban for the Mangs; and 68.84% rural, 31.96% urban for the Chambhars). Moreover, of the total Scheduled Caste workers, roughly 67% are represented in agriculture, with agricultural labourers accounting for over 54% and cultivators 13%.

The population of the areas comprising Maharashtra at the height of the Maratha Empire in 1750, may be estimated to have been 2 million. By 1832, the population of Maharashtra was estimated to be 3.2 million, and by 1872 it had become 5.2 million. If we assume that the proportion of Mahars has remained approximately the same relative to the total population of Maharashtra, then in 1750 Mahars must have numbered around 160,000; in 1832, 260,000; and in 1872, 410,000.

Today as per the 2001 census the Buddhist (Mahar) population has grown upto 56,40,785 i.e. (6.39%). Buddhist (Mahar) derived their livelihood from their traditional occupations such as tanning of hides. They performed agricultural labour for their living and earnings. This community is living along with the other communities in this area.

Maharashtrian society has caste and varna system. The society of Maharashtra is divided into four varnas i.e. Brahmin, Kshatriya, Vaishya and Sudra.

There are three clear distinctions seen among the Maharashtrian society generally known as Marathas, the Brahmins and the Mahars (untouchables). Besides this there are some tribes who are separately identified as Bhills, Ramoshis, Koli, Varlis and Katkaris who are always confined to the agricultural work in the beginning. They were influenced by Chatrapati Shivaji in the 17th century to join military forces.

Knowledgeable, Brahmins continued their dominance in the field of religion and knowledge. In the society they always maintained top position and were closely related with power. Brahmins were also working as merchants, bankers and soldiers in Maharashtra and also village accountants and district accounts. Brahmins were divided into Deshastha and Kayastha.

Similarly, Maratha is an important caste in Maharashtra. Marathas are military caste of Maharashtra which manned the armies and Muslim courts, Shivaji and of the Peshwa and other princes of Maratha confederacy. Marathas were looked on as sudras the fourth class in society. The Marathas were peasants and they are dominant in the state. Marathas were one third of the total population of Maharashtra. Similarly, Mahar was an important and numerous untouchable caste of Maharashtra and they too were martial. Mahar was the village watchman and Mahar gives his help to village headman to maintain peace in village and law and order.

Mahars also served in Military. Before the arrival of British Mahars had an out let from traditional work, in the time of Shivaji as guards, in the hill forts and soldiers in the artillery. Mahars also served in Peshwa army and British army.

Seventy five percent of Bombay Army comprised of Mahars from Maharashtra and they fought many battles besides with British.

Military monument at Koregaon shows their courage and their Maritial traditions.

Thus the Maharashtrian society was divided into many castes. Caste within itself was a bond of union but considering the society as a whole it was a force of disuniting as it split the society into hereditary groups.

Second chapter deals with the Military Culture. How it originated from village community to the State level. The chapter further gives an account of the village life, their administration and socio-economic disparities. By relating this, we are able to discuss defence activities through which military culture has been identified. This chapter also deals with issues, such as, low castes men who participated in the war and militant activities against suppression in Maharashtrian society.

While discussing the above issues, the history of military organizations and its development has been kept in mind throughout the book. The Military, Infantry and Cavalry; its working and their services have been discussed as part of the military culture in detail. The rewards and grants which gave them support to fight for the state and nation has been discussed.

On the basis of this theoretical framework the rest of the other chapters have been co-related and rebuilt to bring out the truth in the book in the final analysis.

After the study of Historical and geographical condition of Maharashtra in the chapter we discuss how Military Culture of Maharashtra originated and had grown in the Maratha period. Here, study of Military culture we take into account a village, district and then state out of which the Military culture of Maharashtra had originated from village community. Village community worked as Government Officials and some castes of village rendered their work to Military services. They protected the village boundaries, these communities called Mahar or untouchable caste of Maharashtra, and some caste like Maratha they also worked like soldiers. These people from village they also served in army's of rulers of these areas and they worked hereditary in military services. Thus we discuss in IInd chapter Village community and Village officials.

In period of our theme, village was the main centre of the socio-economic activities. The material life of the Maharashtrian people was influenced by Gram, Watan, and castes. Village officers in the center of the village i.e. Brahmin, Patil, Kulkarni, Deshmukh, Deshpande, Chaugula and Mahar. In village of Maharashtra there was Balutedari system. Society of Maharashtra was built upon occupation and occupation was divided into castes. Watan was considered very important. In Maharashtra, Varna system prevailed in that time. Except Brahmin nobody had right to take education in the period of our study.

The village communities were developed on the basis of caste system. Caste is unchangeable. He had to do the traditional work of his ancestors and should not take up any other professions, in village communities there were some untouchable caste also survival and they did not have any right to come between 9 a.m. and 12 p.m. in Pune City in Peshwai.

The village community in Maharashtra was economically self-sufficient. There were two principal tenures Mirasi and Upari. The land of the village was divided into fields, gayram and the cultivable land. Every village had fixed boundaries which were carefully marked.

Pattern of the organization of village communities and its officers functions remain unchanged during the period of the different dynasty ruled over the Deccan and continued so in the Maratha period The nature of the duties of the village officer like the headman, clerk and watchman remained as it is.

In this chapter we discuss duties of Patil (the headman), Kulkarni (the clerk), The Chaugula, The Mahar (The watchman) and the Potdar and how they worked.

After studying village life, village community and village official we next see which caste acted as Military caste or races in Maharashtra, here we study the Maratha caste, Marathas were military caste of Maharashtra. Under the head of Maratha so many caste became The Hill Kolis, The Dhangars, The Rajput, The Agris, The Koli, The Bhill, The Ramoshi, The Brahmins, The Mangs, The Berads and the Mahars were the Military races of Maharashtra and these castes served the military during the period of the Marathas. These castes helped Shivaji establish Maratha supremacy over Maharashtra. Information about their caste is given here in detail.

The Military organization of the Marathas of Maharashtra in the early times they must have followed the Chalukaya banner and then Rashtrakuta, Yadava and Silhara dynasties. Marathas reappear on the scene after the fall of the Bahamani Kingdom. Marathas were completely conquered. The physical features of their land formed a natural bulwark, while their villages though few and scattered, were each provided with a defending wall. The Deshmukhes or petty feudal lords could defy an invading army for months in their impregnable strongholds perched on the summit of inaccessible hills. This time idea of nationality was yet unborn, and people were not reluctant to acknowledge the suzerainty of the Muhammadden powers. When King gave guarantee to them peaceful procession of their hereditary lands and rights. People come side with Muhamadden conquerer. The climate and the physical features of the land which engendered courage and endurance in the Maratha made him also self centred and crafty. Marathas lived and died for his watan.

After the dissolution of the Bahamani kingdom the Maratha chiefs began to extend their views and fought civil and military situatios in the new court. Marathas served in Muslim court also.

Marathas were potential soldiers. They could enlist a Bargir and Silkedar. It was in this way in Maharashtra some Maratha families rose to prominence.

The Civil government of the country was subordinated to military needs and the major portion of Maharashtra was held by a number of military leaders serving under these different masters.

In Maharashtra when Chhatrapati Shivaji rose to power. Military culture was built up. Shivaji had a clear conception of military ideas. He approved of unity of command but would not tolerate military interference in civil administration of the country. Shivaji introduced discipline in his army. Shivaji's army was employed in Mulukhgiri or foreign expedition for eight months in the year. Shivaji took care of his army. Shivaji's army successfully fought against four great powers. His army consisted of 1,00,000 soldiers from all castes under the head of Maratha and Mawale. In Shivaji's Army Brahmin could fight shoulder to shoulder with the Mahars an untouchable caste of Maharashtra.

In the village, the police were under the Patil and chief police officer in the rural republics was the Mahar.

In detection of crime the Jaglya or village watchmen's consisting generally from Mahars and other lower castes of society.

Metropolitan police at Poona became a model. In big cities the police was placed under the officer called Kotwal. His duties included regulation of prices and taking of census, and he had to maintain peace and order in the city.

Chhatrapati Shivaji started Infantry and Cavalry in his army. Infantry consisted of 10,000 Mawle and Cavalry consisted of 45,000 Mawle.

The contemporary correspondence of the English factories it appears that during Shivaji's time the infantry preponderated over the cavalry. The infantry continued to maintain its majority in the Maratha army, after Shivaji's death.

In the Peshwa period Cavalry force was far more useful than infantry. The Maratha did not care to enlist as a foot soldier and the infantry consisted almost entirely of outsiders. The Maratha footmen were employed mainly for the suppression of disturbances by the Bhils, Kolis and other turbulent tribes.

Peshwa employed trained battalions in his army. He further employed non Marathas.

The Cavalry of the Peshwa consisted of four classes. (1) The Khasgi Paga (2) The Silhedars (3) The Ekas or Ekandars and (4) The Pendharis.

Hereafter we see expenditure on Military services in time of Shivaji. Of the Cavalry salary given in hone rupees of that time, here Sarnobat, Panchhazari, Hazari, Jamledar, Havaldar and Bargir taking their salary from Shivaji's court.

Then in this chapter, we see salaries of the various officials of cavalry consisting of Sarnobat, Saptahazari, Panchhazari, Hazari, Jumledar, Havaldar, Naik and Civil. The infantry officers were not so well paid as their colleagues in the cavalry. Shivaji was strictly punctual in his payment.

The Maratha state paid special attention to the maintenance of forts and strongholds. Every fort was placed under three officers. These soldiers getting their salaries from Shivaji. Shivaji paid special attention to the construction of new forts and maintenance and repair of old ones.

Shivaji had a naval force, construction of boats and their maintenance as well as the organization of naval force, must have entailed a good deal of expenditure.

Besides the regular pay and allowances, soldiers and officials were given additional allowances for meritorious work. Shivaji conferred pensions, bounties and prizes on those who shed their blood for the cause of the state. Soldiers rewarded with grants of village in Mokasa.

Shivaji departed from the medieval practice of payment in the form of land or estate only with a view to arresting the growth of feudal power.

In a time of Maratha supremacy money spent on arms, ornaments, military equipment, camps etc. Ammunition, cannon, guns, were secretly purchased from foreigners. Shivaji supplied horses to his troops. Shivaji's camp was a simple affair. Shivaji paid moderate salaries to the army, the simplicity in dresses the limited number of weapons most made locally, and the Spartan simplicity of the camps must have minimized the cost of war.

This way in this chapter we see how the Military culture originated from the village of Maharashtra and had grown in state under the leadership of Shivaji after Shivaji this system broke up and new Saranjamshahi of Peshwa rose to power. Peshwa did not take care of the army and soldiers because of that some soldiers and families of Maratha Jagirdar did not serve in his army.

Third chapter deals with the Mahar's origin, growth and tradition. It also discusses their service to village society. This chapter traces the Military services that the Mahars performed during the reign of various rulers. What battles they fought and the cause behind the fighting capabilities has been touched upon. The social suppression under the Peshwai has been discussed in detail in order to understand the resistance power of the community.

This chapter deals with the Mahar's military services in British Army, and how the British employed and used them. Their removal from military service and how they fought for re-enlistment in the army is discussed. Their movement for re-recruitment in army and finally the establishment of Mahar Regiment has been touched upon.

The Mahar is the powerful and ancient community of Maharashtra. According to many historians, scholars, Mahars are the original inhabitants of Maharashtra. Mahars are cultural and civilized people. Mahars are also found in other states of India. Mahars played important role in military services and civil administration in Maharashtra under various rulers of Maharashtra in medieval time.

The names of the Mahars during medieval period were suffixed by Nak, which seems to be the corrupt form of the Nag.

Mahar got so many rewards from rulers for their services. Mughal trusted the Mahars for their unfailing loyalty. Shivaji also trusted Mahars for their loyalty and Shivaji gave the duties to Mahars to watch around the forts and jungles. Shivaji found the Mahars useful. When Shivaji raised a regular standing army Mahars enlisted in the army. Shivaji was not troubled with untouchability. Mahars served in infantry of Marathas.

After Shivaji Mahars continued to be respected for their gallantry honesty and loyalty to the Maratha rulers.

In some villages of Maharashtra, Mahars were Patils i.e. Nagnaik Mahar. During the days of the Maratha ruler Rajaram Maharaj there was a Mahar fighter Sidnak Mahar. Sidnak Mahar was rewarded with village kalambi which stayed with his family for generations.

Here in this chapter we discuss the duties and positions got by the Mahars. Mahars had Patilship, Mahars enjoyed military privileges. Those Mahars holding military rights were known as 'Mete Naik'. Mahars were posted as Killedars (fort keepers) in the period of our study.

Many Battles fought by the Mahars in this time here we mention the Battle of Raighad. In this battle Mahars attacked British army on this fort.

In this Battle Mahars fought continuously for 15 days and they defeated British army.

While attacking the second time on this fort British took help of other Mahar soldiers and they conquered the fort.

In the Battle of Vairatgad, a prominent Mahar sardars named Seti Bin Nagnak who was the Patil of Nagewadi in Wai Taluka Satara District. He was selected by King Rajaram Maharaj to conquer the Vairatgad from Moghal ruler. And Nagnak Mahar conquered that fort and joined it to the Maratha Kingdom.

After Sambhaji, Mahars were helped in building up Maratha rule with their blood and flesh felt they wanted to revive the Maratha rule. Sidnak Mahar and his army of Mahars helped Maratha rulers to establish their rule in territory of Maharashtra. As a reward Sidnak Mahar was given Kalambi as Inam which shows Mahars martial and loyal activities.

Sidnak Mahar's grandson known as Sidnak occupied very high position in the Maratha army. He was not happy with the Peshwa rule because Peshwai became orthodox and they believed in casteism, partially under which the Mahars lost their status and were defeated, since Mahars were on the battlefield.

The Battle of Kharda which is known as the last winning battle of Maratha army in which Mahar soldiers fought besides with Peshwa army under the leadership of Sidnak Mahar.

After Shivaji the Maratha empire lost its clan and strength. There was no unified control. Consideration of nationalism and national patriotism hardly ever entered the thinking of the people. Marathas were separated and they were prepared to serve any master.

Europeans came here as traders but they stayed. In India, their ambitions grew in direct proportion to the decline of the Moghul empire and the disruption of the central and regional political controls.

The English had built fortified factories for themselves in the three important English Presidencies of Madras, Bombay and Calcutta. The English factories in India were placed under these presidencies in 1708. Each Presidency had a separate President who was also the Commander in Chief of such military forces, European and Indian as existed in Presidency. In period of our study French, Portuguese and Dutch also established their factories in India.

French first recruited Indian native people in army. Benoit Dumas formed a force of Indian soldiers in 1740.

In 1742, the infantry in the Bombay Presidency was for the first time, officially spoken of as the Bombay European regiment and its strength.

In the fighting with the British the French used Indian Sepoys. The English saw the advantage and once they had learnt the lesson, they outstripped the French. They never regretted their decision. Major Stringer Lawrence, "the father of the Indian Army" and the first commander-in-chief of all the armies in India, he raised the first new companies of Indian soldiers, called Native Sepoys in January 1748. In Calcutta Robert Clive recruited native people in the army in 1757 and Hindinization of Army began, then in Madras in 1758, and in Bombay under Major William Fraser formed a Bombay Sepoy in 1767 called Bombay Army.

In Bombay Army Mahars of Maharashtra recruited 75% of the total strength of army. The English in Bombay had come in contact with the Mahars and had come to rely on them for household duties as also for military and police services. The loyalty of the Mahars, their dependability and the qualities of their heart and head were recognized by the English. The knowledge of the Mahars of local areas was of great advantage to the English who were new to the land. Mahars showed their merit and gallantry in Bombay army and secured promotions. In Bombay army, Mahaars from Konkan took recruitment in the army. The Mahars rose in rank and increased in numbers forming part of all the twenty or more military regiments of the army and the marine corps.

The year 1768, marked the beginning of a new era in the military organization of the Bombay Army. It was decided to raise two battalions of Sepoys of 1,000 men each with eight European officers and Ten European sergeants to each Battalions. These two battalions formed on 4th August 1768 by amalgamating the existing companies of Indian troops were called 1st and 2nd Battalions of Bombay Sepoys which later were known as the 108th Infantry and 103rd Maratha light Infantry. The Mahars formed part of the original 1st and 2nd Battalions of Bombay Sepoys.

The Marine Battalion of the Bombay Army was raised in 1777. Mahars also served in these Marine Battalion, won a number of awards, and got promotions. Gen. Malcolm confirmed that the Bombay army was composed of all classes, religions and Mahars. Mahar Sepoys were the honour of their Regiments.

In this chapter we also discuss why the people of Maharashtra joined British Military services. We took oral interviews and prepared a questionnaire for that purpose. Her we get some idea as to why these people joined the British Military services. During the Peshwai Hinduism increased and the Brahmin became more orthodox and they followed caste system and untouchability. They denied the untouchables their basic rights. Under the Peshwas, Mahars and other untouchable castes lived outside the village. During the period under review, untouchable Mahars were required to perform many duties. Mahars most important duty was revenue, he watched over the boundaries of the village lands. Mahar was a public messenger and a guide and considered very important by the police. Mahars also swept streets. Forced labour practised in Peshwai, called Vethbegar. In this period Mahars carried certain important duties in the village because of these services Mahars had revenue free Inam land.

This chapter also discusses untouchability under the Peshwas. Untouchability, as practised by the Hindus for centuries, had led to virtual isolation and segregation of a large number of people in their own region. Untouchables carried the badge of inferior status or redemption either in this world or in the next. Manusmritis law was practised by Peshwas in this period. In Manusmriti caste privileges and disabilities are reflected in criminal law. Different punishments are laid down for the same offences for members of different castes.

Untouchables had no right to perform religious rituals, Sanskaras and even the legal rights to redress their grievances.

Mahars are principally the untouchable community in Maharashtra. It is the single largest untouchable community found in Maharashtra. Peshwas suggested and formulated certain codes of behaviour for society at the time of Peshwai. In Pune and the surrounding areas, Mahars did not have any human rights. On this background and on the basis of interview taken of people of Maharashtra we understand that the people of Maharashtra and Mahars joined the British Military services only because of social pattern of Peshwai and their rule.

Forth chapter directly deals with the Koregaon Battle (1st January 1818) and has emerged as the main theme of this book in which the main focus is emphasized on the Koregaon battle. This chapter is divided into the following parts.

The background, the cause of conflict behind the Peshwa and British. Specific emphasis lay upon the internal social situation under the Peshwas. Chapter further deals with direct analysis of war, taking into account the geographical location of the battle and the events leading to the war. Further why the Peshwas were defeated and why the British built the Koregaon monument is discussed in the final analysis of this chapter.

After two hundred years how the Koregaon battle has been viewed by the people. In the final analysis of this chapter various reactions through the questionnaire have been analyzed to arrive at the right conclusion. The issues emerging out of this chapter and its impact on the present generation has been analysed in short.

With the help of interview this martial history of Mahars Military Culture and their service to state has been discussed. Similarly in Chapter IV, Koregaon Battle and its aftermath deals with the Koregaon Battle. This is the main chapter of this book in which the main focus has been emphasized on the battle. This chapter has been divided into background of Battle, Peshwas political conflict with British and social aspect of the people who joined this battle. Mahar's military services in British and their revolt against native rule and finally this chapter deals with the Koregaon Battle.

This chapter also deals with why British built the Koregaon monument and why the people gathered on 1st January every year at Koregaon.

In the background, this part deals with many important happenings which helps to make the chapter strong and logical. The 18th century Maratha polity entered into conflict, confrontation, suspicion, mistrust, treachery and the destruction of law and order situation. After the death of Chhatrapati Shivaji and Sambhaji in Maharashtra, there were two groups that emerged on the platform of Maratha polity, one is Chhatrapati Shahu and other is Tarabai.

In Maharashtra, many Maratha sardars worked under different masters. Many Brahmins like Purushottam Pant and Balaji Vishwanath Bhatt joined Shahu's court. Kanhoji Angre a staunch supporter of Tarabai, also joined Shahu with Dhanaji Jadhav. Peshwa Balaji Vishwanath died in 1720. After his death, his son Balaji Bajirao was appointed as Peshwa. After the death of Shahu in 1749, Balaji Bajirao became the Chief of Maratha polity. His son Vishwasrao died in Battle of Panipat in 1761. Nanasaheb also died after this battle. After his death, his other sone Madhavrao Peshwa was appointed as Peshwa and his uncle Raghunathrao appointed as caretaker of Peshwa. At this time Chitpavan Brahmin, Peshwe opposed by Maratha Sardar Bhosle from Nagpur, Nimbalkar of Paltan and Gopalrao Patwardhan.

At this time conflict between Madhavrao Peshwa and his caretaker uncle, Raghunathrao also emerged. After the death of Madhavrao Peshwa in 1773, Narayanrao Peshwa became the Peshwa of Pune. After nine months only Narayanrao was murdered and Raghunathrao was held responsible who ultimately took shelter of the British and thus the British intervention in Maratha state began. In this time conflict between Deshastha and Konkanastha Brahmin also began.

This chapter deals with the political conflict during this period. Conflict between Chitpavan and Desastha became to the point of breaking the other Sardar's of Maratha from Peshwa. Nizam acquired political rights in some parts of Maharashtra. In 1795 Marathas defeated Nizam in Battle of Kharda. In Maratha polity conflict between Nana Phadnavis and Raghunathrao's son also continued. This way the conflict of political gain continued in Maharashtra. At this time British entered into this conflict. In 1789, they introduced a subsidiary alliance. British isolated French, Tipu, Nizam and Marathas with the help of this policy. Nizam joined with British in 1798. Marathas and Tipu did not join the British. But in 1803 Peshwa took shelter of British and signed the treaty of Bassein.

After signing this treaty, Lord Cornwallis was appointed in Pune as a British Resident. Thus, the Peshwa became powerless, he could not control the Maratha Sardars and Pendharis. These people destroyed the state economy and law and order situation. In 1817, Peshwa signed a new treaty with British by this treaty all his powers were stripped.

After this political changes, the last act organized from the Peshwe camp in Pune was the attack on the British residencies which were burnt simultaneously in Pune and Nagpur. British quickly took major action and wiped out the revolt and this event took the steps towards the battle of Koregaon.

Similarly, in this chapter, we deal with the social aspect and background of the battle which paved the way towards war situation. Koregaon Battle is viewed in this direction. During the period of Peshwai many conflicts were going on like Chitpavan v/s Desastha, Brahmin v/s Maratha. Brahmin and non-Brahmin.

During that time of social, economic, political and cultural devaluation of society began. The lowest of the low specially Mahars were targeted everywhere by the upper castes and policies based on religion were applied strictly by the Peshwe.

Because of need here in this chapter we see the Mahar's role and their activities which helps our theme. Mahars were the untouchable caste of Maharashtra. Caste conflict became sharp during the orthodox rule of Peshwa. Caste gradations and the notions of superiority attached to each higher caste were also the cause of the conflict. The complex among different caste groups as superior or inferior also led to conflict. Every caste had sub-castes in Hindu society.

To preserve the position, status, rights and perquisites in the society, watan was the only source. Sometimes one caste tried to adopt itself to others watan and clashes inevitably arose between them.

The caste conflicts were mainly of conflicts between Brahmin castes, conflicts between Brahmin and non-Brahmin conflict between non Brahmin (Shudra) and conflict between untouchables. This way the society of Maharashtra was full of conflicts during the period of Peshwai.

This chapter also deals with the status of Mahar soldiers and social status of the Mahars during the Peshwe Rule which gave support to recruitment in British army after 1791, and Mahars showed their martial tradition and bravery in the British army. As soldiers, they participated in various battles against native rulers and by the side of the British. In fact, they were helped beyond military requirement. Mahars fought in the Battle of Arcot in 1751, Battle of Plassey in 1754, Third Maratha battle in 1802-03, and battle of Khadaki in 1817 on behalf of the British. Then they fought in the Koregaon Battle. They defeated the huge trained and organized standing army of Peshwa and this was the end of the native rulers and native rule in India. With the help of this background, we study the battle of Koregaon with the help of Geographical conditions of Koregaon. Koregaon village is located in the Sirur Taluka of Pune. In this chapter the actual background of the battle, we take into account. Towards the end of December in pursuit of Bajirao Peshwa, which followed the battle of Kirkee, news reached Colonel Burr, that Bajirao was passing South from Junnar and meant to attack Pune. Colonel Burr sent for help from Sirur. The second battalion of the first regiment Bombay Native Infantry of 500 rank and file under Captain Francis Staunton. This detachment left Sirur for Pune at eight in the evening of the 31st December 1817. After marching all night a distance of twenty-five miles they saw across the Bhima the Peshwas army. The battle started in the morning here we give an account of the whole day's activity of the battle. How the British (Mahar) soldiers who were 500 to 600 fought with 25000 huge army. Many people from the British side fell down, Captain Staunton thought of ending the battle and calling for a ceasefire. But the Mahar soldiers opposed this idea and they told Capt. Staunton that if he wanted a ceasefire he could do so but they would never stop the war with the Peshwa. Because they wanted to destroy the Peshwa rule and this was the time to destroy it. The Mahars fought all day and finally, they defeated the Peshwa army. But historians and scholars say that only these soldiers defended themselves the whole day. This issue also has been consulted in this book. This battle is studied with the help of the Map of Koregaon Battle which gives live information about the activities of soldiers in this battle. In this chapter also we study the result of this battle. After the study of Koregaon Battle, we give a direct analysis which gives more information of Koregaon Battle as viewed by the people of the 21st century with the help of questionnaires.

While concluding it can be stated that there are different methodologies to narrate and analyze history. The Maratha History has been studied by very few historians most of them are interested in warfare and political history of the Marathas, some of them even identified this area as regional history. Our aim is different than the traditional historians. We have tried in this research to give judgement to the area which was neglected.

Similarly, many people have studied military history in the world but very few people have analysed the regional culture which in the final stage promote the military culture as per our hypothesis. We feel that we are successful in proving our hypothesis correct. The Military Culture in Maharashtra developed in a particular situation when there was social-political suppression of the people. The Military Culture of Maharashtra developed clearly due to this factor.

First two chapters we have devoted to the development of Military Culture taking Geography and history in mind. The village community also has been discussed in order to understand the local security aspect which ultimately helped in building up the strong base and fighting ability and military culture. The final two chapters third and fourth we have discussed various theoretical self-level and development of military technique in short actual warfare technique, taking into account to understand the military culture. This chapter also helps to reorganize the book. The fourth chapter is very important. It is considered the main backbone of the entire book. This chapter has been built upon the direct discussion and the oral interviews of various people staying in the vicinity of Konkan battlefield. In fact, I am thankful to those who responded to my call and especially helped in answering my questionnaire. Through the questionnaire, people from Bombay, Pune, Sangli, Solapur and those who had the slightest information about Koregaon Battle came forward and added new and authentic information to this research on which I am able to build this work with full confidence, and write a history which is lost in history. Now peoples have again started to learn this battle with a new dimension of Ambedkarism.

When Aurangzeb killed Chhatrapati Sambhaji Maharaj, scare of Aurangzeb his last ceremony of funeral no one from Maratha Sardars were ready to give their land but Govind Gaikwad Mahar, a friend of Sambhaji Maharaj, and members of Mahar community offered their land for Sambhajis funeral. This was the main cause Peshwa and later Maratha Sardars placed Mahar into untouchable category and committed atrocities because Mahar want family of Shivaji Maharaj became the true rulers of Maharashtra not Peshwa Balaji Vishwanath or his family.

During that time of social, economic, political and cultural devaluation of society began. The lowest of the low especially Mahars were targeted everywhere by the upper castes and policies based on religion were applied strictly by the Peshwe.

The Mahars as untouchables segregated and discriminated in every way of life in the Indian Society. Form the medieval period they began to join Muslim, Maratha and British Army. By their sincerity high ideals honesty and loyalty, they achieved the status of the martial race among the Indian Society.

Finally, I may mention that any military buildup is totally dependent upon social and economic conditions of the people. The people involved in this war when cornered to the extent that they fought back in Koregaon battle. However, fighting with their own countrymen is not a good sign of nationhood. The country men also should also think that they should not create such a situation that our own countrymen will force our target particular section of the society to fight with. For hope that this book will help to wind up the gap between the people those who are residing in the country. Defeat of the huge Peshwa army of 25,000 trained personnel by only 500 Mahar soldiers should make Indians think seriously about the socio-economic system prevailing in India then and even now. Perhaps, we cannot blame the Mahars who were ruthlessly suppressed overs the years by our own countrymen. If one cannot live honourably and peacefully in the country, people will revolt.

BIBLIOGRAPHY

Primary Sources (Unpublished.)

Petitions

Petitions from – Shivram Janba Kamble and 500 Mahars of Pune, w.d. Accompaniment to the Government resolution Gen. Dept. No.5789 dated 25th October, 1904, available in the *Khairmode Collection,* University of Bombay, Fort Library.

Reply to the Petition by Shri J. Sladen, Acting Secretary, Government of Bombay, Gen. Dept. No.5789, Bombay Castle 25th October, 1904. Vol.No.134, J.D. No. 1799, M.S.A., *Bombay Archives,* Mumbai.

Petition by Shri Shivram Janba Kamble to the Secretary of State for India, *Khairmode Collection,* University of Bombay, fort Library, 1910.

Published Sources

The Report of the Reform Committee (Franchise) Vol. II, Government of India, 1919.

The Eden Commission (1879)

The Esther Committee (1920)

The Peel Commission (1859)

Indian Sandhurst Committee (Skin Committee) (1927).

Ministry of Defence Archives, India, New Delhi.

Dr. B. R. Ambedkar, Writings and Speeches, Vol. I to XVIII, Government of Maharashtra, Mumbai, 1979 to 2003.

Source Material on Dr. B. R. Ambedkar, and the Movement of the Untouchables, Vol. I, Govt. of Maharshtra, Mumbai, 1982.

The Army of India and it's Evolution, Government of India, Publ, Delhi, 1924.

Census of India, 1971, 1991 and 200l.

Gazetteer of Bombay Presidency Vol. XI, *Satara,* Government Central Press, Bombay, 1885.

Gazetteer of Bombay Presidency, Vol. XVIII, Part I, *Poona District,* Government Central Press, Bombay, 1885, Vol. XVIII Part-II, Bombay 1885, Vol. XVIII, Part-III, Poona District, Bombay, 1885.

Gazetteer of India, District Series, XX Poona District, Bombay Presidency, Govt. Central Press, Mumbai, 1954.

Gazetteer of India, Indian Union, vol. II, *History and Culture* Ministry of education and Social Welfare, New Delhi, 1973.

Imperial Gazetteers of India, Provincial Series, Bombay Presidency. Vol. V, Superintendent, Government Printing, Calcutta, 1909.

Maharashtra State Gazetteer, History Part I, *Ancient Period,* Bombay Directorate of Government. Printing Stationery and Publication, Bombay, 1967.

Maharashtra State Gazetteer, History Part II, *Medieval Period,* Bombay Directorate of Government Printing Stationery and Publication, Bombay, 1967.

Maharashtra State Gazetteer, History Part III, *Maratha Period,* Bombay Directorate of Government Printing Stationery and Publication, Bombay, 1968.

Maharashtra State Gazetteer, Maharashtra Land and its People, Government Central Press, Bombay, 1968.

Maharashtra State Gazetteer, Poona District, Government of Maharashtra, Government Central Press, Bombay, 1954.

Official Government Records

Military Letters from the Court of Directors to the Government of India, 1790-1859, 96 volumes, National Archives of India, New Delhi.

Military letters from the Government of India to the Court of Directors, 1780-1859, 134 volumes. Military Consultations, National Archives of India, New Delhi.

Home Department Public Proceedings, 1780-1800, 27 volumes, National Archives of India, New Delhi,

General Orders Commander-in-Chief, 1816-1859, 102 volumes, National Archives of India, New Delhi.

Military Proceedings, 1799-1859, 1,600 volumes, National Archives of India, New Delhi.

Foreign Department Secret Consultations, 1800-1850, National Archives of India, New Delhi.

Bombay Government Consultations: Public Diaries for the years 1750, 1751, 1753, 1757, 1760, 1766-70, 1772-79, 1782, 1784., Maharashtra State Archives, Mumbai.

Military Department, Bombay Castle, Vol. 13/1891. No. 01009/24-C.

General Department, No. 5789 Vol. No.134, T.D.No.1799.

Revenue Department, Bombay Castle, Vol. 77/1895.

Vol. 77/1896.

At Maharashtra State Archives, Mumbai.

Factory Records, Surat Factory, Vol.105, File 172.

Vol.88, File 32,36, 37.

Vol.107, File 177.

Vol.108, File 34-35.

Maharashtra State Archives, Mumbai.

Military Department Diaries l805 to l873, Maharashtra State Archives, Mumbai.

Poona Residency, 34 volumes, 38-69, Maharashtra State Archives, Mumbai.

Bombay Army List, 1851-1939, Maharashtra State Archives, Mumbai.

Indian Army – 1849-1937; 1947-1951, Maharashtra State Archives, Mumbai.

Official Correspondence

Letter from the Commander, Zhob to L.T. Col. Dyke, the Briish and Indian Officers, NCO's and Men of the Battalion. Dl.Loralabi 7th October 1920, Head Quarters Zhob; Loralabi No.23/49/Z.O. Unpublished Handwritten Notes, Kharmode Collection, University of Bombay, Library.

Letter from D. Saired Col. Commanding Head Quarters Zhob Loralabi No. 23/50/Z.O., dated 7th October, 1920, to the Gen. Staff, 2nd Indian Battalion B.N.Quetta, unpublished copy of letter, Kharmode Collection, University of Bombay, Library.

Letter from G.O.C. 2nd Indian Battalion to the Gen. of Gen. Staff, Simla No.353/8/G.S., dated 26 October, 1920, Kharmode Collection, University of Bombay, Library.

Letter from Army Headquarters, India, (Adjustant General Branch) Simla No. A/15369/I/A.G.-67, dated 13th September, 1922, Kharmode Collection, University of Bombay, Library.

Letter from Dr. B. R. Ambedkar to the Hon. Sir, Regenald Maxwell, Home Minister of the Viceroy's Executive Council dated 10th January 1943, National Archives, New Delhi.

Reply to the letter of Dr. B. R. Ambedkar, dated 10th January, 1943 *from Hon. Sir Regenald Maxwell,* Home Minister of the Vicetory's Executive Council, New Delhi, dated 14th January, 1943, National Archives, Delhi.

Poona Residency Correspondence, Poona Affairs, Elphinstone's Embassey, Part I-II, Maharashtra State Archives, Mumbai.

Microfilms

Bombay Deccan Ryot Commission of Report of the Committee on the Ryot in Poona, Ahgmednagar, and Bombay, Vol. II Documentation Co., Switzerland, 1875-1876.

Blacker, V, *The Mahratta Wars,* 1816, 1817, 1818 and 1819 , Memoir Operations of the British Army in India, Parbury and Accer, London, 1821.

Enthoven, R.V., *Tribes and Castes of Bombay,* Vol.3, Inter Documentation Co., Switzerland, 1920-22.

Official Publications

Annual Registers, of the years 1815,1816, 1817, 1818, 1819.

The East India Register and Directory, 1816,1817,1818, 1819.

Encyclopedias

Bhide, G.R., *Abhinav Marathi Dnyankosha,* Vol. I-IV, G.R. Bhide Publication, Kolhapur, 1963, 1965, 1967, 1977.)

Buckland C.E., *Dictionary of Indian Biography,* Swan Son & Co. Ltd., London, 1906.

Chitrav, S., *Bharatvarshiva Anachina Charitrakosha,* Pune, 1946.

Joshi, Mahadevshastri P., *Bharatiya Sanskritikosh,* Bharatiya Sanskriti Mandal, Pune, 1972.

Kelkar, Y.N., *Atihasik Shabdakosh,* Vol. I, II. Thokal Prakashan, Pune, 1962.

Kelkar, V.S., *Maharashtriya Dnyankosh,* Vol. I to XV, Maharashtriya Dnyankosh Mandal, Nagpur, 1925.

Molesworth, J.T., *A Dictionary of English and Marathi,* Part I, II, Second edition, enlarged and revised by T.Comdy, Bombay, 1873.

Molesworth, J.T., *Marathi-English Dictionary* corrected reprint, Shubhada Saraswat, Pune, 1975.

Chronological Tables

Modak, B.P., *Shaka Va Sana Yanchi Tithi Va Tarikh Vara*, Jantri, Printed by Chitrashala Press, Pune and Vidyavilas Press, Kolhapur, 1889.

English (Travels, Records, Reports, etc.)

Buchanan Francis, *A Journey from Madras Through the Countries of Mysore, Canara and Malbar.* Vols. I, III, 2nd ed., Higginbotham andCo., 165, Mount Road, Madras, 1870.

Dubois Abbe J.A., *Hindu Manners Customs and Ceremonies,* Translated by Beaucham H.K., Reprinted in India by Shree Publishing House, Delhi, 1991.

Elliot Sir H.M. and Dawson John, *The History of India as told by its own Historians,* Vols. VII and VIII, lst ed., Kitab Mahal Pvt., Ltd., Allahabad, 1974.

Elphinstone Mountstuart, *Territories Conquered from the Peshwa. A Report,* First Reprint, Oriental Publishers, Delhi, 1973.

Frobes James, *Oriental Memoirs,* Vols. I-II, 2nd ed., 1834, Richard Bentley, New Burlington Street, London.

Forrest George W., *Selections from the Minutes and Other Official Writings of the Honourable Mountstuart Elpohinstone,* Richard Bently and Sons, London., 1884,

Goodine R.N., *A Report on the Deccan Village Communities,* Bombay, 1852.

Jenkins Richard, *Report on the Territories of the Rajah of Nagpur,* at Government Press, Nagpur, 1827, Reprinted 1923

Malcom Sir John, *A Memoirs of Central India,* Vols. I-II, Parbury, Allen and Co., Leaden Hall Street, London, 1832.

Rawlinson H.G. and Patwardhan R.P. (Ed.), *A Source Book of Maratha History,* Calcutta, 1978.

Sen S.N., *Foreign Biographies of Shivaji,* K.P. Bagachi & Co., Calcutta, 1927.

Secondary Sources

Books in English

Ackworth, H.A., *Ballads of the Marathas*, Longmans Green & Co., London, 1894.

Agarwal, C.B., *The Harijans in Rebellion: Case for the Removal of Untouchability,* Popular Prakashan, Bombay, 1934.

Alexander, Cunningham, *The Ancient Geography of India,* Bharatiya Publishing House, Varanasi, 1975.

Alexander, K.C., *Social Mobility,* Deccan College, Post-Graduate and Research Institute, Pune, 1968.

Alexander, Robertson, *The Mahar Folk,* YMCA, Publishing House, Calcutta, 1938.

Altekar A.S., *A History of Village Communities in Western India,* Oxford University Press, Bombay, 1927.

Ambedkar, B. R. , *Annilihation of caste: with a reply to Mahatma Gandhi,* Bhusan Press, Bombay, 1936.

--, *Mr. Gandhi and the Emancipation of the Untouchables,* Thacker & Sons, Bombay, 1943.

--, *What Congress and Gandhi have done to the Untouchables?* Thacker & Co., Bombay, 1945.

--, *Who were the Sudras,* Thacker & Co., Bombay, 1946.

--, *States and Minorities,* Thacker & Co., Bombay, 1947.

--, *The Untouchables,* Amrit Book Co., New Delhi, 1948.

--, *The Buddha and his Dhamma,* Siddharth College Publication I, Bombay, 1957.

--, *Ranade, Gandhi and Jinnah,* Thacker & Co., Bombay, 1943. Reprinted by Bheem Patrika Publications, Jullundur, 1964.

Andhare Wink : *Land and Sovereignty in India*, Cambridge Univ. Press, Cambridge, 1986.

Andre, Bateille (ed), *Caste, Old and New,* Asia Publishing House, Bombay, 1969.

Apte, B.K., *A History of the Maratha Navy and Merchantships,* State Board for Literature and Culture Government of Maharashtra, Mumbai, 1973.

Arthur Crawford C.M.G., *Our Troubles in Poona and the Deccan,* West-Minister Archibald Constable and Co., London, 1897.

Arnold, T.W., *Legacy of Islam,* Oxford, 1931.

Arnold, F., Veith von Golssenau, *Warfare: Relation of War to Society,* trans. By f. Fitzerald, 1939.

Ashraf K.M., *Life and the Conditions of the People of the Hindustan,* Munshiram Manoharlal Oriental Publishers, Delhi, 1970.

Baden-Powell, B.H., *The Origin and Growth of Village Communities in India,* Swen Sanneshein & Co.Ltd., New York, 1899.

Bailey F.G., *Caste and Economic Frontier,*Manchester University, Manchester, 1957.

--,*Tribe, Caste and Nation,* Manchester University Press, Manchester, 1960.

Ball, Hatcheet, K., *Social Policy and Social Change in Western India, 1817-1830,* Oxford University Press, London, 1957.

Bal Krishna, *Shivaji the Great,* Modern Publishers & Distributors, Delhi, 1985.

Banaji D.R., *Slavery in British India,* D.B. Taraporevala Sons & Co., Kitab Mahal, Hornby Road, Bombay, 1944.

Banerjee, P.D., *A Handbook of the fighting races of India,* Thacker & Co., Calcutta, 1899.

Barnabas, A.P. and Mehta, S., *Caste in Changing India,* Everest Press, New Delhi, 1967.

Barber, Bernard, *Social Stratification,* Harcourt, Brace & Co., New York, 1957.

Bava Sunder Singh, Lt. Col.(Rtd.), *Tradition Never Dies, The Genisis and Growth of the Indian Army,* Lalwani Publishing House, Bombay, 1946.

Behene N.K., *The Background of Maratha Renaissance in the 17th Century,* The Bangalore Press, Bangalore, 1946.

Bendrye V.S., *Maharashtra of Shivashahi Period* Phoenix Publication, Pune, 1946.

Bern, Major H. Von Dach, *Total Resistance, Swiss Army Guide in Guerrilla Warfare and Underground Operations,* ed. By R.K. Brown, Boulder, Colo, n.d.c. 1965.

Bhagwandas, *Thus Spoke Ambedkar* (Vol.I and Vol.II), Bheem Patrika Publications, Jullunder City, 1963.

Bhagat, K.A., *A Decade of Indo-British Relations,* Popular Book Depot, Bombay, 1959.

Bhandarkar, R.G.S, *Early History of the Dekkan,* Asian Eductional Services, New Delhi, 1985.

Bhattacharya, S.C., *Some Aspects of Indian Society,* Firma K.L.M. Pvt., Calcutta, 1978.

Bhattacharya, P.K.,*British Residents at Poona,* Progressive Publishers, Calcutta, 1948.

Bhatt and Vanaramai A., *The Harijans of Maharashtra,* All India harijan Sevak Sangh, Delhi, 1941.

Bhat B.V., *Maharashtra Dharma,* Satakaryotcjaka Sabhga, Dhule, 1925.

Bhave V.L. and Tulpule S.G. (Ed.), *Maharashtra Saraswat,*Popular Prakashan, Bombay, 1963.

Bombay Gazetteer, *Bombay Gazeteer,* Vol.VII, 1884-85.

Bose, P.,*A History of Hindu Civilization, Vol.I & II, During British Rule,* Jadunath Seal Hare Press, Calcutta 1894.

Borale, P.T., *Segregation and Desegregation in India: A Sociological Study,* Manaktalas, Bombay, 1968.

Broughton, T.D., *Letters from A Maratha Camp, During the year 1809,* Descriptive of ceremonies of the Maratha, Bagachi & Co., Calcutta, 1977.

Burton, R.G., *The Maratha and Pindhari War,* Seema Publications, Delhi, 1975.

Cadel (Sir) Patric, *History of the Bombay Army,* Green & Co., London, 1938.

Cambridge, R.O., *Account of the War in India between the English and the French on the Coast of Coromandel from the year 1761, etc.,* London, 1762.

Candler, Edmund, *The Sepoy,* John Murray, London, 1919.

Chanana Dev Raj, *Prachin Bharatatil Gulamgiri,* Translated in Marathi by Ganesh Thite, Lokyangmaya Graha, Bombay.

Chaplin William, *Report exhibiting a view of the Fiscal and Judicial system of administration introduced into the conquered Territory above the Ghauts.*

Chitnis, K.N., *Glimpses of Maratha Socio-Economical History,* Atlantic Publishers Distributors, New Delhi, 1994.

Choksey, R.D., *The Last Phase-Selection from the Deccan Commissioners File (Peshwa Daftar), 1815-1818,* K.B.Dhate Prakashan, Mumbai, 1947.

Choksey, R.D., *Economic Life in Bombay Deccan,* Choksey Pub., Poona, 1935.

Chopra, Pri and Das (ed), *Social, Cultural and Economical History of India,* 3 Vols. Macmillion Co., London, 1954.

Clause Witz Von (J.J.Grahm, Translator), *On War,* Vol.III, Routledge & Legan Poul, London, 1968.

Chopra, P.N., *Select Papers from British Royal Archives,* Konark Publishing Pvt.Ltd., New Delhi, 1998.

Cohen, Stephen, P., *The Indian Army, It's Contribution to the Development of the Nation,* University of California Press, Berkely, Los Angles, 1971.

Das, Maj. Gen. Chand N., *Tradition and Customs of the Indian Armed Force,* Vision, New Delhi.

Das S.T., *Studies in Defence Strategy,* Sagar Publications, New Delhi, 1978.

Dastane, Santosh, *Glimpses of Maharashtra,* Dastane Ramchandra & Co., 1993.

Deodhar Y.N., *Nana Phadnis,* Popular Prakashan, 1st. ed., Bombay, 1962.

Deopujari, M.B., *Shivaji and the Maratha Art of War,* Vidarbha Samshodhan Mandal, Nagpur, 1973.

Deshpande, C.D., *Geography of Maharashtra (India the Land People),* National Book Trust, New Delhi, 1971.

Deshpande, C.D., *Western India, A Regional Geography,* Students Own Book Depot, Dharwar, 1948.

Desai, Sudha V., *Social Life in Maharashtra under the Peshwas,* Popular Prakashan, Bombay, 1980.

Divekar, V.D., *Survey of Material in Marathi on the Economic and Social History of India,* B.I.S.M., Pune, 1981.

Douglas, James, *Bombay and Western India,* S.L.Martson & Co., London, 1893.

Drewitt, F.G.D., *Bombay in the Days of George IV,* Longmans Green & Co., London, 19007,

Duff, J.G., *History of the Maratha's,* Vol. I, II, III, reprint, Karam Publication, Delhi, 2000.

Dutta, N.K., *Origin and Growth of Caste in India,* Firma K.L. Mukhopadheyay, Vol.l, 2nd ed., Calcutta, 1968.

Dutta, R.C., *A History of Civilization in Ancient India,* Vols.I-II, Based on Sanskrit Literature, Vishal Publishers, Delhi., 1898-90.

--, *Epochs of Indian History* (Ancient India), Longmans Green & Co., London, 1913.

Dutta, B., *Indian Art in Relation to Culture,* Navbharat Publishers, Calcutta, 1956.

Edwards S.M., *The Gazetteer of Bombay City and Island,* Times Press, Bombay, 1909.

Elphinsone, M., *The History of India,* Murray & Co., London, 1889.

Elphinstone, M., *Territories Conquered from the Paishwa: Report,* Oriental Publishers, Delhi, 1973.

Forbes, James, Oriental Memoirs, Vols.I, II, 2nd edn. R. Bentley & Co., London, 1834.

Fukazawa, Hiroshi, *The Medieval Deccan,* Oxford University Press, 1991.

Fuller JFC (Maj. Gen.), *The Conduct of War,* Army Publishers, Delhi, 1960.

Gadgil, D.R., *Poona, A Socio-Economic Survey, Part I,* Gokhale Institute of Politics & Economics, Poona, 1945.

Gavali P.A., *Society and Social Disabilities under the Peshwas,* National Publishing House, New Delhi, 1988.

Ghurye G.S., *Caste and Race in India,* Popular Prakashan, Pune, 1932.

Ghurye, G.S., *Caste, Class and Occupation,* Popular Prakashan, Pune, 1932.

Giles, L., *Sun Tzu or The Art of War,* trans. From the Chinese, London, 1910.

Gokhale, B.G., *Buddhism in Maharashtra,* Popular Prakashan, Bombay, 1976.

Gould Harold, A., *The Adaptive Functions of Caste in Contemporary Indian Society,* Assam Survey, III(9), 1963, pp.427-38.

Griffiths, S.B., *Sun Tzu*, trans. *Art of War,* Oxford, 1963.

Griffiths, Ralph T.H., (ed),*he Hymns of the Rgveda,* Vol.I, II, The Chowkhamba Sanskrit Series Office, Varanasi, 5th Ed., 1971.

Guha, J.P. Ed., *James Grant Duff History of the Marathas,* Vol.I, Associated Pub. House, New Delhi, 1971.

Gune V.T., *The Judicial System of the Marathas,* Deccan College, Poona, 1953.

Gunnar Lathmar, *The Origin of the Inequality of the Social Classes,* London, 1938.

Gupta, P.C., *Bajirao II and the East India Co., (1796-1818),* Oxford University Press, London, 1931.

Guevara, Ernesto Che and Mao Tse Tung, *On Guerrilla Warfare,* with a foreward by Capt. B..Liddell Hart, London, 1961; Introduction to Mao by Brig-Gen. S.B.Griffith; Introduction to Guevara by Major Harries Clichy Peterson, New York, 1962.

Hart, Ernest, *Explanatory Note on Indian Arms: Empire of India Exhibition,* London, Illustrate Official Cat.,1895.

Hasting Warren, *Historical Document of British India,* Anmol Publications, New Delhi, (Reprinted), 1985.

Heathcote T.A., *The Indian Army, 1822-1922,* The Garrison of British Imperial India, David & Charles, London, 1974.

Hutton, J.H., *Caste: In India,* Oxford University Press, Bombay, 1977.

Issac, Harold, *India's Ex-Untouchables,* John Day & Co., New York, 1965.

Jackson Maj. D., *India's Army,* Sampson Low, London, 1940.

Jatava, Daya Ram, *Social Philosophy of B. R. Ambedkar,* Phoneix Agency, Agra, 1965.

--, *Political Philosophy of B. R. Ambedkar,* Phoneix Publishing Agency, Agra, 1965.

--, *Poverty within Poverty,* Sterling Publishers, New Delhi, 1979.

Johari, R.C., *Western Army Thought,* Chandraprakash & Brothers, Delhi, 1972.

Kale, D.V., *Social Life and Manners in Maharashtra (1750-1800),* Mss of thesis, Bombay University, Bombay, 1927.

Kamble, B. R., Studies *in Shivaji and his times,* Shivaji University Publications, 1982.

Kamble, B. R. , *Caste and Philosophy in Pre-Buddhist India,* Parimal Prakashan, Aurangabad, 1979.

Kamble N.D., *Atrocities on Scheduled Castes in Post-Independent India* (from 15 August 1947 to 15 August 1979), Ashish Publishing House, New Delhi, 1981.

--, *The Scheduled Castes,* Ashish Publishing House, New Delhi, 1981.

--, *Bonded Labour in India,* Uppal Publishing House, New Delhi, 1982.

--,*Deprived Caste and their struggle for equality,* Ashish Publishing House, New Delhi, 1983.

Kane, P.V., *History of the Dharmashastra Ancient and Medieval Religious & Civil Law,* Government Oriental Series, B.No.6, Poona, 1930.

Kantak, M.R., *First Anglo-Maratha War he Last Phase, (1780-1783),* Popular Prakashan, Pune, 1989.

Karve, Iravati, *Hindu Society: An Interpretation,* Sangam Press, Pune, 1961.

--, *Maharashtra Land and It's People,* Government of Maharashtra Publication division, Bombay, 1965.

Karve, Iravati & Damle, *Group relation in Village, Community,* Deccan College, Pune, 1963.

Keer, Dhananjaya, *Dr. Ambedkar, Life and Mission* (2nd ed.), Popular Prakashan, Bombay, 1962.

Kelkar, N.C., and Apte, D.V. (Ed.), *English Records on Shivaji,* Vols. I-II, Shivacharitra Karyalaya, Poona, 1931.

Kincaid C.A., and Parasnis D.B., *A History of he Maratha People,* Vols. I-II, Oxford University Press, London.

Kosambi D.D., *The Culture and Civilization of Ancient India in Historical Outline,* 4th ed., Vikas Publications, Bombay, 1976.

Kosambi D.D., *History and Society; Problems of Interpretation,* University of Bombay (Department of History), Bombay, 1985.

Kothari, Rajni (ed), *Caste in Indian Politics,* Allied Publishers, New Delhi, 1970.

Krishnarau, A.K., *Life of Shivaji Maharaj,* Manoranjan Press, Bombay, 1921.

Kulkarni A.R., *Maharashtra in the Age of Shivaji,* 1st ed. Popular Prakashan, Poona, 1969.

--,*The Marathas* , Books & Books Publishers, New Delhi, 1996.

Kumar Ravindra, *Western India in the Nineteenth Century,* University of Toronto Press, London, 1968.

Lawrence (Sir) Henry, *Essays Military and Political, Written in India,* W.H.Allen, London, 1859.

Leader W.F. (Lieut.) *Discription and History of Purandhar,* Karandikar Rajahansa Co., Poona, 1935.

Limaya D.H., *Aspects of India's Military and Defence,* New Book Co., Bombay, 1941.

Lioyd and Susane Rudalphe, *Politics and the Military in New States,* Chandeler Sen Francisco, 1962.

Lohia, Rammanohar, *The Caste System,* Navahind, Hyderabad, 1964.

Longer Victor, *Forefront For Ever History of Mahar Regiment,* The Mahar Regimental Center, Sagar, M.P., 1981.

Louis Maheu., *Social Movement and Social Classes,* Sage Publication Ltd., New Delhi, 1995.

Lovet A.C., (Major), *The Armies of India,* Adam & Charles Block, London, 1911.

Luttwak Edward N., *Strategy, The Logic of War andPeace,* Harvard University Press, London, England, 1987.

Lynch, Owen, N., *The Politics of Untouchability,* Columbia University Press, New York, 1969.

Liddell-Hart, Basil H., *Strategy, The Indirect Approach,* 3rd edn., New York, 1954.

--, *The Revolution in Warfare,* 1946.

Linebarger, Paul, M.A., *Psychological Warfare,* Washington, D.C., 1955.

Macdonald, *Memoir of the Life of the Late Nana Parnavis,* Reprinted of 1851, Oxford University Press, 1927.

Macmillan Michael, *The Last of the Peshwas,* Blackie & Son Ltd., London, 1907.

Macmunn Lient, Gen. Sir, George, *The Martial Races of India,* Sampson Law, London, 1933.

Mahajan T.T., *Maratha Administration in the 18th Century,* Commonwealth Pub., New Delhi, 1990.

Mahar J., Michael (ed), *The Untouchables in Contemporary India,* The University of Arizona Press, Tucson, USA, 1972.

Mahar, Pauline, M., *Changing Caste Ideology in a North Indian Village,* Asia Publishing House, Bombay, 1958.

Majumdar, D.N., *Caste and Communication in an Indian Village,* Asia Publishing House, Bombay, 1958.

Majumdar B.N. (Lt. Col.), *The Little Ward Army,* Eductional Stores, New Delhi, 1967.

Majumdar, R.C., & N.G. Dighe, *The Martha Supremacy,* Bharatiya Vidya Bhavan, Bombay, 1977.

Maxmuller F.,(ed), *Sacred Books of the East* (English translation of Sanskrit Works by various Scholars), *The Laws of Manu, Vol. XXV,* Motilal Banarasidas, Delhi, 1975.

Monier-Williams, M., *A Sanskrit English Dictionary,* Motilal Banarasidas, Delhi, 1899, Reprint, 1981.

Mann H.H., *Land and Labour in a Deccan Village,* 1917, Oxford University Press, Oxford.

Mann Harold, H., *Social Framework of Agriculture,* Daniel Thorner, Bombay, (ed), Vora, 1916.

Manson's Phillip, *A Matter of Honour,* Holt, Reinhart, 1974.

Nadkarni R.V., *The Rise and Fall of the Maratha Empire,* Bombay, Popular Prakashan, Bombay, 1966.

Naravane M.S., *Forts of Maharashtra,* Asia Publishing House, , New Delhi, 1995.

Naravane M.S., *Battles of Medieval India (AD 1295-1850)* APH Publishing Corpn, New Delhi, 1996.

Nasution, Abdul Haris, *Fundamentals of Guerilla Warfare,* with an introduction by Otto Heilbrunn, New York, 1965.

Omvedt, Gail, *Cultural Revolt in a Colonial Society,* Scientific Society Education Trust, Bombay, 1976.

Pagadi Setu, Madhav Rao, *18th Century Deccan,* Popular Prakashan, Bombay, 1963.

Pagadi Setu Madhavrao, *Chhatrapati Shivaji,* Continental Prakashan, Pune, 1974.

Pagadi Setu Madhavrao, *Shivaji, National Book Trust,* India New Delhi, 1983.

Pagadi Setu Madhav Rao, *Studies in Maratha Histoy, Vol.I,* Shivaji University, Kolhapur, 1971.

Palsokar R.D. (Col.) *Shivaji The Great Guerilla,* Spicer College Press, Pune, 1973.

Panikkar, K.M., *Geographical Factors in Indian History,* Bombay, 1959.

Pant, G.N., *Studies in Indian Weapons and Warfare,* New Delhi, 1970, Mentions 65 Centres of Arms Collection in India. The Saga of Indian Arms, in JIH, *Golden Jubilee Volume,* 1973.

Paranjape B.G., (ed), *English Records on Shivaji Vol. 1 and 1,* Shivacharitra Karalayala, Pune, 1931.

Parasnis D.B., *Poona in Bygone Days,* The Times of Press, 1921.

Patvardhan, Sunanda, *Change among India's Harijan, Maharashtra A Case Study,* Orient Longmans, New Delhi, 1973.

Pawar A.G., *Maratha History, Seminar Papers,* Shivaji University Press, lst ed. Kolhapur.

Phadke Y.D., *Social Reform Movement in Maharashtra,* Maharashtra Information Center, New Delhi, 1989.

Phatak N.R., *The First Maratha War,* Aryabhanu Press, Kolhapur, 1928.

Pitre K.G. (Brig), *A Short History of Warfare in India,* Pune, 1994.

Prabhu P.H., *Hindu Social Organization,* Popular Prakashan, Bombay, 1961.

Prasad Nandan, *The Military History of India,* K.P. Bagachi, Calcutta, 1976.

Puri R.C., (Translator and Editor), *Shivaji the Great Patriot,* Metropolitan Book Co., Pvt., Ltd., New Delhi, 1980.

Raghuvanshi V.P.S., *Indian Society in the 18th Century,* Associated Publishing House, Delhi, 1969.

Ranade, M.G., *Rise of the Maratha Power,* Pundalkar & Co., Bombay 1900.

Roger Banmant, *Sword of the Raj, The British Army in India, 1774 to 1947,* Bobbs-Marrill, New York, 1977.

Robbin, Jeanette, *Dr. Ambedkar and His Movement,* Dr. Ambedkar Publishing Society, Hyderabad, 1964.

Russel, R.V., *Introductory Essay's on Caste, In the Tribes and Caste of the Central Provinces of India,* Vol.I to IV, London, 1916, (Reprint, 1975).

Russell, R.V. and Hiralal, *The Tribes and Caste of the Central Provinces of India,* 4 vols. Reprint, Cosmo Publication, Delhi,1975.

Sanjana, J.E., *Caste and Outcaste,* Thacker & Sons, Bombay, 1946.

Sardesai G.S., *New History of the Marathas,* 3 Vols. Pheonex Publication, Bombay. 3rd ed., 1971.

--,*Main Currents of Maratha History,* M.C. Sarkar and Sons, Calcutta, 1926.

--*Shivaji Souvenior,* Dhamale Prakashan, Bombay, 1927.

--, (ed), *English Records of Maratha History,* Popular Press, Bombay, 1950.

Sarkar Jadunath, *Shivaji and his Times,* S.N. Sarkar & Sons, Calcutta, 1929.

Sarkar Jadunath, *Military History of India,* M.C. Sarkar & Sons, Pvt. Ltd., Calcutta, 1960.

Sarkar Jadunath, *Shivaji and His Times,* Oriental Longman Ltd., Bombay, 1st ed., 1973.

--,*House of Shivaji,* S.N. Sarkar & Sons, Calcutta, 1940.

Saxena K.M.L., *Military System of India, 1850 to 1900,* Sterling Publishers Ltd., New Delhi, 1974.

Sen Surendranath, *Administration System of the Marathas,* K. Bagachi & Co., Calcutta, 1976.

Sen S.N. (Ed.), *Foreign Biographies of Shivaji,* K.P. Bagachi & Co., Calcutta 1931, Reprint 1976-77.

Sen S.N., *Administrative System of the Marathas,* 1st ed., 1925, Calcutta, 3rd ed., K.P.Bagachi & Co. Calcutta, 1976.

--,*Military System of the Marathas,* Orient Longmans, Bombay 1st Ed., 1928.

Sen Surendranath, *Siva Chhatrapati,* K.P. Bagachi & Co., Calcutta, 1920.

Sharma, D.T., *Maratha History (Re-examined) 1295 to 1707,* Karnatak Publishing House, Bombay, 1944.

Sharma, Gautam (Maj.), *Indian Army Through the Ages,* Allied Publishers Pvt. Ltd., Bombay, 1966.

Shekspher e Colonel, L.W., *A Land History of Poona and its Battlefield,* Macmillan & Co., Ltd., London, 966.

Sherwani, Harunekhan, *The Bahamani's of the Deccan,* Hyderabad, 1963.

Singh (Brig.) Rajendra, *History of the Indian Army, Army Educational Stores, New Delhi, 1963.*

Singh Jodh (Maj) *War, Principles, Tactics an Strategies,* Surjett Publications, Delhi, 1980.

Singh Saint Nihal, *India's Fighter's,* Sampsonlow, London, 1948.

Spate, O.H.K., *India & Pakistan,* Methuen & Co., Ltd., London, 1954.

Takakhav N.S., *Life of Shivaji,* Vol. I and II, Sunita Publications, Delhi, 1985.

Temple Richard, *Oriental Experience,* John Murray Albemarle Street, London, 1883.

Temple, R., *The Maratha Nationality, in Shivaji and the Rise of Marathas,* K.P. Bagachi & Co., Calcutta, 1953.

Thapar Romila, *History of India,* Romila Thapar Books, Australia, 1966.

Thorat, MajorGeneral, S.P.P., *The Regimental History of the Machine Gun Regiment,* The Army Press, Dehradun, 1954.

Tikekar S.R. (Ed), *Sardesai Commemoration Volume,* Dhawale Prakashan, Bombay, 1938.

Tikekar, S.R., *Maharashtra; The Land its People and their culture,*Maratha Information Center, New Delhi, 1966.

Toynbee, Arnold, J., *A study of History,* Oxford University Press, London, 1940.

Vagts, Alfred, *A History of Militarism,* Meredian Book, New York, 1959.

Varda, Ahmed & Bhatt, *Race, Caste and Politics,* Saga Publishers, New York, 1972.

Vas & Parasnis, *Sanada & Patre,* Purushottum Vishram Mauji, Bombay, 1913.

Verma S, *Mountstuart Elphinstone in Maharashtra,* Bagachi & Co., Calcutta, 198l.

Verma Virendra, *Shivaji A Captain of War with a Mission,* Youth Education Publication, Poona, 1976.

Vidyarthi, P.L., *Leadership in India,* Asia Publishing House, Bombay, 1967.

Weber, Max, *The Sociology of Religion,* Translated by Ephraim Fischoff, Boston Press, Boston, 1963.

Westcott, G., *Kabir and the Kabir Panth,* Susil Gupta Limited, Calcutta, 1953.

Wilkinson, T.A., and Thomas, M., (ed), *Ambedkar and the Neo Buddhist Movement,* The Christian Literature Society, Madras, 1972.

William, H.H., *Glossary of Judicial and Revenue Terms,* Vol.II, East India Co., London, 1855.

Wiser, W.H., *The Hindu Jajmani System,* (3rd ed), Lucknow Publishing Hose, Lucknow, 1969.

Yazdani G., *The Early History of the Deccan, Vol. I & II,* Oxford University Press, London, 1916.

Zelliot, Eleanor, *Caste in Indian Politics,* ed. By. Rajani Kothari, Orient Longmans Ltd., New Delhi, 1970.

Marathi Secondary Sources

Marathi Books

Aavalaskar S.V., *Rayagadachi Jivan Katha,* 1st ed., Maharashtra Sahitya Va Sanskratik Mandal, Mumbai, 192.

Acworth H.A. and Shaligram S.T. (Eds), *Itihas Prasidha Purusande Va Striyanche,*Powade, Bombay, 1891.

Abhyankar, M.G., Lt. Col., *Marathyanchye Yuddhashasta,* Maratha Itihas Vyakhanmala, Shivaji University, Kolhapur, 1983.

Amatya Ramchandrapant, *Ajnapatra,* Rao V.D. (ed), lst ed., Rajwade Samshodhan MSandal, Dhule, 1955.

Ameen, Sayeed, *Mahapurush Chatrapati Shivaji,* Sayeed meen Prakashan, Sangli, 1974.

Apte, D.V.and Oturkar, R.V., *Maharashtracha Patra-rup Itihas (1624-1859),* Pune Anath Vidyarthigriha, Pune, 1941.

Apte, D.V. (ed), *Maharashtra Itihas Manjiri,* Chitrashala Press, Poona, 1923.

Apte, D.V., and Oturkar R.V. *Maharashtracha Patraroopa Itihas,* Poona, 1963.

Apte, D.A., Oturkar R.V., *Sadhan Parichav Arthath Maharashtracha Patrarup Itihas,* Loksangraha Chapkhana, Pune, 1862.

Apte, D.V., Divekar S.M., (ed) *Shree,* Shiv Bharat, B.I.S.M., Pune, 1927.

Apte D.V., Kelkar N.C. (ed) *Shivkalin Patrasar-Sangraha* Vol.I & II, Shree Shivcharitra Karyalaya, Pune, 1930.

Athawale, Sadashiv, *Shivaji Ani Shivyug,* Ajab Pustakalaya, Kolhapur, 1971.

Athawale, Sadashiv, and Sasvadkar, *Marathi Sattecha Vikas Va Rhos,* Sadhana Prakashan, Pune, 1974.

Atre, T.N., *Gav-Gada,* Published by H.V., Mote, Bombay, 1959.

Bendrye, V.S., *Chhatrapati Rajaram Maharaj* (1970), Lokavangmaya Graha, Bombay.

Bhagvat A.N., *Sataracha Pratinidhi Ghamacha Itihas,* Vol.I-III, Published by Aoundha Sansthana (1924-29).

Bhalerao, Shreenivas, *Nagvanshiyano Tumchi Asmita Geli Kulthe?* Siddharth Prakashan, Pune, 2002.

Bharat Itihas Sanshodhak Mandal, Series, *Siva-Charitrya Sahitya* (various editions) 13 vols., Poona, 1910-1965.

-- *Aitihasik Sankirna Sahitya* (various editions), 12 vols. Poona, 1929-1967.

Bhave V.K., *Musalman Purva Maharashtra,* Vol.II Lokjivan, Poona, 1947.

--,*Sivaraj Va Sivakal,* Kesari Press, Poona, 1957.

--,*Peshwekalin Maharashtra,* Bharatiya Itihas Anusandhan Parishad, New Delhi, 1976.

Bhave, L.V., *Maharashtra Saraswat Part I, II,* 3rd Ed. Thane, 1922.

Bhave, V.K. ,*Musalman Purva Maharashtra,* Modern Printing Press, Pune, (Shake 1868), 1946.

Bhave, V.K., *Peshwekalin Maharashtra,* G.B. Joshi, Anand MudranMandir, Pune, 1935.

Chafekar N.G., *Peshwaichya Sawalit,* Laxman Narayan Chaphekar, Arya Sanskruti Mudranalaya, Pune, 1859.

Chapekar N.G., *Peshwaicha Savalit,* Arya-Sanskriti Press, Poona, 1937.

Chitnis K.N., *Madhyayugin Bharatiya Sankalapana Va Sanstha,* Poona, 1976.

Chitnis, M.R., *Sakakarte Sivaji Maharaj Hyanche Saptaprakarnatmak Charitra,* Herwadkar R.V., (ed), Venus Prakashan, Poona, 1967, 1st Ed.

--,*Thorale Shahu Maharaj Yanche Charitra,* Sane K.N.(ed), 3rd ed. Poona, 1924.

Chaudhari A.P., Mandhare, D.A., *Bharatiya Sainya Itihas,* Vol. 1,2, Archana Prakashan, Jalgao, 1984.

Deshpande, P.N., *Marathyancha Uday Ani Utkarsha,* Moghe Prakashan, 1974.

Devale, S.R., *Maharashtratil Kille,* Shrelekhan Vachan Bhandar, Pune, 1981.

Divekar, S.M. (ed), *Kavindra Parmanand Vircahit, Shree Shiv Bharat,* Mumbai, 1927.

Divekar S.N. (Ed.), *Parnala-parvata-grahanakhyan,* Kalyan, 1927.

Divekar S.M. and Apte D.V. (Ed), Parmanand, *Sivabharat,* Divekar S.M. and Apte D.V. (Ed), B.I.S.M., Puraskrita, Poona, 1927.

Gaghbatta, *Shivaji-Prasasti,* Fourth Sammelan Vrtta, B.I.S.M., Poona, Shake 1838, (1916).

Gaikwad, Shankarrao, *Vijastambha,* Prerna Prakashan, Pune, 1994.

Gaikwad, Sardesai, Thorat, *Marathekalin Sanstha Va Vichar,* M.V. Phadke & Co., Kolhapur, 1982.

Gaikwad, Sardesai, Hanmane, *Aitihasik Kagadpatre Va Sthale Yancha Abhyas,* Phadke Booksellers, Kolhapur, 1980.

Gautam, Munshilal, *Samajik Kranti Ke Agredut Bhimsainik, Master, R.N. Chavan,* Shreenivas Mudranalaya, Nagpur, 1992.

Gavli, P.A., *Marathyancha Itihas,* Kailas Publication, Aurangabad, 1999.

Gavli P.A., *Peshwekalin Samaj Va Jatiya Sangharsha,* Prachar Prakashan, Kolhapur, 1982.

Ghanekar, P.K., *Athato Durga Jidnyasa,* Snehal Prakashan, Pune, 1991.

Gupte, Dr. Parshuram, *Gurrila Yuddha Karma,* Prakash Book Depot Bareli, 1983.

Hanvate, Prem, *Shivrayanche Nishthavanth Muslim Sainik,* Lokayat Prakashan, Vardha, 2003.

Hanumante Raghunath, *Rajvaryasaharak Kosa* (including Siva-Charitra Pradip) Divkar S.M. and Apte D.V., (ed), B.I.S.M., Poona, 1925.

Ingle Ramchandra T, *Maharancha Sanskritik Itihas,* Abhijeet Prakashan, Nagpur, 1987.

Jadhav, T.V., *Shivrayancha Athawava Pratap,* Manorama Prakashan, Mumbai, 1995.

Jadhav, V.T., *Maharashtracha Mahar,* Sugat Prakashan, Nagpur, 1980.

Joshi, A.B., and Chandarkar (Ed.), *Sri-SivasahicaLekhanalankar,* Poona, 1934.

Joshi, P.V., *Parakiyanchya Drishtikonatun Shivaji,* Mehta Publishing House, Pune, 1976.

Joshi N.V., *Pune-Vamana,* Khanolkar G.D. (ed), Sahitya Sahakar, Bombay, 2nd ed., 1971.

Joshi S.M. (Ed), *Sivakalin Patrasar Sangraha,* Vol. III (1937), Siva-charitra Karyalaya, Poona.

Joshi, S.N. (ed), *Shivkalin Patra-sar Sangraha,* Vol.l, III, B.I.S.M., Pune, 1937.

Joshi, S.N. (ed), *Krishnaji Appaji Sabhasad Virachit Chatrapati Shivaji Maharaj Yanchi Bakhar,* Chitrashala Prakashan, Pune, 1960.

Joshi S.N., *Marathekalin SamajDarshan,* Chitrashala Press, Poona, 1960.

Joshi S.N., *Sabhasad Bakhar,* Chitrashala Press, Pune, 1960.

Johari, R.C., *Pashchatya Sainya Itihas,* Chandraprakash & Brothers, Hapud (U.P.), 1977.

Kale, Y.M. (ed), *NagpurcarBhonslanchi Bakhar,* Madhya Prant Sanshodhan Mandal, 2nd ed., Nagpur, 1936.

Kamble, N.D., *Mahar Regiment Ek Shoryagatha,* Naudini, T. Goli, Kolhapur, 1986.

Kamble, N.D., *Maharancha Sainiki Itihas,* Anand Prakashan, Aurangabad, 1981.

Kanetkar Y.G., *Sakharambapuche Charitra,* Chitrashala Press, Poona.

Khabde, Dr. Dinkar, *Marathyancha Itihas,* Kailas Publications, Aurangabad, 1987.

Khairmode, C.B., *Ashprushyancha Lashkari Pesha,* Maharashtra Rajya Sahitya Ani Sanskriti Mandal, Mumbai, 1992.

Karve Iravati, *Marathi Lokanchi Sanskriti,* Maharashtra Rajya Prakashan, Mumbai.

Karve Iravati, *Maharashtra Ek Abhayas,* Maharashtra Sahitya Parishad, Pune, 1971.

Kathare Anil, *Shivkal Va Peshvekalatil Maharancha Itihas,* Kalpana Prakashan, 2002.

Kathare Anil, *Marathekalin Sarkari Adhikari Ani thyanche Gairvartan,* Sugava Prakashan, Pune, 1995.

Keer Dhananjaya, *Dr. Ambedkar,* Popular Prakashan, Bombay, 1962.

Kelkar, N.C., Apte, D.V. (ed), *Shiv-charitra Nibandhavali,* Shree Shivcharitra Karyalaya, Pune, 1929.

Kelkar N.C. and Apte D.V. (ed), *Shivakalin Patrasar Sangraha,* Vols. I-II, Poona, 1930.

Khairmode, C.B., *Amratnak* (2nd ed.), (in Marathi), Maharashtra Dalit Sahitya Sangh, Varali, Bombay, 1961.

--,*Dr. Bheemrao Ramaji, Ambedkar Charitra Khand,* Vol.I (3rd Ed), (in Marathi), Pratap Prakashan, Goregaon, Bombay, 1978.

--,*Dr. Bheemrao Ramaji Ambedkar Charitra Khand, Ambedkar,*Vol.I, Y.B. Amebdkar, 1952, Vol.II, Bombay, Bauddhajan Panchayat Samiti, 1958, Vol. III, Pratap Prakashan, Bombay, 1964, Vols. IV and V, Dr. Ambedkar Education Society, 1966, 1968 (in Marathi), Bombay.

Kharat, Shankarrao, *Maharashtratil Maharancha Itihas,* Dr. Shakuntala Kharat, Pune, 2003.

Kharat, Shankar Rao, *Ashprashacha Mukti Sangram* (in Marathi), Lokhande Prakashan, Pune, 1965.

--,*Daundi,* Continental Publishers, Pune, 1965.

Khare, G.H., *Shiv-charitra Sanshodhan Vritta,* Vol.I, II and III, Rajyabhiskk, Pune, 1953.

Khare, G.H., *Sguvocgarutra Vritta Sangraha,* Vol.II, B.I.S.M., Pune, 1939.

Khare , G.H., *Hingane Daftar,* Vols. I-II, B.I.S.M., Publications (1945-47).

Kosare, H.L., *Prachin Bharatatil Nag,* Dnyan Pradeep Prakashan, Nagpur, 1989.

Kulkarni, A.R., & Khare, G.H., (ed), *Marathyancha Itihas,* Vol. I-III, Continental Prakashan, Pune, 1984, 1985, 1986.

Kulkarni, S.R., *Shivkalin Rajniti ani Ranniti,* Popular Prakashan, Mumbai, 1994.

Limye Raja, Capt., Ranraj, *Shivrayanchya Yuiddhakatha,* J.K. Publications, Nashik, 1992.

Limye aja Capt, *Yuddha Ek Kala,* Dilipraj Prakashan, Pvt.Ltd., Pune, 1999.

Malshe S.G., (ed), *Marathi Vangmayacha Itihas, Vol. I-II,* Maharashtra Sahitya Parishad, Pune, 1982.

Mangudkar M.P.,*Mahatma Phule Ani Satyashodhak Chalval,* Sangam Publication, Pune.

Manu, *The Manusmriti,* Nene, Gopalshastri (Ed), The Chowkhamba Sanskrit Series Office, Varanasi, 2nd ed. 1970.

Mate, S.M., *Ashprushthancha Prashna,* Loksangraha Chhapkhana, 624, Sadashiv Peth, Pune, 1933.

Mirashi, V.V., *Satvahana and Prachin Kshatrapa Yancha Itihas, Ani Koriv Lekh,* Maharashtra Rajya Sahitya Mandal, Bombay, 1979.

Modak, Capt., G.V., *Pratapgadache Yuddha,* N.N.Datar & Sons, Pune, 1927.

Nannavare, K.K., *Vatandar Maharanchi Sanskriti,* Anand Prakashan, Aurangabad, 1995.

Navalkar, H.N., *Shivram Janba Kamble, Yanche Charitra, Ani Pune Parvati Satyagrahacha, Sankshipta Itihas,* Sugava Prakashan, Pune, 1997.

Nischalpuri, *Sivarajyabhiseka-Kalpatra,* B.I.S.M., Quarterly, *Shake* 1851 (1929), Apte D.V. and Dixit K.N. (Ed).

Oturkar R.V. (Ed), *Peshwekalin Samajik Va AthikPatravavahar* (1723-1854), B.I.S.M., Poona, 1950.

Pagadi, Setu Madhavrao, *Marathyanche Swatantraya Yuddha,* Joshi Ani Lokhande Prakashan, Pune, 1962.

Pawar A.G., (Ed), *Tarabai-Kalin Kagad Patre,* Vols. I-III, Shivaji University Publication, Kolhapur, 1969.

--*Jijabai-Kalin Kagad Patre,* Shivaji University Publication, Kolhapur, 1978.

Pawar, J.B., *Marathi Sattecha Uday,* C. Jamnadas and Co., Mumbai, 1978.

Pande, Dr. Ram Bapu, *Yuddha Adhyan, Ek Siddharth,* Chandraprakash & Co., Raibarchi, 1999.

Pindye Jairam, *Radha-madhav-vilas-can put,* Rajawade V.K. (D), Poona, 1922.

Pitre, Dr. K.G. (Brig), *Marathyancha Yuddha Itihas,* Continental Prakashan, Pune, 2000.

Purandare, K.V., Joshi, S.N. (Ed), *Marathyanchya Itishasachi Sandhane,* 25 Vol. Rajwade, Sanshodhan Mandal, Dhule, 1941.

Rajbhoj P.N., *Lashkari Pesha,* Ashok Press, Shanivar Peth, Pune, 1933.

Rajwade, V.K., *Marathanchya Itihasachi Sadhane,* V.G. Vijapurkar, Kolhapur, 1900.

Rajwade, V.K., *Marathyanchya Itihasachi Sadhane,* Maharashtra Sahityaparishad, Pune, 1909.

Rajawade, V.K. (Ed), *Marathyancha Itihasachi Sadhane,* 27 vols., vol. 25th edited by Purandhare K.V. and Joshi S.N. vol. 26th ed. By Mehendal K.C. vol. 27th ed. By Joshi M.L.

Rajawade, V.K., *Marathyanchya Itihasachi Sadhane,* 8, Vol. B.I.S.M., Pune.

Ranade, M.G., *Marathi Sateecha Udaya,* Maharashtra Rajya Sahitya Ani Sanskriti Mandal, Bombay, 1964.

Sabhasad, *Sabhasad Bakhar,* Joshi S.N. (Ed), 1st Ed., Poona, 1960.

Sahastrebuddhe P.G., *Maharashtra Sanskriti,* Continental Prakashan, Pune, 1979.

Sardesai, G.S., (Ed), *Selections from the Peshwa Daftar,* 45 vols., Government of Bombay Publication (1930-1934).

Sardesai, G.S., Kale, Y.M., and Kulkarni K.P. 9Ed), *Aitihasik Patravyavahar,* Samartha Bharat, Poona, 1933.

--*Aitihasik Lekh,* Patre, Yadi etc. Chitrasala, Poona 1930.

Shejwalkar T.S., *Panipat,*1971, Joshi Lonkade, Prakashan, Poona, 1961.

Shinde, M.K. (Captain), *Prachin, Arvachin Yudhatantra & Parchure,* Prakashan Mandir, Mumbai, 1980.

Shinde, V.R., *Bharatiya Ashprushateche Praghaver,* Nav Bharat Granthamala Office, Nagpur, 1933.

Singh, Dr. Lallanji, *Kautilya Ka Yuddhadarshan,* Prakash Book Depot, Bareli, 1984.

Shiv-Charitra SahityaVol. IV, B.I.S.M., Pune. 1934.

Vol. V,"" 1942.

Vol.VI," " 1937.

Vol. VII"" 1937

Vol. VIII"" 1942.

Vol. XI"" 1957-58.

Vad, G.C., and Parasnis D.B. Sane, Marate and Joshi (Ed.), *Selections from the Satara Rajas and the Peshwas Diaries,* 9 Vols, Poona, 1906-11).

Vad, G.C., Mawjee, P.V. and Parasnis, D.B.(ed), *Sanads and Letters,* Poona, 1913.

-- *Decisions From the Shahu and Peshwa Daftar,* Government of Bombay, 1909.

Vaidya, S.L., (Ed), *Vaidya Daftaraiun Niwadtele Kagad,* 5 vols. B.I.S.M., Pune.

Newspapers, Periodicals, Journals.

Bahishkrut Bharat

Bombay Chronicle

Bombay Courier

Bombay Gazette

Bombay Native Observer

Bombay Darpan

Dnyan Prakash

Janata

Kesari

Maharashtra Times

Poona Observer

Sudhakar

Somuvamshya Mitra

The Times of India.

www.ingramcontent.com/pod-product-compliance
Lightning Source LLC
LaVergne TN
LVHW010652110826
845149LV00014B/3056

* 9 7 8 8 1 9 3 4 8 5 6 0 6 *